INTELLIGENCE COOPERATION UNDER MULTIPOLARITY

Non-American Perspectives

Edited by Thomas Juneau, Justin Massie, and Marco Munier

While counterterrorism has been the primary focus of the defence and security policies of major Western countries in the last two decades, recent years have seen the re-emergence of states as the major threat. *Intelligence Cooperation under Multipolarity* offers a timely analysis of the challenges and opportunities for intelligence cooperation, characterized by the re-emergence of great power competition, particularly between the United States, China, and Russia.

This collection explores foreign policy and national security tools and partnerships that have emerged as the United States, typically an international leader, experiences internal and external shocks that have rendered its role on the international stage more uncertain. The book focuses on non-American perspectives in order to understand how America's allies and partners have adjusted to global power transitions. Drawing on contributions from leading intelligence and strategic studies scholars and professionals, *Intelligence Cooperation under Multipolarity* aims to broaden and deepen our understanding of the consequences of the power transition on national security policies.

THOMAS JUNEAU is an associate professor in the Graduate School of Public and International Affairs at the University of Ottawa.

JUSTIN MASSIE is a professor of political science at the Université du Québec à Montréal and co-director of the Network for Strategic Analysis.

MARCO MUNIER is a PhD candidate in political science at the Université du Québec à Montréal.

Intelligence Cooperation under Multipolarity

Non-American Perspectives

EDITED BY THOMAS JUNEAU,
JUSTIN MASSIE, AND MARCO MUNIER

UNIVERSITY OF TORONTO PRESS
Toronto Buffalo London

© University of Toronto Press 2024
Toronto Buffalo London
utorontopress.com

ISBN 978-1-4875-5074-5 (cloth)   ISBN 978-1-4875-5079-0 (EPUB)
ISBN 978-1-4875-5075-2 (paper)   ISBN 978-1-4875-5077-6 (PDF)

Library and Archives Canada Cataloguing in Publication

Title: Intelligence cooperation under multipolarity : non-American perspectives / edited by Thomas Juneau, Justin Massie, and Marco Munier.
Names: Juneau, Thomas, editor. | Massie, Justin, editor. | Munier, Marco, editor.
Description: Includes bibliographical references and index.
Identifiers: Canadiana (print) 20230523501 | Canadiana (ebook) 20230523536 | ISBN 9781487550745 (cloth) | ISBN 9781487550752 (paper) | ISBN 9781487550790 (EPUB) | ISBN 9781487550776 (PDF)
Subjects: LCSH: Intelligence service – International cooperation. | LCSH: National security – International cooperation. | LCSH: Security, International – International cooperation. | LCSH: Multipolarity (International relations)
Classification: LCC JF1525.I6 I48 2024 | DDC 327.12 – dc23

Cover design: Val Cooke
Cover image: Liu Zishan/Shutterstock.com

We wish to acknowledge the land on which the University of Toronto Press operates. This land is the traditional territory of the Wendat, the Anishnaabeg, the Haudenosaunee, the Métis, and the Mississaugas of the Credit First Nation.

University of Toronto Press acknowledges the financial support of the Government of Canada, the Canada Council for the Arts, and the Ontario Arts Council, an agency of the Government of Ontario, for its publishing activities.

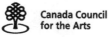

Contents

Acronyms vii

Introduction 3
MARCO MUNIER, THOMAS JUNEAU, AND JUSTIN MASSIE

1 Intelligence Adaption from the Cold War to the
Resurgence of Great Power Politics 19
DAMIEN VAN PUYVELDE

2 Intelligence Demands Linked to European Autonomy in Trade,
Technology, and Security 39
BJÖRN FÄGERSTEN

3 Transatlantic Intelligence Sharing and Cooperation:
Existing Challenges and Opportunities 61
ADRIANA SEAGLE

4 Don't Hold Back: Canadianize 83
THOMAS JUNEAU AND STEPHANIE CARVIN

5 Intelligence Cooperation in Historical Perspective:
From Cold War Bipolarity to the Multipolar Present 101
REG WHITAKER

6 Australia's National Intelligence Community:
Challenges and Opportunities in a Multipolar World 117
PATRICK F. WALSH

vi   Contents

7   Enhanced ISR: The Paradox of Pursuing Strategic Advantage
and Strategic Stability   137
NANCY TEEPLE

8   In Search of Trust: Challenges in UN Peacekeeping-Intelligence   167
SARAH-MYRIAM MARTIN-BRÛLÉ

Conclusion   185
DANIEL JEAN

Contributors   193

Acronyms

A4P	Action for Peacekeeping initiative
ABM	anti-ballistic missile
AI	artificial intelligence
ASAT	anti-satellite
ASEAN	Association of Southeast Asian Nations
ASIS	Australian Secret Intelligence Service
AUKUS	Australia, UK, US
BCRA	Bureau Central de Renseignement et d'Action
BECA	Basic Exchange and Cooperation Agreement
BIS	Bureau of Industry and Security
CAF	Canadian Armed Forces
CAI	Comprehensive Agreement on Investment
CBSA	Canada Border Services Agency
CCP	Chinese Communist Party
CFINTCOM	Canadian Forces Intelligence Command
CFIUS	Committee on Foreign Investment in the US
CFSP	Common Foreign and Security Policy
CIA	Central Intelligence Agency
CIRO	Cabinet Research and Intelligence Office
COMCASA	Communications Compatibility and Security Agreement
COREPER	Committee of Permanent Representatives
CPTPP	Comprehensive and Progressive Agreement for Trans-Pacific Partnership
CSE	Communications Security Establishment
CSIS	Canadian Security Intelligence Service
CSO	Commonwealth SIGINT Organization
CSU	Charles Sturt University
CTBT	Comprehensive Test-Ban Treaty
CTG	Multilateral Counterterrorism Group
CVO	Centre for Monitoring and Operations
DARPA	Advanced Research Projects Agency
DGSE	Direction Générale de la Sécurité Extérieure
DGSI	Direction Générale de la Sécurité Intérieure

viii Acronyms

DND	Department of National Defence
DO	Direction Opérationnelle
DPA	Department of Political Affairs
DPI	Department of Public Information
DPKO	Department of Peacekeeping Operations
DPO	UN Department of Peace Operations
DR	Direction du Renseignement
DRM	Direction du Renseignement Militaire
DSS	Department of Safety and Security
DT	Direction Technique
ECTC	European Counter Terrorism Centre
EDF	European Defence Fund
EDF	European Development Fund
EEAS	European External Action Service
EEC	European Economic Community
ESPAS	European Strategy and Policy Analysis System
EC	European Commission
EU	European Union
EUGS	EU Global Strategy
EUMM GEORGIA	EU Monitoring Mission in Georgia
EUNAVFOR	EU Naval Force Somalia
EUROPOL	European Union Agency for Law Enforcement Cooperation
EUTM MALI	European Union Training Mission Mali
FBI	Federal Bureau of Investigation
FDI	Foreign Direct Investment
FINTRAC	Financial Transactions and Reports Analysis Centre of Canada
FLQ	Front de Libération du Québec
FOIP	free and open Indo-Pacific
FRA	European Union Agency for Fundamental Rights
GAC	Global Affairs Canada
GBMD	ground-based midcourse defence
GEOINT	geospatial intelligence
GIDE	Global Information Dominance Experiments
GSRP	Global Security Reporting Program
HDR	higher degree research
HIPPO	High-Level Independent Panel on Peace Operations
HQ	headquarters
HR	High Representative
HUMINT	human intelligence
IAEA	International Atomic Energy Agency
IALP	Intelligence Analyst Learning Program
IARPA	Intelligence Advanced Research Projects Activity
IAS	Intelligence Assessment Secretariat
IC	intelligence community
ICBM	road-mobile intercontinental ballistic missiles
ICC	International Criminal Court

IIR	Independent Intelligence Review
INF	intermediate nuclear forces
IntCen	EU Intelligence Analysis Centre
IntDir	EU Military Staff Intelligence Directorate
IS	Islamic State
ISED	Innovation, Science, and Economic Development
ISR	Intelligence, Surveillance, and Reconnaissance
ITAC	Integrated Terrorism Assessment Centre
ITAR	International Traffic in Arms Regulations
JADC2	Joint All Domain Command and Control
JEIS	Joint EU Intelligence School
JMAC	Joint Mission Analysis Centre
JOC	Joint Operations Centre
MAD	mutually assured destruction
MINUSCA	United Nations Multidimensional Integrated Stabilization Mission in the Central African Republic
MINUSMA	United Nations Multidimensional Integrated Stabilization Mission in Mali
MONUSCO	United Nations Organization Stabilization Mission in the DR Congo
NATO	North Atlantic Treaty Organization
NIC	Australia Intelligence Community
NISAB	National Intelligence Science and Advisory Board
NORAD	North American Aerospace Defence Command
NPR	Nuclear Posture Review
NPT	Non-Proliferation Treaty
NSIC	National Strategic Intelligence Course
OCHA	Office for the Coordination of Humanitarian Affairs
OHCHR	Office of the High Commissioner for Human Rights
ONI	Office of National Intelligence
ONUC	UN Operation in the Congo
OSS	Office of Strategic Services
PCO	Privy Council Office
PESCO	Permanent Structured Cooperation
PHAC	Public Health Agency of Canada
PNR	passenger name record
PPE	personal protective equipment
PQ	Parti Québécois
PRC	People's Republic of China
QUAD	Quadrilateral Security Dialogue
RCMP	Royal Canadian Mounted Police
SAGE	situational awareness and geospatial
SatCen	EU Satellite Centre
SIAC	Single Intelligence Analysis Capacity
SIGINT	signals intelligence
SIS II	Schengen Information System II
SOCMINT	Social media intelligence
SRSG	Special Representative of the Secretary-General

x Acronyms

SSBN	Soviet ballistic missile submarines
START	New Strategic Arms Reduction Treaty
STEM	science, technology, engineering, and mathematics
STRATCOM	Strategic Command
TCC	troop and police contributors
TFEU	Treaty on the Functioning of the European Union
TOR	terms of reference
TTP	Trans-Pacific Partnership
UAV	unmanned aerial vehicle
UN	United Nations
UNDP	UN Development Programme
UNMISS	United Nations Mission in South Sudan
UNOCC	UN Operations and Crisis Centre
UNPROFOR	United Nations Protection Force
USNORTHCOM	US Northern Command
USSR	Union of Soviet Socialist Republics
WADA	World Anti-Doping Agency
WMD	weapons of mass destruction

INTELLIGENCE COOPERATION UNDER MULTIPOLARITY

Introduction

MARCO MUNIER, THOMAS JUNEAU,
AND JUSTIN MASSIE

In March 2021, Japan and Germany signed an intelligence-sharing agreement as part of a shared effort to counter Chinese behaviour in the South and East China Seas.[1] Why did Tokyo and Berlin pursue such an arrangement? As questions mount about the capacity of the United States to support the rules-based international order – indeed, about the Americans' very reliability – many of Washington's traditional allies and partners have come to realize that they need to adapt.[2] That means developing new foreign policy and national security partnerships. One of those initiatives has been undergoing a quiet revolution in recent years, albeit with little public or academic discussion: intelligence cooperation.

The academic literature on intelligence cooperation is limited and has mostly focused on the United States, with only a handful of studies on other countries.[3] It has also focused largely on the past, albeit important moments in that past, such as the two world wars, the Cold War, and the war on terror.[4] In a recent analysis of intelligence cooperation studies, Pepijn Tuinier found that the topic has been neglected. In the two most prominent journals in the field, for example, intelligence cooperation was the subject of only 4.5 per cent of all articles between 1991 and 2019, and most of those focused on the Cold War.[5]

In light of all this, the present volume addresses the challenges the new international environment poses to intelligence cooperation. It focuses on non-US perspectives in order to examine specifically how America's allies and partners have adjusted to the transition in global power. It features leading intelligence and strategic studies scholars and professionals and fills a gap in Intelligence Studies by focusing on how US allies and partners address challenges and seek opportunities for intelligence cooperation in an era of intensifying great power competition.

The Challenges of a Power Transition

The decline of US hegemony and the rise of China are leading to a power transition from West to East.[6] As US president, Donald Trump accelerated this transition by constantly questioning the utility of military alliances, free trade agreements, and the place of the United States in the international order, thereby undermining the durability of the US-hegemonic international order. At the same time, the rapid growth in China's economic, military, and diplomatic power has led it to increasingly challenge the existing order and US leadership. In response, the United States has redirected its attention to the Indo-Pacific to uphold its primacy in the region.[7] This attention shift may have helped create a window of opportunity for Vladimir Putin to order an all-out invasion of Ukraine with the goal of re-establishing Russia's imperial control over its western neighbour. We have now entered an era marked by intensifying great power competition, during which we can expect deterrence measures, increasing levels of confrontation, and heightened risks of grey-zone and armed conflict.

The future of the US-led order rests in great part on one of its core features, namely its uniquely vast alliance system. The fate of that system hinges as much on US leadership – what the United States will or will not do – as on its allies' followership – what those allies will or will not do. In his assessment of the future of the international order, John Ikenberry has identified several scenarios, which revolve around whether the decline of the United States is leading to a search for alternatives or strengthening a desire to preserve the existing order.[8] It is anticipated that if the power transition leads to a search for alternatives, the United States will pursue retrenchment and its allies will seek security hedging. This may involve the latter engaging with US competitors, such as China, or strengthening allied military and security capabilities, both nationally and collectively, such as through the European Union. This path could accelerate a decrease in cooperation with the United States. On the other hand, if there is a common desire to maintain US hegemony, we should expect to see the emergence of guardians of the liberal international order, that is, actors willing to play a greater role in upholding the rules-based order, with the support of the United States. In this scenario, US allies would shoulder a greater share of the economic, political, and military costs of US hegemony and band together to confront the rise of revisionist states. There is evidence of both scenarios, with the UK and Australia tightening their security and technology bonds with the United States in the face of a growing Chinese threat and with France doubling down on its third-way strategy in the Indo-Pacific.

China today is challenging the international status quo by pursuing aggressive actions in the South China Sea, promoting a new financial order, and establishing a new Silk Road.[9] Chinese influence, moreover, is spreading among US allies and partners such as Japan, South Korea, India, Indonesia, and New Zealand. Meanwhile, the COVID-19 pandemic has exacerbated competition between the great powers and provided China with additional opportunities to further spread its influence at the expense of Western democracies.[10] The EU, though still a close ally of the United States, is not blind to the decline of US power and the challenge this represents for the liberal international order.

Many European countries recognize that the world has become more multipolar and that China, and Russia as well, pose challenges.[11]

Indeed, Russia is seeking to take back what it perceives as its rightful place in a multipolar world while trying to become a power pole of its own.[12] Its broad objective is to have the international order shift away from the universalism of the Western model by promoting multiple political forms as well as historical and cultural particularities. To that end, Russia does not hesitate to work with other actors that are also critical of the current international order.[13] Russia's heavy involvement in the war in Syria, officially to fight against the Islamic State but in practice to prop up its ally, the regime of Bashar al-Assad, illustrates its ambition, as does its spreading influence in West Africa and Turkey. As a result, NATO's attention is being increasingly stretched, with its members debating whether to focus on defending their territory against the Russian threat or pursuing a global role for NATO to help sustain the existing order in the face of Chinese encroachments. Russia's invasion of Ukraine in February 2022 demonstrates Moscow's bellicosity and disregard for the rules-based international order. In the face of this aggression, there has been an outpouring of support for the Ukrainian people in the form of economic, humanitarian, and military aid to help the country counter the Russian invasion.

Intelligence cooperation was key in the lead-up to the war and has done much to influence its conduct. The United States, as well as other states, accurately anticipated Russia's attack and operational plans and rushed to alert Kyiv, its allies, and the international community of what was about to happen. In a departure from standard practice, it released classified information for the purpose of exposing Russia's false pretext for war; it also helped Kyiv plan a defence against the aggressor and set out to build an international coalition to support Ukraine and punish Moscow.[14] European and Ukrainian officials had been more sceptical about Russia's intentions, arguing that it was not amassing enough troops to achieve its objectives of regime change and occupation of Ukraine.[15] But the extent of intelligence sharing by Washington, as well as the clarity of that intelligence, eventually proved convincing. The US intelligence community had gathered "extraordinary detail" about Russia's war plans, including its operational strategy, military funding, and positioning of troops and weaponry.[16] In contrast, Moscow's own intelligence assessments of Ukrainian willingness to fight and the West's determination to support Kyiv militarily were fundamentally flawed.[17]

Yet very few intelligence services expected that Russia would fail to subdue Ukraine. In the United States, only the State Department's Bureau of Intelligence and Research anticipated the level of Ukrainian resistance; that was because it factored in Ukrainian public opinion polls, which demonstrated strong anti-Russian sentiment and a willingness to engage in armed combat, including in eastern Ukraine.[18] But it has been Washington's intelligence sharing with the

Ukrainian military, whether obtained through space-based imagery, tactical drones, or human sources, that has proved instrumental to Kyiv's military successes so far.[19] Furthermore, the protection of Ukraine against future Russian aggression will require establishing deep and permanent intelligence cooperation between Ukraine and its allies. The Working Group on International Security Guarantees for Ukraine, co-chaired by the Head of the Ukrainian President's Office Andriy Yermark and former Danish prime minister and NATO Secretary General Anders Fogh Rasmussen, has concluded that "Ukraine and guarantors will need to have a mechanism of collecting, exchanging, processing, and analyzing intelligence, including for the purpose of early detection regarding preparations for an armed aggression."[20]

The emergence of multipolarity has also led to an increase in conflicts in cyberspace and a growing resort to espionage and foreign influence operations. It is true that these are relatively old methods and practices, but Russia, China, and other powers such Iran and North Korea have been using them increasingly aggressively. Information manipulation, in particular, is now a common tactic in the competition among great and regional powers, either to erode trust in democratic systems or to promote an alternative, authoritarian model.[21] In an extensively researched report, for example, Paul Charon and Jean-Baptiste Jeangène-Vilmer have demonstrated that Chinese "influence operations have hardened considerably in recent years and its methods increasingly resemble those employed by Moscow."[22]

Similarly, the cyber domain has become a crucial space for destabilization operations and espionage. Russia, in particular, favours a hybrid warfare model, with the aggressive use of cyberattacks.[23] For example, its annexation of Crimea in 2014 began with propaganda and a series of cyberattacks aimed at paralysing Ukrainian government networks.[24] Operations in cyberspace have the advantage of being less risky, as personnel can remain safe in their home countries, with access to more targets than have their human intelligence counterparts.[25] China is a newer player in cyberspace than Russia and is working to match the United States and Russia in this field.[26] It is preparing to use cyberattacks in the event of conflict with the United States as a means to disable, destroy, or deny access to cyberspace infrastructure.[27] That said, cyberespionage targets not only adversaries but allies as well. For example, France claims that the United States and China are the main cyberattackers of French businesses, and Germany accuses France and the United States of being the main economic spies among friendly countries. In addition, the United States has carried out numerous cyberattacks against countries such as Russia, North Korea, China, Iran, and Syria.[28]

Finally, clandestine foreign influence is a growing concern. China, in particular, controls various interest groups in Western democracies, monitors the Chinese diaspora and overseas discourse on China, and attempts to silence dissidents by various means.[29] Combating foreign espionage and interference is now a top priority for Western intelligence services. The director of the Canadian Security Intelligence Service, David Vigneault, declared in 2018 that "traditional interference by foreign spies remains the greatest danger."[30]

Intelligence Cooperation in Theory and Practice

Why do states cooperate in intelligence affairs? And how? A state can use intelligence to maximize the impact of its foreign policy by identifying the capabilities, characteristics, and vulnerabilities of others; to gain a strategic advantage by revealing the intentions of others; and to protect its national security and its citizens.[31]

Intelligence cooperation holds a central place in the intelligence world, yet there is limited academic literature specifically on intelligence cooperation under multipolarity. Austin Gee and Robert Patman, in one rare example, have shown that the growth in aggressive Chinese operations has led to more extensive intelligence exchanges within the Fives Eyes as well as to an extension of Fives Eyes cooperation to other countries, such as Germany and Japan.[32] Yet Jan Ballast notes that even at a time when new challenges are emerging, NATO members are still often reluctant to share intelligence within the alliance, preferring bilateral arrangements instead.[33] The challenge posed by the new strategic environment is that states do not agree on strategic priorities, nor do they all share the same threat perceptions. Terrorism brought states together, whereas the challenges posed by multipolarity are more difficult to identify, as can be seen in the divergent views about how to deal with the rise of China. However, when states go rogue, turning to brute military force to challenge the rules-based order, greater cooperation is to be expected among status quo powers, the invasion of Ukraine providing a clear example. But if Svendsen is right when he says that the changing strategic environment is having an impact on the nature and forms of intelligence cooperation,[34] then the war in Ukraine will be accompanied by new challenges.

Nevertheless, intelligence cooperation has a long history and has been common in the twentieth and twenty-first centuries. As Michael Herman writes, allies have always shared intelligence in wartime, and intelligence sharing has always been a feature of diplomacy, even among rivals.[35] An obvious reason for such cooperation is, as Lefebvre points out, that "no one agency can do and know everything."[36] Jeffrey Richelson identifies two broad benefits from intelligence cooperation: it provides access to information that would otherwise be unavailable, and it can influence the behaviour of other states in a desired direction.[37] We propose a third category, namely that it offers efficiencies through sharing of the costs associated with intelligence.

In the first situation, cooperation between the Soviet Union and the United Kingdom and United States allowed the Soviets to gain access to privileged intelligence about German capabilities and intentions during the Second World

8   Marco Munier, Thomas Juneau, and Justin Massie

War. In exchange, the Soviets provided information on Japanese capabilities and intentions.[38] Similarly, Canada spied on Castro's Cuban regime during the 1960s and 1970s and provided the intelligence it gathered to the Americans. Following the diplomatic rupture between Cuba and the United States, Washington had asked Canada and the United Kingdom to provide intelligence on the Cuban regime. Canada was in a privileged position, as it had maintained diplomatic and trade relations with Cuba.[39] Another example of this form of cooperation is the relationship between the Australian Secret Intelligence Service (ASIS) and the CIA in the 1960s. When the CIA withdrew from Cambodia in 1965, ASIS took over that particular file and provided intelligence on that country to the CIA.[40] More recently, Ukraine benefited considerably from US intelligence on Russian intentions and war plans, which helped it prepare to defend itself.

In the second situation, a state can share intelligence with another state in the hope of influencing its behaviour. Just before the Second World War, for example, after the Soviet Union signed a non-aggression pact with Hitler, the United Kingdom shared intelligence it had obtained through the ULTRA project (which deciphered encrypted enemy communications) indicating that the Germans intended to invade Russia. Churchill strongly desired that the Soviets join the war against Nazi Germany. Unfortunately, it seems that Stalin either did not receive all of that information or did not want to accept what it told him.[41] The intelligence the United States shared with its allies and the international community regarding the alleged existence of weapons of mass destruction in Iraq after 9/11 provides another example of a state sharing intelligence – erroneous in this case – in an attempt to influence the perceptions and behaviour of others. With regard to the war in Ukraine, the United States was attempting to disrupt Russia's war plans when it disclosed classified information about Russia's intentions and operational tactics.

In the third situation, intelligence cooperation can be a means to share the costs of an intelligence operation or program. For example, the UKUSA arrangement "provided for SIGINT burden-sharing among the 'Five Eyes' in terms of geographic coverage and targeting."[42] Similarly, the French attempted to create a European SIGINT capability based on the development of satellites. While most of its costs were covered by France, the idea was to share the financial burden with allies, including Italy and Spain.[43] Looking ahead, the West should expect to be solicited by Ukraine to share the costs of its intelligence agencies to strengthen their capacity and reach vis-à-vis the existential threat it faces.

While there are important benefits to sharing intelligence, there are also risks.[44] One of the greatest risks is that doing so may compromise methods or sources. And there is always the risk that the information could be disclosed to a third party. That is why many sharing agreements, formal or informal, include a non-disclosure clause. As noted by Richelson, "all other things being equal, the wider the dissemination of information, the greater the chance of its unauthorized disclosure."[45] Another risk is that the country sharing its information may intentionally select it to deceive or influence the receiving country. Shared information, moreover, can be used for other purposes than the original one. For example, Israel used US intelligence to target Iraq's Osirak nuclear reactor in 1981.[46] Another problem with intelligence sharing is what might be called the "confirmation loop." In this situation, shared intelligence may become difficult to identify or trace and may be inadvertently recycled to confirm other assessments. The impression then is that the assessments have been confirmed by several separate sources, when in fact they are based on a single source. Lastly, there is a risk that classified information may be leaked to the media. When Edward Snowden leaked classified US documents, for example, he exposed activities not only of the US intelligence community but also of allies, including Canada.[47]

In addition to the risks outlined here, there are several other constraints when it comes to cooperation. Differences in threat perceptions or strategic or political interests, as well as legal issues related to, for example, a country's reputation for respecting human rights, can constrain intelligence cooperation.[48] As the threat posed by rising powers grows, however, these divergences tend to dissipate. As Pierre Morcos argues regarding the so-called diverging views between France and the United States over China, Paris has hardened its position on China in recent years and "is now ready to serve as a counterweight to China's rise." Morcos notes that while Paris may not always see eye-to-eye with Washington, as the AUKUS crisis abruptly showed, France sees value in increasing its cooperation with the United States, including in terms of intelligence sharing, joint exercises, and contingency planning.[49]

In practice, intelligence cooperation can take several forms. First, a distinction must be made between formal and informal cooperation.[50] The first refers to a formal intelligence-sharing agreement between two (sometimes several) countries. The second refers to intelligence sharing without a formal agreement. The second distinction is based on the nature of the relationship, that is, on whether the cooperation is transactional or relational.[51] In transactional cooperation, something is expected in exchange for information; it typically involves an *ad hoc* exchange or what is commonly called a *quid pro quo*. In relational cooperation, the exchange of intelligence is less delimited and more regular and generally extends over time, without necessarily an expectation of immediate reciprocity. The essential factors in transactional cooperation are the intrinsic value of what is exchanged and the mutual gains from that exchange. In relational cooperation, by contrast, the "intrinsic value gain is supplemented – and sometimes even outweighed – by the benefits accruing to or extracted from the larger political relationship."[52] Finally, we can distinguish between bilateral and multilateral intelligence sharing. Bilateral cooperation is often preferred, because multilateral cooperation involves a greater risk that information will be disclosed.[53]

Among these forms of intelligence cooperation, all combinations are possible. For example, the Club of Berne, which brings together the heads of the security and intelligence services of the EU states, is a relational, informal, multilateral forum. Participants exchange views on security and intelligence issues related to the EU, and they share information, although they are not required to. The most important and institutionalized intelligence partnership is the 1946 UKUSA agreement, which has evolved into the Five Eyes. In this partnership, bilateral cooperation has been transformed into multilateral cooperation, but bilateral agreements still exist. Initially, the BRUSA agreement of 1943 was a formal and bilateral signals intelligence (SIGINT) partnership between the United Kingdom and the United States. The subsequent 1946 UKUSA agreement, besides outlining US–British SIGINT cooperation, contains the proviso that intelligence can be shared with the British dominions, including Canada, Australia, and New Zealand. At the same time, the Commonwealth SIGINT Organization (CSO) agreement between the United Kingdom, Canada, Australia, and New Zealand was created.

Several factors promote or facilitate intelligence cooperation. Stephen Lander and Michael Herman write that political relations and foreign policy set the context for intelligence cooperation. Thus, if an intelligence cooperation relationship is truly extensive and robust, it is because the broader political relationship between the states is robust.[54] Cultural factors can also facilitate intelligence cooperation. The cultural ties that bind the Anglosphere countries have, notably, helped cement cooperation among the Five Eyes. As Hager Ben Jaffel argues, despite Brexit, the United Kingdom will continue to cooperate with other EU countries, because cooperative practices are deeply rooted on both sides.[55] Furthermore, trust is important, even essential, when it comes to sharing information.[56] Trust plays a significant role in determining the degree and extent of cooperation but is not a *necessary* element of intelligence sharing. In several situations, political or strategic interests outweigh considerations of trust or even amity. When the British decided to share intelligence on German intentions toward the Soviet Union during the Second World War, trust did not play a significant role, and the strategic interest in having the Soviets fight Germany was clear. Jennifer Sims also points out that intelligence sharing can take place between adversaries if the parameters of a specific issue make it necessary. For example, Israel maintains regular relations with the intelligence services of many Arab countries, even adversaries, while US intelligence offered immunity to some of Hitler's collaborators in exchange for intelligence on the Soviet Union.[57]

The war on terror has globalized intelligence cooperation, between allies but also among rivals and even enemies. Indeed, the terrorist threat has brought

Introduction   11

many countries together under a common banner. And while military tools are essential in the fight against terrorism, intelligence is also at the heart of counterterrorism, both offensively to identify and target terrorist groups and defensively to prevent attacks and protect citizens and institutions. As pointed out by Martin Rudner, "the dynamics of [intelligence agencies'] comparative advantage[s], coupled with the synergy of cooperation, have since 9/11 led to the building of a coalition of unprecedented scope and interaction in the intelligence domain, directed specifically against international Islamicist terrorism."[58]

Pathways to Intelligence Cooperation

Adam Svendsen identifies four main drivers of the globalization of intelligence cooperation. First, the increased volume of intelligence needed requires some degree of burden sharing. Second, operational imperatives, particularly in Iraq and Afghanistan, have lowered the formal barriers to cooperation. The third driver is fear of future major attacks, which might be averted through information sharing. And finally, preventive and pre-emptive strategies require a common baseline of presumptions. "These pressures appear to not only outweigh counterintelligence concerns about security, but to be reshaping the patterns of cooperation."[59] As an example, the United States and the United Kingdom have cooperated in clandestine operations in Afghanistan against the terrorist group al-Qaeda, and some unfriendly countries such as Iran, Syria, and Libya have shared intelligence with the West.[60] However, intelligence cooperation is not equal everywhere. While the United Nations has a growing need for intelligence, the issue is a delicate one. The UN wants to avoid being blamed for espionage against one of its members. The organization must thus find a way to balance its intelligence needs with the political constraints it faces.[61] As Svendsen writes, "the globalization of intelligence [cooperation] is a response to the changing nature of the operational environment."[62] Thus, it is not surprising that the changing strategic environment during the war against the Islamic State impacted intelligence cooperation.[63]

The case studies in this volume offer insights into how the return of great power competition is affecting patterns of intelligence cooperation. Kenneth Waltz famously wrote that in response to changes in the balance of power, states respond by engaging in internal or external balancing, or both.[64] States engage in balancing behaviour in an effort to "amass military might so as to deter another's aggression or prevail in a conflict should deterrence fail."[65] In the international relations literature, this has implied that internally, states balance by increasing their own capabilities, especially by procuring more weapons; externally, they balance by forming security alliances. This logic can be transposed to the realm of intelligence. At the onset of the war on terrorism after the 9/11 attacks, for example, the United States and its allies and partners responded to the emergence of a new threat at these two levels. Internally, they developed their capabilities by creating new intelligence agencies focused on the new threat, providing existing ones with greater resources or expanded mandates, and enhancing coordination among them all. Externally, they broadened existing intelligence alliances and partnerships and created new ones.

This book sets out to explore such pathways to novel patterns of intelligence cooperation in response to more recent changes in the international environment – the return of great power competition, mounting uncertainty surrounding the United States, the rise of China, and Russia's revanchism. Externally, as chapters in this volume demonstrate, America's allies and partners have deepened their cooperation and also sought to build new partnerships. Similarly, at the internal level, some US allies and partners have sought to boost their intelligence capabilities, notably in Europe and in Canada, as some of our chapters demonstrate. For these states, this is both an end in itself and a means to an end: by expanding their internal capabilities, US allies position themselves to gain more, by having more to offer, from existing and new cooperation agreements. Many have, in practice, done both, generating new means internally and building partnerships abroad.

Plan of the Book

This book provides an overview of the challenges and opportunities for intelligence cooperation in a multipolar world. The war on terrorism certainly continues, but intelligence services in the United States and those of its allies have come to focus much more in recent years on the activities of hostile great powers – Russia and China – and less on non-state actors. The book focuses, more specifically, on how US allies have been adjusting to this shifting international environment.

In chapter 1, Damien van Puyvelde argues that intelligence organizations have always operated in an international environment marked by self-help and anarchy, but Western agencies also face the constraints posed by liberal democratic norms and rules, especially since the end of the Cold War. Yet the study of intelligence has been built mainly on realist assumptions. Understanding how intelligence services have adapted to the return of great power politics requires pluralist conceptions that overcome paradigmatic divides between realism and liberalism. The chapter illustrates the relevance of a realist-liberal framework by examining the transformation of France's intelligence services in the face of renewed great power competition.

In chapter 2, Björn Fägersten discusses the EU's desire to achieve strategic autonomy, which requires significant intelligence capabilities for both member countries and the EU as a whole. As the author explains, the rise of China and technological rivalries have strengthened the desire of EU countries to achieve the strategic autonomy they have been seeking for several decades. He asserts that strategic autonomy – that is, conducting a foreign and security policy independent of the United States – must be achieved in at least four areas: decision-making, operational, commercial, and technological. He notes that the EU's search for autonomy will lead to further intelligence cooperation.

In chapter 3, Adriana Seagle examines the extent to which transatlantic intelligence sharing can go beyond counterterrorism and law enforcement cooperation to focus on pressing geopolitical challenges arising from the New Silk Roads and failed states. She notes that traditionally, intelligence cooperation between the United States and the EU has been impacted by a lack of trust, different understandings of secrecy and civil liberties, changes in US security policies, and, above all, different threat perceptions. She argues that there is room to reinvent transatlantic intelligence sharing around issues such as cyber, trade, and climate change.

In chapter 4, Stephanie Carvin and Thomas Juneau point out the pros and cons of Canadianizing intelligence in a context where Canada receives more intelligence than it provides within the Five Eyes. They show that information obtained from allies may not reflect Canadian needs, priorities, and interests. However, they note that in recent years, efforts have been made to Canadianize the collection and analysis of foreign intelligence, to further dilute it in the decision-making process, and to focus specifically on Canadian needs and interests.

In chapter 5, Reg Whitaker takes a historical perspective on Canadian intelligence cooperation from the Cold War to today's multipolarity. He highlights Canada's early steps in intelligence cooperation with its traditional allies as well as the many mistakes and scandals that have marked the history of Canadian intelligence. Like Thomas Juneau and Stephanie Carvin, he argues that Canadian intelligence is more focused on Canadian interests than in the past. He stresses that while traditional intelligence cooperation with the Five Eyes will continue, Canadian intelligence will need to diversify its intelligence cooperation with other countries and non-governmental actors, especially regarding subjects such as pandemics and climate change.

In chapter 6, Patrick Walsh addresses the profound changes underway in the Australian intelligence community by asking two key questions: How can the Australian intelligence community's reform agenda provide opportunities to strengthen intelligence cooperation through the traditional Five Eyes partnership? And how do the reform initiatives provide that community with a platform to build greater intelligence cooperation that is mutually beneficial through less "traditional pathways," such as through the newly reinvigorated Quadrilateral Security Dialogue – a forum among Australia, India, Japan, and the United States that shares and promotes liberal and democratic values in the Indo-Pacific?

In chapter 7, Nancy Teeple shows how attempts to dominate the field of intelligence, surveillance, and reconnaissance can provoke counter-responses and

14 Marco Munier, Thomas Juneau, and Justin Massie

even preventive actions by strategic competitors of the United States, notably China and Russia. US superiority in intelligence, surveillance, and reconnaissance leads competitors like Russia and China to rely on hybrid measures when targeting US informational and cyber capabilities.

In chapter 8, Sarah-Myriam Martin-Brûlé contextualizes the need for and the development of a peacekeeping-intelligence policy and doctrine at the UN while highlighting the challenges of designing and implementing guidelines in the absence of consensus on how to define the concept. She addresses the intelligence versus transparency paradox that arises when mechanisms are being created for "all the countries in the world" to share classified information.

The book concludes with a synthesis by Daniel Jean, former National Security and Intelligence Advisor to the Prime Minister of Canada. He argues that intelligence cooperation is more than ever required for US allies in a multipolar world marked by a geopolitical and geo-economic US–China confrontation as well as by Russian hybrid warfare. Intelligence agencies, however, must recognize that they no longer have a monopoly on the collection, assessment, and dissemination of intelligence; they must now engage with the private sector and civil society. Success is vital, for failures to anticipate threats and mistakes no longer have limited consequences.

NOTES

1 "Japan, Germany hold 1st security talk to deter China," *The Independent*, 13 April 2021, https://www.independent.co.uk/news/japan-germany-hold-1st-security-talk -to-deter-china-germany-japan-foreign-ministry-east-xinjiang-b1830611.html.
2 See, for example, Ivan Krastev and Mark Leonard, "The Crisis of American Power: How Europeans See Biden's America," *European Council on Foreign Relations*, 19 January 2021, https://ecfr.eu/publication/the-crisis-of-american-power-how -europeans-see-bidens-america.
3 Adam D.M. Svendsen, "Connecting Intelligence and Theory: Intelligence Liaison and International Relations," *Intelligence and National Security* 24, no. 5 (2009): 704, 707.
4 See, for example, David Stafford and Rhodri Jeffreys-Jones, eds., *American–British– Canadian Intelligence Relations 1939–2000* (London: Frank Cass, 2000); Charles Cogan, "American–French Intelligence Relations and the French Nuclear Deterrent," *Journal of Intelligence History* 3, no. 1 (2003): 55–60; Hugues Canuel, "French Aspirations and Anglo-Saxon Suspicions: France, Signals Intelligence and the UKUSA Agreement at the Dawn of the Cold War," *Journal of Intelligence History* 12, no. 1 (2013): 76–92; Don Munton, "Intelligence Cooperation Meets International Studies Theory: Explaining Canadian Operations in Castro's Cuba," *Intelligence and National Security* 24, no. 1 (2009): 119–38; Tore Vestermark, "International Liaison in the

Afghan Theatre of War: Strategic Interests and Hierarchical Relations," *International Journal of Intelligence, Security, and Public Affairs* 19, no. 2 (2017): 112–33; Owen L. Sirrs, "The Perils of Multinational Intelligence Coalitions: Britain, America, and the Origins of Pakistan's ISI," *Intelligence and National Security* 33, no. 1 (2018): 36–47; Adam D.M. Svendsen, *Intelligence Cooperation and the War on Terror: Anglo-American Security Relations after 9/11* (London: Routledge, 2010); and Adam D.M. Svendsen, *The Professionalization of Intelligence Cooperation: Fashioning Method out of Mayhem* (New York: Palgrave Macmillan, 2012).

5 Pepijn Tuinier, "Explaining the Depth and Breadth of International Intelligence Cooperation: Towards a Comprehensive Understanding," *Intelligence and National Security* 36, no. 1 (2021): 116–38.

6 Justin Massie and Jonathan Paquin, "Introduction: America's Allies Coping with US Relative Decline," in *American's Allies and the Decline of US Hegemony*, ed. Justin Massie and Jonathan Paquin (London: Routledge, 2020), 1–2.

7 Joshua R. Itzkowitz Shifrinson, "Neo-Primacy and the Pitfalls of US Strategy toward China," *Washington Quarterly* 43, no. 4 (2020): 79–104.

8 G. John Ikenberry, "American Decline, Liberal Hegemony, and the Transformation of World Politics," in *Coping with Geopolitical Decline*, ed. Frédéric Mérand (Montreal and Kingston: McGill-Queen's University Press, 2020), 231–43.

9 Srdjan Vucetic, "China's Counter-Hegemony? Evidence from 'Making Identity Count,'" in *American's Allies and the Decline of US Hegemony*, ed. Justin Massie and Jonathan Paquin (London: Routledge, 2020), 50.

10 Stefanie von Hlatky et al., "The Geopolitical Impacts of COVID-19," *Policy Brief* no. 1, Network for Strategic Analysis, June 2020, https://ras-nsa.ca/publication/the-geopolitical-impacts-of-covid-19; Marco Munier, "Transatlantic Relations during a Pandemic: Cooperation or Competition?," *Hot Takes*, Network for Strategic Analysis, 14 August 2020, https://ras-nsa.ca/publication/transatlantic-relations-during-a-pandemic-cooperation-or-competition.

11 Caterina Carta, "Making Sense of the Future: European Discourse on Global Power Transition," in *American's Allies and the Decline of US Hegemony*, ed. Justin Massie and Jonathan Paquin (London: Routledge, 2020), 194–212.

12 Fyodor Lukyanov, "Russian Dilemmas in a Multipolar World," *Journal of International Affairs* 63, no. 2 (2010): 30.

13 Elena Chebankova, "Russia's Idea of the Multipolar World Order: Origins and Main Dimensions," *Post-Soviet Affairs* 33, no. 3 (2017): 217–34.

14 Associated Press, "U.S. intel accurately predicted Russia's invasion plans. Did it matter?," MSNBC, 25 February 2022.

15 The head of France's Directorate of Military Intelligence, General Eric Vidaud, was sacked for that miscall.

16 Shane Harris et al., "Road to war: US struggled to convince allies, and Zelensky, of risk of invasion," *Washington Post*, 16 August 2022: https://www.washingtonpost.com/national-security/interactive/2022/ukraine-road-to-war.

16   Marco Munier, Thomas Juneau, and Justin Massie

17   Greg Miller and Catherine Belton, "Russia's spies misread Ukraine and misled Kremlin as war loomed," *Washington Post*, 19 August 2022, https://www.washingtonpost.com/world/interactive/2022/russia-fsb-intelligence-ukraine-war.

18   Katie Bo Lillis and Natasha Bertrand, "US intelligence community launches review following Ukraine and Afghanistan intel failings," CNN, 13 May 2022, https://www.cnn.com/2022/05/13/politics/us-intelligence-review-ukraine/index.html.

19   Julian E. Barnes and Helene Cooper, "Ukrainian officials drew on US intelligence to plan counteroffensive," *New York Times*, 10 September 2022, https://www.nytimes.com/2022/09/10/us/politics/ukraine-military-intelligence.html.

20   Kyiv Security Compact, *International Security Guarantees for Ukraine: Recommendations*, Kyiv, 13 September 2022, https://www.president.gov.ua/storage/j-files-storage/01/15/89/41fd0ec2d72259a561313370cee1be6e_1663050954.pdf.

21   See, for example, Mario Baumann, "'Propaganda Fights and 'Disinformation Campaigns': The Discourse on Information Warfare in Russia–West relations," *Contemporary Politics* 26, no. 3 (2020): 288–307; Alexander Lanoszka, "Disinformation in International Politics," *European Journal of International Security* 4 (2019): 227–48.

22   Paul Charon and Jean-Baptiste Jeangène Vilmer, *Les opérations d'influence chinoises: Un moment machiavélien* (Paris: Institut de recherche stratégique de l'École militaire, 2021), https://www.irsem.fr/rapport.html.

23   See Aaron Franklin Brantly, *The Decision to Attack: Military and Intelligence Cyber Decision-Making* (Athens: University of Georgia Press, 2016), 123; Michael Warner, "A Matter of Trust: Covert Action Reconsidered," *Studies in Intelligence* 63, no. 4 (2019): 33–41.

24   Peter Gill and Mark Phythian, *Intelligence in an Insecure World* (Cambridge: Polity Press, 2018), 120.

25   See Herbert Lin and Amy Zegart, eds., *Bytes, Bombes, and Spies: The Strategic Dimensions of Offensive Cyber Operations* (Washington, D.C.: Brookings Institution Press, 2018).

26   Jack A. Jarmon, *The New Era in US National Security: An Introduction to Emerging Threats and Challenges* (Lanham: Rowman and Littlefield, 2014), 136.

27   Adam Segal, "US Offensive Cyber Operations in a China–US Military Confrontation," in *Bytes, Bombs, and Spies: The Strategic Dimensions of Offensive Cyber Operations*, ed. Herbert Lin and Amy Zegart (Washington, D.C.: Brookings Institution Press, 2018), 319.

28   Jarmon, *The New Era in US National Security*, 139.

29   Stephanie Carvin, *Stand on Guard: Reassessing Threats to Canada's National Security* (Toronto: University of Toronto Press, 2021), 202–19.

30   David Vigneault, "Remarks by Director David Vigneault at the Economic Club of Canada," Canadian Security Intelligence Agency, 4 December 2018, https://www.canada.ca/en/security-intelligence-service/news/2018/12/remarks-by-director-david-vigneault-at-the-economic-club-of-canada.html.

31 Stephen Lander, "International Intelligence Cooperation: An Inside Perspective," *Cambridge Review of International Affairs* 17, no. 3 (2004): 481.

32 Austin Gee and Robert G. Patman, "Small State or Minor Power? New Zealand's Five Eyes Membership, Intelligence Reforms, and Wellington's Response to China's Growing Pacific Role," *Intelligence and National Security* 36, no. 1 (2021): 34–50.

33 Jan Ballast, "Merging Pillars, Changing Cultures: NATO and the Future of Intelligence Cooperation within the Alliance," *International Journal of Intelligence and CounterIntelligence* 31, no. 4 (2018): 735–36.

34 Adam D.M. Svendsen, "The Globalization of Intelligence since 9/11: The Optimization of Intelligence Liaison Arrangements," *International Journal of Intelligence and CounterIntelligence* 21, no. 4 (2008): 662.

35 Michael Herman, *Intelligence Power in Peace and War* (Cambridge: Cambridge University Press, 1996), 200.

36 Stéphane Lefebvre, "The Difficulties and Dilemmas of International Intelligence Cooperation," *International Journal of Intelligence and CounterIntelligence* 16, no. 4 (2003): 534.

37 Jeffrey T. Richelson, "The Calculus of Intelligence Cooperation," *International Journal of Intelligence and CounterIntelligence* 4, no. 3 (1990): 311.

38 Bradley F. Smith, *Sharing Secrets with Stalin: How the Allies Traded Intelligence 1941–1945* (Lawrence: University Press of Kansas, 1996).

39 Don Munton, "Intelligence Cooperation Meets International Studies Theory: Explaining Canadian Operations in Castro's Cuba," *Intelligence and National Security* 24, no. 1 (2009): 119–38.

40 Richelson, "The Calculus of Intelligence Cooperation," 311.

41 Smith, *Sharing Secrets with Stalin*, 11–12.

42 Martin Rudner, "Hunters and Gatherers: The Intelligence Coalition against Islamic Terrorism," *International Journal of Intelligence and CounterIntelligence* 17, no. 2 (2004): 198.

43 Rudner, "Hunters and Gatherers," 204–5.

44 For an extensive review of the potential costs of intelligence sharing, see Richelson, "The Calculus of Intelligence Cooperation," 315–18; Lefebvre, "The Difficulties and Dilemmas," 534–536.

45 Richelson, "The Calculus of Intelligence Cooperation," 315.

46 Jennifer E. Sims, "Foreign Intelligence Liaison: Devils, Deals, and Details," *International Journal of Intelligence and CounterIntelligence* 19, no. 2 (2006): 204.

47 "Whistleblower Edward Snowden's impact on Canada," *CBC News,* 21 February 2014, https://www.cbc.ca/news/canada/whistleblower-edward-snowden-s-impact -on-canada-1.2546624.

48 Lefebvre, "The Difficulties and Dilemmas," 534–35.

49 Pierre Morcos, "France's Shifting Relations with China," *War on the Rocks*, 4 January 2022, https://warontherocks.com/2022/01/frances-shifting-relations-with-china.

50 Morcos, "France's Shifting Relations with China," 533.

18   Marco Munier, Thomas Juneau, and Justin Massie

51 Timothy W. Crawford, "Intelligence Cooperation," in *The International Studies Encyclopedia*, ed. Robert A. Denemark (Oxford: Wiley Blackwell, 2010), 3790. See also Robert O. Keohane, "Reciprocity in International Relations," *International Organization* 40, no. 1 (1986): 1–27.
52 Crawford, "Intelligence Cooperation," 3791.
53 Lefebvre, "The Difficulties and Dilemmas," 532.
54 Lander, "International Intelligence Cooperation," 486; Herman, *Intelligence Power in Peace and War*, 215.
55 Hager Ben Jaffel, *Anglo-European Intelligence Cooperation: Britain in Europe, Europe in Britain* (London: Routledge, 2020).
56 Lefebvre, "The Difficulties and Dilemmas," 529; Chris Clough, "*Quid Pro Quo*: The Challenges of International Strategic Intelligence Cooperation," *International Journal of Intelligence and CounterIntelligence* 17, no. 4 (2004): 603.
57 Sims, "Foreign Intelligence Liaison," 204–6.
58 Rudner, "Hunters and Gatherers," 216.
59 Svendsen, "The Globalization of Intelligence since 9/11," 662.
60 Vestermark, "International Intelligence Liaison," 124–5; Rudner, "Hunters and Gatherers," 217.
61 Clough, "*Quid Pro Quo*," 608.
62 Svendsen, "The Globalization of Intelligence Since 9/11," 662.
63 See Adam D.M. Svendsen, "Developing International Intelligence Liaison against Islamic State: Approaching 'One for All and All for One'?" *International Journal of Intelligence and CounterIntelligence* 29, no. 2 (2016): 260–77.
64 Kenneth Waltz, *Theory of International Politics* (New York: McGraw-Hill, 1979).
65 Joseph M. Parent and Sebastian Rosato, "Balancing in Neorealism," *International Security* 40, no. 2 (2015): 56.

1 Intelligence Adaption from the Cold War to the Resurgence of Great Power Politics

DAMIEN VAN PUYVELDE

This chapter seeks to bridge the gap between Intelligence Studies and International Relations and show that similar assumptions about the role of the state drive orthodox intelligence scholarship and realist theories of international relations. The first section links the pre-eminence of the realist frame in intelligence scholarship to the significance of power competition during the Cold War, a period that fundamentally shaped modern intelligence organizations and affected the ways in which scholars have thought about intelligence. The second section explores the extent to which the fall of the Soviet Bloc, the rise of global interdependencies, and the requirements of counterterrorism have forced intelligence services to engage in organizational and operational changes. Some of these changes are best explained by moving beyond realism. The third section explores the relationship between intelligence and repertoires of power in the twenty-first century, a period marked by the prospect of a return of great power competition. The chapter argues that intelligence organizations operate in a world best described in terms of elements of realism and persistent liberal dynamics, with the result that they must engage in a broad spectrum of operations and practices that are sometimes difficult to reconcile. Building on the case of France, the final section asserts that if the challenges Western intelligence services face are comparable in nature, they are very different in their degree of significance. Importing lessons from international relations theory can help intelligence scholars understand the conditions and range of adaptations intelligence services are engaged in, but this effort requires a conceptually flexible approach that overcomes paradigmatic divides.

Intelligence Power in the Cold War Era

In 1949, intelligence practitioner Sherman Kent argued that intelligence aims to protect "the nation and its members from malefactors who are working to our national and individual hurt."[1] This view, which ties intelligence to national

20   Damien Van Puyvelde

interests, largely dominates the field of Intelligence Studies and echoes realist views that the international order is shaped by self-help and anarchy.[2]

Both realism and traditional approaches to Intelligence Studies take the nation-state as a referent object of security. Strategic intelligence is thus defined as "knowledge vital for national security" and identified as "a form of state power in its own right."[3] This view of intelligence builds on the assumption that the international system is shaped by state-based competition, which implies self-interested behaviours and cost–benefit calculus.[4] As former US officials Shulsky and Schmitt put it, "intelligence is part of a struggle between two countries ... as much a struggle with an enemy as is armed combat."[5] This realist conception of intelligence activities has solid historical foundations. From the former spies of the kings to the operational and strategic use of intelligence in armed conflict, the history of espionage maintains a rich relationship with international configurations based on power politics.[6] In the course of the twentieth century, technological progress and the growth in communication and mobilities helped turn intelligence into a vital tool for the defence of strategic interests.[7] Even if their significance for the outcome of the conflicts is still a matter of debate, signals intelligence (SIGINT), cryptography, and covert operations contributed to the war efforts during the two world wars of the twentieth century.[8] If those wars helped drive the emergence of permanent intelligence services, it was the Cold War that fostered their institutionalization and subsequent theorization as actors and vectors of power rivalries.

This state-centric approach tends to conceptualize intelligence in political and strategic terms and to overlook its inner administrative workings. Intelligence organizations have a degree of autonomy vis-à-vis the state and maintain interorganizational exchanges at the national and international levels that do not necessarily align with overt foreign policy positions. Developing a more nuanced understanding of the contemporary challenges faced by intelligence organizations requires a dialogue between strategic considerations and a range of phenomena that characterize (intelligence) administrations, including bureaucratization, rivalries, and individual and group psychology.[9]

Intelligence cooperation illustrates the challenge that realists face when trying to explain the existence of alliances and long-term relationships among states. Realists conceive of intelligence services as being primarily focused on the defence of their self-interests, so that they engage in cooperation only when it serves their own purposes. Realists give too much importance to short-term incentives[10] and tend to identify cost–benefit calculus as the driving factor in cooperation.[11] The bilateral and multilateral arrangements that have thrived among intelligence organizations as a result of counterterrorism policies – from the Club de Berne to the Maximator alliance – shed light on the nature and scale of this practice.[12] In the past two decades, this issue has attracted growing academic interest. Today, a burgeoning literature provides both enlightening theoretical frameworks and empirical cases for understanding the dynamics and history of intelligence cooperation.[13]

Scholarship on intelligence cooperation is one of the most promising approaches to linking the study of intelligence to that of international relations theory.[14] The pre-eminence of the realist frame in this body of literature is a result of various factors, including the significance of the Cold War in the study of intelligence. Modern intelligence organizations were shaped by the Cold War in ways that continue to affect how scholars and practitioners think about intelligence.

The antagonism between the United States and the Soviet Union turned intelligence into both an essential cog in the "organized knowledge" of contemporary Western states (intelligence as information) and a vehicle for deploying *power* policies through covert operations.[15] The realist theory of the balance of power asserts that states ensure their security by preventing other states from gaining enough power to dominate all the others. In line with this theory, the posture of nuclear deterrence and the ability to defend the integrity of the state rested for both great powers on the ability to collect reliable intelligence with which to assess the adversary's capabilities and monitor its behaviour.[16]

To protect one's own secrets goes hand in hand with the capacity to steal the other's secrets, especially those that can offer a strategic advantage. Power competition and the balance of power elevated the role of strategic intelligence.[17] Intelligence collection sources enabled Western services to monitor the evolution of the military capabilities of the Soviet Union and to sometimes provide, thanks to formidable sources, information of true strategic value.[18] One famous example is the use of U-2 spy plane imagery and agent in place Oleg Penkovsky to spot and analyse the deployment of Soviet missiles in Cuba in 1962.[19] These sources helped the United States monitor the Soviet Union's strategic posture and analyse Soviet intentions. In the end, the Cold War shaped intelligence organizations to such a great extent that a widely shared understanding of what intelligence is still consists in defining it by its function: to provide policymakers with raw or analysed information likely to help reduce the level of uncertainty in decision-making.[20]

The Cold War also helped establish covert action as a core element of the intelligence playbook.[21] Shaped by ideological confrontation between liberal democracies and people's democracies, the struggle to preserve and extend respective spheres of influence mobilized a whole spectrum of interventions, from propaganda to paramilitary actions.[22] The stakes associated with high-intensity conflicts in a context of nuclear deterrence pushed the two sides to invest resources in lower-intensity actions that they did not acknowledge publicly. From the overthrow of Mohammad Mossadegh in Iran in 1953 to the Bay of Pigs invasion in 1961 and the use of "active measures" by the Soviet Union and its satellites, covert action represented a key lever of power politics.[23] On both

22   Damien Van Puyvelde

sides of the Iron Curtain, the power rivalry of the Cold War placed intelligence at the forefront of the defence of strategic interests. Intelligence progressively became the actor, *par excellence*, of the realist theory of international relations.

The Cold War underscored the importance of the security apparatus for identifying and preventing adversary penetrations.[24] Historically, counter-intelligence developed together with the institutionalization of intelligence. In the context of the Cold War, however, counter-intelligence became even more central to intelligence organizations, and this had consequences for their daily functioning. Counter-intelligence consists in disrupting foreign espionage attempts and tends to reinforce the control of intelligence officers by internal security offices.[25] The intensification of security measures creates stovepipes and diffuses a collective mindset of suspicion and distrust. James Jesus Angleton, chief of counter-intelligence for the Central Intelligence Agency (CIA) from 1954 to 1974, epitomized the paranoia that arises from a tendency to see traitors and double agents everywhere.[26] The centrality of counter-intelligence materializes in the structures and daily work of intelligence administrations. The "need to know" principle means that the whole organization is structured so that intelligence officers only have access to the information and classified documents that directly relate to their working subject. This comes with a strict traceability of documents and of their readers, with strong respect for hierarchy and compartmentalization of units and the information to which they have access. The threat of foreign espionage that was so prominent in the context of the Cold War strengthened the "security state" and shaped the daily practices of modern intelligence organizations.[27]

Dialogue between intelligence and international relations theories has remained relatively scarce. Yet similar assumptions about the state drive orthodox intelligence scholarship and realist theories of international relations. The practice of espionage is historically associated with the state, and the Cold War shaped modern intelligence organizations in ways that reinforced the prominence of the state. The fall of the Soviet Union, however, brought about changes in intelligence organizations that challenged this paradigm. Specifically, the rising prominence of non-state actors in the post–Cold War era changed the ways in which intelligence organizations worked and consequently affected their study.

Intelligence in an Age of Terror

The end of the Cold War paved the way for an international order dominated by one superpower. A unipolar moment created room for the United States to propagate liberal political and economic norms and play the role of "global policeman."[28] The fall of the Soviet Union initially raised questions about the role of intelligence services. Some commentators openly wondered about the continuing need for government intelligence agencies. Yet as CIA director James Woolsey famously pointed out during his nomination hearing, the fall of the Soviet "dragon" had revealed "a jungle filled with a bewildering variety of poisonous snakes. And in many ways, the dragon was easier to keep track of."[29] Power had become more diffuse, threats had apparently multiplied, and scholarly understanding of security matters had broadened.[30]

The disappearance of the Soviet arch-enemy raised questions about the role and meaning of intelligence.[31] The sudden collapse of an international order dominated by power politics plunged many intelligence organizations in an identity crisis. In the Netherlands and the United States, some commentators even came to advocate for the outright dismantling of intelligence services.[32] The Cold War mindset was so deeply ingrained in intelligence organizations that their very purpose seemed to have vanished. Yet the void left by the fall of the Soviet Union was soon filled by a variety of threats. The proliferation of criminal networks and hubs of organized violence, persisting and emerging civil wars, and the rise of irregular warfare, as well as societal security concerns, broadened the security agenda.[33] This new disorder seemed to challenge the dominance of the realist paradigm.[34]

The accelerating pace of globalization in the late twentieth century brought about the emergence of an array of non-state actors in the international system. The liberalization of the world economy created new financial and economic opportunities but also hastened the breakdown of poorly governed states and stimulated the proliferation of grey zones and criminal networks.[35] Civil wars and uncontrolled areas created safe havens for armed groups, some of them driven by radical ideologies. The US embassy bombings in Dar es Salaam and Nairobi in 1998 sounded the alarm that radical jihadism was emerging as a threat.[36] The 9/11 attacks, now viewed by some as the greatest intelligence failure in US history, launched a two-decade-long "global war on terrorism," prompting Western intelligence services to reorganize themselves so as to focus their activities on counterterrorism.[37]

Technological progress and the rise of multinational corporations posed a further challenge to states, by weakening some of the levers of national authority and empowering a broader variety of interests.[38] Growing interdependencies have provided new types of non-state actors with the means to influence state behaviour. Developments in cyberspace, for example, have facilitated access to information sources, besides diffusing means of investigation that had been associated with state agencies during the Cold War. Investigative capacities associated with open source intelligence (OSINT) – epitomized by the investigative group Bellingcat – are eroding the dominance of government intelligence services in producing knowledge about threats to national and international security.[39] All of this illustrates what the liberal theorist James Rosenau calls the "revolution of individual capacities by technological democratization."[40]

24   Damien Van Puyvelde

Intelligence services have to adjust constantly to shifts in the threat environment. The rise of non-state actors has forced those services to restructure and change their processes in order to keep abreast of the fluid, decentralized, and adaptive threats they face. Because of the fluidity and porosity of non-state actors, information must flow quickly; the administrative silos inherited from the Cold War are no longer tenable. The "need to know" principle is vital to the protection of national security, but it implies practices of compartmentalization that make it harder to share and quickly disseminate information. Adapting to non-state threats requires bureaucratic decompartmentalization and efficiency in the exploitation and analysis of intelligence. In a sharp break from the collective psychology of generalized suspicion that marked the Cold War, the CIA rethought its organization in 2013, establishing *mission centres* designed to bring together technical and all-source analysts and operational officers.[41] These changes have been so consequential for the practices and inner workings of intelligence services that those services can now be viewed "less as exponents of realism and more as the smooth and experienced exemplar of liberal institutionalism."[42]

The transnational character of non-state actors has led to a dispersal of relevant information among competent administrations. In the United States in the lead-up to 9/11, and in France in November 2015, inadequate intelligence-sharing between services responsible for domestic intelligence and security (the FBI in the United States, the DGSI in France) and those in charge of foreign intelligence (CIA, DGSE) contributed to a more general failure to anticipate and thwart terrorist attacks. When threats are situated precisely at the junction of domestic and foreign intelligence, bureaucratic conflicts are more likely to cause problems. The same target – a senior terrorist leader, for example – can fall under different jurisdictions depending on whether that person is located in a conflict zone (military intelligence), in a foreign country (foreign intelligence), or within the country (domestic intelligence). Yet their status can change very quickly. The flexibility of modern threat actors has thus created a need for intelligence organizations to cooperate at the national and international levels in order to anticipate and counter threats to national security effectively.[43]

Intelligence cooperation has expanded over the past two decades so that it now constitutes a network of shared interests among services that realist representations had failed to explain. In an environment dominated by transnational threats, cooperating and circulating information is vital to national security.[44] In 2002, US Deputy Secretary of State Richard Armitage pointed out that "the most dramatic improvement in intelligence collection and sharing has come in bilateral cooperation with other nations."[45] Increased cooperation has provided researchers with a growing body of empirical material to study over the past two decades.[46] The international configuration of the past twenty years has challenged the dominance of the realist paradigm and provided opportunities for dialogue among intelligence scholars and liberal theorists.[47]

Economic globalization and the centrality of counterterrorism have transformed the paradigm on which state intelligence used to be based. The end of the Cold War not only encouraged a broadening of security matters[48] but also turned intelligence into a tool for managing insecurity. As David Omand notes, security is now defined by the "confidence that the risks, whether they result from organized threats or impersonal hazards, are being managed to a point where everyday life – and investment in the future – can safely continue."[49] Today, as the prospect of great power rivalry rises, intelligence organizations are being challenged to adapt once again.

Intelligence and Power in the Twenty-First Century

China's economic rise, Russia's displays of influence in the Middle East and Africa, and the growing assertiveness of regional powers such as Iran and Turkey all seem to point to a revival of power politics. The renewed prospect of power competition has reoriented intelligence priorities over the last few years, but the dynamics inherited from the post–Cold War order have not faded away. Intelligence organizations are now confronted by a broad spectrum of traditional and less traditional threats, which come with contradictory organizational imperatives.[50]

The Cold War rested on nuclear deterrence as well on technological and ideological competition. Power rivalries in the early twenty-first century rest on similar incentives, but their background is different. Today, economic interdependence, financial capacities, technological development, and cooperation in defence and intelligence matters are essential instruments of power.[51] Defending capitalist interests and conglomerates from predatory activities, property theft, and economic espionage has become a core activity for intelligence services. Economic intelligence is important because it contributes to technological development, which in turn determines intelligence capacities and brings about means of influence. Security and espionage issues related to the deployment of 5G perfectly illustrate this: the Chinese company Huawei is suspected of conducting espionage for the Chinese Communist Party (CCP) through its deployment of 5G technology in other countries.[52] Technological and digital development has evolved into a new arena in power politics. From information warfare to hacking and dedicated offensive capabilities, cyberspace has opened a new playground for states to project influence.[53]

The return of power competition has brought old-style challenges to intelligence services besides adding to the threats generated by high levels of social and economic interdependency. Radical Islamists using terrorism and irregular warfare will continue to preoccupy intelligence services in the coming years.[54] Organized crime, drug trafficking, and irregular migration will continue to draw the attention of intelligence and security services, especially in a context in which rising demographic challenges and intensified climate change are reinforcing their underlying causes.[55] The information age has broadened access to offensive and investigative capacities for an array of non-state actors, thus eroding the dominance of state intelligence services in producing and collecting information on security issues.[56] In the contemporary era, intelligence services need to adapt to short-term technological and media-driven incentives that affect policy-makers' expectations and, in turn, their operational capacities.[57]

While the return of power competition is breathing new life into the realist perspective in Intelligence Studies, liberal theorists' emphasis on states' dependencies on domestic and international civil societies remains highly relevant. The rise of China and the prospect of renewed power politics should not overshadow the persistence of transnational dynamics. Non-state actors, economic globalization, and digitization remain decisive features of the international order. The realist paradigm overlooks the broad range of features affecting the international landscape today, but that does not mean it is irrelevant. Paradigmatic divides tend to obscure the complexity of the challenges confronting states and their intelligence apparatuses, because they are often conceived in ways that are mutually exclusive.[58] The current international landscape to which intelligence organizations are adapting calls for the use of concepts from both realist and liberal theories. The renewed prospect of power politics requires a diversification of intelligence activities and of the ways scholars of Intelligence Studies and international relations construe their role.

Today's international environment, characterized as it is by the coexistence of realism and liberalism, has significant organizational and operational implications for intelligence services. Strategic competition in the international arena is bringing to the fore two key intelligence disciplines: counter-intelligence and political intelligence. Counter-intelligence was a cornerstone of intelligence activities during the Cold War; over the past two decades, however, human and financial capabilities devoted to it have substantially decreased and have been transferred to counterterrorism divisions. The return of power politics is realigning intelligence priorities, prompting a re-evaluation of how resources are allocated and organized internally. The threat from espionage, whether institutional, military, technological, or economic, is pushing intelligence services to once again strengthen their counter-intelligence and security capabilities. Similarly, political intelligence, which never disappeared, has returned to the fore. Developing a deep understanding of the organization, structure, and inner workings of adversarial states can help us understand their intentions, anticipate their strategic decisions, and direct intelligence collection capabilities accordingly. This realignment should provide policy-makers with the sound analysis and assessments they expect.

The types of intelligence needed in times of power rivalries differ from those needed in a context dominated by irregular threats. Counterterrorism tends to

Intelligence Adaption   27

orient requirements toward operational and tactical intelligence. SIGINT, IMINT, and Social Media Intelligence (SOCMINT) help in mapping networks and locating targets.[59] Counter-intelligence and political intelligence tend to rely more on human intelligence. The capacity to gather intelligence on the adversary's human intelligence operations often comes from one's own capacity for those same operations. Technological capabilities can help identify and control sources, but in the end, the level of access that human intelligence allows matters most. The challenge is that the closed, controlled nature of authoritarian regimes complicates access to human sources. In China, Russia, Iran, and even Turkey, intelligence work carried out from embassies by declared officers is almost impossible because of individual surveillance by local counter-intelligence services.[60] In these countries, developing HUMINT under non-official cover remains a highly perilous endeavour. Shifts in power competition affect the relative importance of the means agencies deploy to collect relevant intelligence.

The resurgence of great power competition has also affected intelligence analysis, most notably by reinvigorating policy-makers' interest in strategic and anticipatory intelligence. Strategic assessments differ markedly from the typical products of counterterrorism activities and are playing an increasingly prominent role in informing and eventually defining state policies against other states. Well-placed sources occasionally provide raw information that bears strategic significance, but good use of open-source intelligence (OSINT) corroborated by secret sources can provide authorities with more robust strategic assessments that help reduce the uncertainty they may face when making difficult foreign policy choices. Such strategic analysis has to be conducted while counterterrorism requirements remain high. Yet the practices associated with political and counterterrorism intelligence follow contradictory administrative imperatives. The need for both decompartmentalization and the rapid dissemination of information associated with counterterrorism is now deeply rooted in the organization and functioning of Western intelligence services. A whole generation of intelligence officers has been trained in and acculturated to administrative practices shaped by the centrality of counterterrorism. For this generation of professionals, adapting to the tightening of individual and collective security practices required by the return of state-led espionage is a fierce and frustrating challenge.

At the practical level, one can imagine that the target-centric work of counterterrorism intelligence easily adapts to the fastidious filing practices of counterintelligence. Yet the analytical capacities and expertise needed to produce strategic intelligence require more generalists and call for an adjustment of career paths. For intelligence organizations, power competition has added requirements to assess the long-term strategic intentions of adversarial states to the tactical intelligence and analysis needed in the fight against terrorism and non-state actors.[61] The character of intelligence collection and analysis, and even the profiles of intelligence officers, vary in each case. As a result, the

28   Damien Van Puyvelde

paradigm in which intelligence services now evolve leaves them torn between contradictory necessities.

Tough administrative challenges lie ahead to diversify intelligence activities and master an ever-wider operational spectrum. To embrace and theorize contemporary intelligence organization similarly requires scholars to bridge paradigmatic divides between schools of thought. To make this case for a broadening of the lens we use to study intelligence, the last section of this chapter zooms in on the case of France.

The Transformation of French Intelligence

The case of France offers an opportunity to test the relevance of the combined use of realism and liberalism developed in this chapter. Although Western intelligence services are preoccupied by roughly the same array of threats, national conditions mean that intelligence organizations adapt in their own ways to changes in their environment. The focus of much of the intelligence literature on the United States has limited our understanding of intelligence and supports the dominance of the realist understanding. Committed to defending its strategic autonomy even while relying heavily on cooperation, the French intelligence community provides a different empirical starting point for reflecting on intelligence and international relations.

The integration of intelligence into the French policy-making process is relatively new.[62] French public opinion and policy-makers have long distrusted and disdained their intelligence services.[63] The conviction of the Jewish army officer Alfred Dreyfus in 1894 on the basis of documents forged by the army's Deuxième Bureau is often used as a starting point to explain the French people's suspicion of intelligence.[64] After the Second World War, French communists accused the Free French intelligence services of the Bureau Central de Renseignement et d'Action (BCRA) of having been infiltrated during the war by the far-right paramilitary organization "La Cagoule."[65] This story, and the ruthless use of paramilitary forces during France's wars of decolonization in Indochina and Algeria, left a mark on French attitudes toward intelligence. Together with the activities of networks in France's African sphere of influence, this history reinforced the image of dirty tricks that continues to stain the national reputation of the French services to this day. Since then, scandals related to the assassination of an opponent of the Moroccan king Mehdi Ben Barka in 1965 and the failed covert action to sink Greenpeace's *Rainbow Warrior* in 1985 have only reinforced these representations.[66]

It is mainly the fight against terrorism that has pulled French intelligence out of this historic condition. Over the past decade, transnational threats have fostered the development of a French intelligence community. The French intelligence services had historically been divided between the Ministry of the

Interior and the Ministry of Defence; in recent years, the successive reforms of 2008,[67] 2011,[68] 2013, and 2015 have developed a French intelligence community and provided its activities with a comprehensive legal framework. The "normalization" of intelligence in France through successive laws can also be viewed as an effect of the diffusion of liberal democratic norms.

The centrality of counterterrorism and transnational threats has left a strong mark on the organization and practices of the French intelligence community. The DGSE and the DGSI are the products of a complex history that long precedes the post-Cold War era.[69] Since then, the transformation they have undergone has considerably affected the way they work. Waves of attacks by Salafi jihadists triggered the need for new intelligence legislations and massive investments in human resources and technical capabilities. The budget of the Direction Générale de la Sécurité Extérieure (DGSE), in charge of foreign intelligence, has grown from €460 million in 2008 to €880 million in 2021.[70] Between 2009 and 2015, the DGSE recruited 770 new employees, and its domestic intelligence counterpart, the DGSI, has recruited 1,200 new officers. The reliance on high-tech intelligence in counterterrorism has transformed approaches to analysis, which now focus on gathering information about specific individuals and networks rather than producing strategic assessments. The organizational culture of most French intelligence services is now shaped by a young generation of officers more familiar with and attuned to rapid information flow. Cooperation at the national level is now easier, as officers often move from one service to another.

The resurgence of power competition has required the French intelligence community to strike a balance between the political desire for strategic autonomy and requirements for international cooperation. For French intelligence, counterterrorism policies have brought about political recognition and underscored the need to cooperate nationally and internationally and to establish platforms for intelligence-sharing and joint operations.[71] It seems, though, that the international consensus over counterterrorism slowly diminishes as different threats arise. Renewed power rivalries are prompting a new transition phase for French intelligence services.

After twenty years of the "war on terrorism," the emergence of China is shifting the priorities of the US intelligence community.[72] The US "pivot to Asia" and the withdrawal from long wars in Afghanistan and Iraq are together relegating counterterrorism to fifth place on the list of US intelligence priorities.[73] By contrast, France's proximity to jihadists' theatres of operations in the Sahel and the Near East has compelled French services to maintain the fight against terrorism as a higher priority.[74] The US withdrawal from various zones of jihadist presence, where "their support to French operations is crucial," has reduced the high-tech intelligence collection capacities from which France long profited.[75] French intelligence services therefore need to compensate on their own for the loss of key intelligence collection platforms. Because the French community is smaller, it faces a much stronger need to prioritize than a great intelligence power like the United States. France cannot spy on all fronts and is not part of the Five Eyes. French intelligence organizations have to compromise to address the broad range of requirements spawned by an international order that has both realist and liberal characteristics.

The way France has organized its foreign intelligence agency illustrates its desire to achieve a form of strategic autonomy. France is one of the few great intelligence powers that has embedded its technical and cyber capabilities within its external service. The DGSE's Technical and Innovation Directorate (DTI) has been a key component of the French intelligence service since the Second World War. In the words of then Director General Bajolet, the DGSE is unique in "bringing together within the same service the collection capabilities (human, technical and operational), analysis, dissemination and covert action."[76] This "integrated model" provides a degree of autonomy that rests on its ability to keep technological collection capabilities close to the human intelligence operations of the Research and Operations Directorate (DRO). The most recent reform of the DGSE (2022) has reinforced this model, which enables greater coordination between intelligence collectors by facilitating integrated operational manoeuvres and more efficient sharing of information. This approach further facilitates organizational reactiveness to crises thanks to a dedicated monitoring centre; it also increases fluidity in the conduct of covert operations.[77] French intelligence officials view this "integrated" approach as a core institutional capacity to confront the resurgence of power politics. For the past two decades, policy-makers have consistently invested in the development of the intelligence community to support French autonomy in defence and security matters.[78]

French policy-makers are well aware that pursuing autonomy is not enough to confront contemporary threats; it must be accompanied by the development of strong bilateral cooperation and partnerships. The quest for autonomy through a strengthening of national capabilities is a logical consequence of the renewed power competition that realist theorists have long identified. Economic, technological, and human interdependencies, however, have grown so strong that the possibility of navigating alone cannot even be considered. During the Cold War, French foreign and defence policy sought to develop a "third way" between the United States and the Soviet Union. The collapse of the latter and the interdependencies that resulted from European integration and economic globalization have transformed France's strategic posture.[79] Given the renewed prospect of great power rivalry, bilateral and multilateral relations among intelligence services continue to be developed along the whole spectrum of cooperation.[80] From exchanges of analyses and assessments to the sharing of raw intelligence up to fully joint human intelligence operations, cooperation remains an operational necessity for French intelligence services.[81]

The broadening of the intelligence agenda, from counterterrorism to political intelligence, counter-intelligence, and cyber operations, is expanding international intelligence cooperation.

The information age has also increased the need for intelligence services to develop partnerships with the private sector.[82] Internal innovation is no longer sufficient to cope with the speed of technological development and increased volumes and diversity of data. French intelligence services are also affected by the rise of "big data." Like others, they have invested significant resources in the hardware and software necessary to leverage the ubiquity of data.[83] For example, in 2020 the Direction du Renseignement Militaire (DRM) benefited from a €3 million budget increase to develop partnerships with the private sector aimed at acquiring artificial intelligence capabilities for the exploitation of geospatial intelligence (GEOINT).[84] Technological developments are affecting all the layers of cyberspace and have confronted countries like France with the need to develop new cooperation with industry in a range of areas.[85]

While the French intelligence services have sought to strengthen their capacity for offensive cyber operations and the prevention of information manipulation,[86] they still need to adapt their organization to the ongoing reassertion of realist principles associated with the resurgence of power competition.[87] The war in Ukraine has vigorously demonstrated the need to strengthen the autonomous capacities of strategic analysis. Public communication strategies such as those used by the US and British intelligence communities in the context of the war in Ukraine are as much a way to expose the truth as a means to influence other countries' assessments and diplomatic choices. For France, independent intelligence collection and autonomous assessment capacities are crucial for the defence of strategic interests and the establishment of sound diplomatic policies. Caught between the needs for strategic autonomy and essential cooperation, French intelligence services are engaged in a quick and massive movement of modernization. Policy-makers will also need to adapt to evolving intelligence capabilities and use them to their fullest potential.

Conclusion

Power politics has shaped the rise and fall of intelligence services throughout history. Contemporary intelligence organizations are the heirs of the Cold War, and most of the literature dedicated to their study is built on realist assumptions about power. Yet the past two decades have brought about changes in the international order that have transformed the principles and functioning of Western intelligence organizations. After two decades of focus on terrorist threats, the resurgence of power politics should not be interpreted as a return to Cold War imperatives. Instead, this international configuration is bringing a new set of challenges for intelligence organizations, one that is already prompting them

32   Damien Van Puyvelde

to adapt to multiple and sometimes irreconcilable needs. Intelligence organizations face a global situation characterized by elements of realism together with the persistence of liberal dynamics, and this requires them to master a broad operational spectrum.

NOTES

1 Sherman Kent, *Strategic Intelligence for American World Policy* (Princeton: Princeton University Press, 1971), xxi.
2 Realism is not a unified theory. For an overview of the main assumptions associated with proponents of realism, see Jack Donnelly, *Realism and International Relations* (Cambridge: Cambridge University Press, 2009); and Christian Reus-Smit and Duncan Snidal, *The Oxford Handbook of International Relations* (Oxford: Oxford University Press, 2010). On the realist approach to intelligence cooperation, see Jennifer E. Sims, "Foreign Intelligence Liaison: Devils, Deals, and Details," *International Journal of Intelligence and CounterIntelligence* 19, no. 2 (2006): 196; and James Igoe Walsh, *The International Politics of Intelligence Sharing* (New York: Columbia University Press, 2009).
3 Michael Herman, *Intelligence Power in Peace and War* (Cambridge: Cambridge University Press, 1996).
4 Kenneth N. Waltz, *Realism and International Politics* (New York: Routledge 2008).
5 Abram N. Shulsky and Gary J. Schmitt, *Silent Warfare: Understanding the World of Intelligence* (Washington, D.C.: Potomac Books, 2002).
6 Christopher Andrew, *Secret World: A History of Intelligence* (New Haven: Yale University Press, 2018).
7 Michael Warner, *The Rise and Fall of Intelligence: An International Security History* (Washington, D.C.: Georgetown University Press, 2014).
8 David Kahn, "The Rise of Intelligence," *Foreign Affairs*, September–October 2006, https://www.foreignaffairs.com/articles/2006-09-01/rise-intelligence.
9 Sébastien Laurent, "Pour une autre histoire de l'État," *Vingtieme Siecle. Revue d'histoire* 83, no. 3 (2004): 180.
10 On alliance theory, see George Liska, *Nations in Alliance: The Limits of Interdependence* (Baltimore: Johns Hopkins University Press, 1962); Ole R. Holsti, P. Terrence Hopmann, and John D. Sullivan, *Unity and Disintegration in International Alliances: Comparative Studies* (Hoboken: John Wiley and Sons, 1973); and Stephen Walt, *The Origins of Alliances* (Ithaca: Cornell University Press, 1990).
11 Pepijn Tuinier, "Explaining the Depth and Breadth of International Intelligence Cooperation: Towards a Comprehensive Understanding," *Intelligence and National Security* 36, no. 1 (2021): 116–38.
12 Bart Jacobs, "Maximator: European Signals Intelligence Cooperation, from a Dutch Perspective," *Intelligence and National Security* 35, no. 5 (2020): 659–68; Aviva

Guttmann, "Combatting Terrorism in Europe: Euro-Israeli Counterterrorism Intelligence Cooperation in the *Club de Berne* (1971–1972)," *Intelligence and National Security* 33, no. 2 (2018): 158–75.

13 See, for example, Adam D.M. Svendsen, "Connecting Intelligence and Theory: Intelligence Liaison and International Relations," *Intelligence and National Security* 24, no. 5 (2009): 700–29; Walsh, *The International Politics of Intelligence Sharing*; Sophia Hoffman, "Circulation, not Cooperation: Towards a new Understanding of Intelligence Agencies as Transnationally Constituted Knowledge Providers," *Intelligence and National Security* 36, no. 6 (2021): 807–26.

14 Svendsen, "Connecting Intelligence and Theory."

15 Maurice Pearton, *The Knowledgeable State: Diplomacy, War, and Technology Since 1830* (New York: HarperCollins, 1982).

16 Richard Ned Lebow and Janice Gross Stein, "Deterrence and the Cold War," *Political Science Quarterly* 110, no. 2 (1995): 157–81.

17 Jefferson Adams, *Strategic Intelligence in the Cold War and Beyond* (New York: Routledge, 2014).

18 Andrew Rathmell, "Towards Postmodern Intelligence," *Intelligence and National Security* 17, no. 3 (2002): 87–104.

19 James G. Blight and David A. Welch, "The Cuban Missile Crisis and Intelligence Performance," *Intelligence and National Security* 13, no. 3 (1998): 173–217.

20 Loch K. Johnson, "National Security Intelligence," in *The Oxford Handbook of National Security Intelligence*, ed. Loch K. Johnson (Oxford: Oxford University Press, 2010).

21 Odd Arne Westad, *The Cold War: A World History* (New York: Basic Books, 2017).

22 On covert action, see Rory Cormac, *Disrupt and Deny: Spies, Special Forces, and the Secret Pursuit of British Foreign Policy* (Oxford: Oxford University Press, 2018); and Rory Cormac, Calder Walton, and Damien Van Puyvelde, "What Constitutes Successful Covert Action? Evaluating Unacknowledged Interventionism in Foreign Affairs," *Review of International Studies* 48, no. 1 (2022): 111–28.

23 John Prados, *Presidents' Secret Wars: CIA and Pentagon Covert Operations from World War II through the Persian Gulf* (Lanham: Rowman and Littlefield, 1996); Thomas Rid, *Active Measures: The Secret History of Disinformation and Political Warfare* (New York: Macmillan, 2020).

24 Stephen J. Cimbala, *The Politics of Warfare: The Great Powers in the Twentieth Century* (University Park: Pennsylvania State University Press 1996), 117.

25 Hank Prunckun, *Counterintelligence Theory and Practice* (Lanham: Rowman and Littlefield, 2019).

26 David Martin, *Wilderness of Mirrors: Intrigue, Deception, and the Secrets That Destroyed Two of the Cold War's Most Important Agents* (New York: Lyons Press, 2003); David Robarge, "Moles, Defectors, and Deceptions: James Angleton and CIA Counterintelligence," *Journal of Intelligence History* 3, no. 2 (2003): 21–49.

27 David Omand, *Securing the State* (London: Hurst, 2010).

34   Damien Van Puyvelde

28 Stephen Wertheim, *Tomorrow, the World: The Birth of US Global Supremacy* (Cambridge, MA: Harvard University Press, 2020).
29 James Woolsey, Testimony before the Select Committee on Intelligence of the United States Senate, 103rd Congress, 1st session, 2–3 February 1993, 76.
30 Loch K. Johnson, *Bomb, Bugs, Drugs, and Thugs: Intelligence and America's Quest for Security* (New York: NYU Press, 2002).
31 James Bamford, *Body of Secrets: Anatomy of the Ultra-Secret National Security Agency* (New York: Doubleday, 2001), 553.
32 Daniel Patrick Moynihan, *Secrecy: The American Experience* (New Haven: Yale University Press, 2012); Richard J. Aldrich, "Beyond the Vigilant State: Globalization and Intelligence," *Review of International Studies* 35 (2009): 889–902.
33 Keith Krause and Michael C. Williams, "Broadening the Agenda of Security Studies: Politics and Methods," *Mershon International Studies Review* 40, no. 2 (1996): 229–54.
34 Mary Kaldor, *New and Old Wars: Organized Violence in a Global Era* (Stanford: Stanford University Press, 2012).
35 Gaidz Minassian, *Zones grises – Quand les états perdent le contrôle* (Paris: CNRS Éditions, 2018).
36 Marc Hecker and Elie Tenenbaum, *La guerre de vingt ans. Djihadisme et contre-terrorisme au XXIème siècle* (Paris: Robert Laffont, 2021).
37 Gregory Treverton, *Intelligence for an Age of Terror* (Cambridge: Cambridge University Press, 2011).
38 Johan Eriksson and Giampiero Giacomello, *International Relations and Security in the Digital Age* (New York: Routledge, 2010).
39 Eliot Higgins, *We Are Bellingcat: An Intelligence Agency for the People* (London: Bloomsbury, 2021).
40 James Rosenau, *Turbulence in World Politics. A Theory of Change and Continuity* (Princeton: Princeton University Press, 1992); James Rosenau and J.P. Singh, *Information Technologies and Global Politics* (Albany: SUNY Press, 2002).
41 Stephen Slick, "Measuring Change at the CIA," *Foreign Policy*, 6 May 2016, https://foreignpolicy.com/2016/05/04/measuring-change-at-the-cia.
42 Richard Aldrich, "Dangerous Liaisons: Post-September 11 Intelligence Alliances," *Harvard International Review* 24, no. 3 (2002): 49–54.
43 Svendsen, "Connecting Intelligence and Theory"; Tuinier, "Explaining the Depth and Breadth."
44 William Rosenau, "Intelligence Cooperation and the War on Terror: Anglo-American Security Relations after 9/11," *Intelligence and National Security* 28, no. 6 (2013): 913–14.
45 Richard Armitage, testimony before the United States Senate Joint Intelligence Committee on Intelligence Sharing and the 11 September 2001 Attacks (19 September 2002), quoted in Derek S. Reveron, "Old Allies, New Friends: Intelligence-Sharing in the War on Terror," *Orbis* 50, no. 3 (2006): 455.

46 For a recent addition to the literature on bilateral cooperation, see Michael Smith, *The Real Special Relationship* (London: Simon and Schuster, 2022). For a more original case of bilateral cooperation, see, for example, Sobukwe Odinga, "'We recommend compliance': Bargaining and Leverage in Ethiopian–US Intelligence Cooperation," *Review of African Political Economy* 44, no. 153 (2017): 432–48.

47 Tuinier, "Explaining the Depth and Breadth."

48 Herman, *Intelligence Power in Peace and War*, 125.

49 Omand, *Securing the State*, 9.

50 Office of the Director of National Intelligence, *2021 Annual Threat Assessment of the U.S. Intelligence Community*, https://www.dni.gov/index.php/newsroom /reports-publications/reports-publications-2021/item/2204-2021-annual-threat -assessment-of-the-u-s-intelligence-community.

51 Pierre Buhler, *La puissance au XXIème siècle* (Paris: CNRS Éditions, 2019).

52 Calder Walton, "China Will Use Huawei to Spy Because So Would You," *Foreign Policy*, 14 July 2020, https://foreignpolicy.com/2020/07/14/britain-boris-johnson -china-will-use-huawei-to-spy-because-so-would-you.

53 Damien Van Puyvelde and Aaron Brantly, *Cybersecurity: Politics, Governance and Conflict in Cyberspace* (Cambridge: Polity, 2019).

54 Coordination nationale du renseignement et de la lutte antiterroriste, *Stratégie Nationale du Renseignement*, 2019, https://www.sgdsn.gouv.fr/publications /strategie-nationale-du-renseignement-juillet-2019.

55 Bertrand Badie, *Inter-socialités* (Paris: Éditions CNRS, 2020).

56 Paul Charon, Fabien Laurençon, and Clément Renault, "OSINT: développement & usages dans la pratique du renseignement," *Hérodote* 186 (2022).

57 Joshua Rovner, "Think Small: Why the Intelligence Community Should Do Less about New Threats," *War on the Rocks*, 16 June 2021, https://warontherocks.com/2021/06 /think-small-why-the-intelligence-community-should-do-less-about-new-threats.

58 Raymond Aron, *Peace and War: A Theory of International Relations* (Piscataway: Transaction, 2003).

59 Robert M. Clark, *Intelligence Analysis. A Target-Centric Approach* (Washington, D.C.: CQ Press, 2007).

60 Kyle S. Cunliffe, "Hard Target Espionage in the Information Era: New Challenges for the Second Oldest Profession," *Intelligence and National Security* 36, no. 7 (2021): 1018–34.

61 Michael Handel, "Intelligence and the Problem of Strategic Surprise," *Journal of Strategic Studies* 7, no. 3 (1984): 229–81.

62 Olivier Chopin, "Intelligence Reform and the Transformation of the State: The End of a French Exception," *Journal of Strategic Studies* 40, no. 4 (2017): 532–53; Olivier Forcade and Bertrand Warusfel, *Le droit du renseignement*, Actes de Colloque de l'Académie du renseignement (La documentation française, 2020).

63 Jean Guisnel, Rémy Kauffer, and Roger Faligot, *Histoire politique des services secrets français* (Paris: La découverte, 2013).

36   Damien Van Puyvelde

64   Gérald Arboit, "Les services spéciaux du temps de l'affaire Dreyfus," *Après-demain* 37, no. 1 (2016): 10–11.

65   Sébastien Albertelli, *Les services secrets du Général de Gaulle* (Paris: Perrin, 2009).

66   Jean-Christophe Notin, *Le maître du secret* (Paris: Tallandier édition, 2018).

67   Décret n° 2008–609 du 27 juin 2008 relatif aux missions et à l'organisation de la direction centrale du renseignement intérieur, https://www.legifrance.gouv.fr/loda /id/JORFTEXT000019078545/.

68   Arrêté du 9 mai 2011 pris en application du troisième alinéa du I de l'article L. 2371–1 du code de la défense, https://www.legifrance.gouv.fr/loda/id /JORFTEXT000023976427/2021-07-20/.

69   Guisnel, Kauffer, and Faligot, *Histoire politique des services secrets français*.

70   Projet de loi de finances pour 2021 : Défense : Environnement et prospective de la politique de défense, *Sénat*, 19 November 2020, http://www.senat.fr/rap/a20-140 -5/a20-140-51.pdf.

71   Direction générale de la sécurité intérieure, "DGSI, chef de file de la lutte antiterroriste en France," *Revue Défense Nationale* 813, no. 8 (2018): 20–2.

72   Peter Martin and Nick Wadhams, "CIA Weighs Creating Special China Unit in Bid to Out-Spy Beijing," *Bloomberg*, 12 August 2021, https://www.bloomberg.com /news/articles/2021-08-12/cia-weighs-creating-special-china-unit-in-bid-to-out -spy-beijing.

73   "Transcript: NPR's Full Conversation with CIA Director William Burns," *NPR* 22 July 2021, https://www.npr.org/2021/07/22/1017900583/transcript-nprs-full -conversation-with-cia-director-william-burns.

74   Coordonnateur National du Renseignement et de la lutte antiterroriste (CNRLT), *Stratégie Nationale du Renseignement*, July 2019, https://www.economie.gouv.fr /files/20190703-cnrlt-np-strategie-nationale-renseignement.pdf?v=1570010606.

75   See, for instance ,Philippe Chapleau, "Sahel: les soutiens britannique et américain à Barkhane maintenus pour l'instant," *Ouest-France,* 24 April 2020; "Florence Parly à Washington pour retenir les Américains dans le Sahel," *Le Point*, 27 January 2020, https://www.lepoint.fr/afrique/florence-parly-a-washington-pour-retenir-les -americains-dans-le-sahel-27-01-2020-2359821_3826.php.

76   Bernard Bajolet, "La DGSE, modèle français d'intégration," *l'ENA hors les murs*, no. 442 (2014).

77   Arrêté du 10 mars 2015 portant organisation de la direction générale de la sécurité extérieure, https://www.legifrance.gouv.fr/loda/id/JORFTEXT000030375775. The DGSE was reorganized in 2022: Arrêté du 13 juillet 2022 portant organisation de la direction générale de la sécurité extérieure, https://www.legifrance.gouv.fr/jorf/id /JORFTEXT000046048881.

78   Alexandre Papaemmanuel and Floran Vadillo, *Les espions de l'Elysée. Le président et les services de renseignement* (Paris: Tallandier, 2019).

79   Alice Pannier and Olivier Schmitt, *French Defence Policy Since the End of the Cold War* (New York: Routledge, 2020).

80 Yvan Lledo-Ferrer, "La coopération internationale, une source de renseignement à part entière?," *Revue Défense Nationale* 842 (2021): 13–17.

81 Benjamin Oudet, "Les coopérations internationales françaises de renseignement face aux nouvelles menaces," *Les Champs de Mars* 30, no. 1 (2018): 27–35.

82 Damien Van Puyvelde, *Outsourcing US intelligence: Contractors and Government Accountability* (Edinburgh: Edinburgh University Press, 2019).

83 Damien Van Puyvelde, Stephen Coulthart, and M. Shahriar Hossain, "Beyond the Buzzword: Big Data and National Security Decision-Making," *International Affairs* 93, no. 6 (2017): 1397–416.

84 Laurent Lagneau, *Le renseignement militaire muscle ses capacités d'analyse de l'imagerie satellitaire avec l'intelligence artificielle*, Opex360, 8 July 2021, http://www.opex360.com/2021/07/08/le-renseignement-militaire-muscle-ses-capacites-danalyse-de-limagerie-satellitaire-avec-lintelligence-artificielle.

85 US Department of State, "United States and France Strengthen Relationship on Cyber Policy," Office of the Spokesperson, 9 February 2018, https://2017-2021.state.gov/united-states-and-france-strengthen-relationship-on-cyber-policy/index.html.

86 Ministère des Armées, "Le commandement de la cyberdéfense," État-Major des Armées, 26 January 2022, https://archives.defense.gouv.fr/ema/nos-organismes/comcyber/le-commandement-de-la-cyberdefense/comcyber.html.

87 Thibault Menut, "L'Agence nationale de lutte contre les manipulations de l'information, nouvelle arme anti-fake news du gouvernement," *Portail de l'IE*, 3 June 2021, https://portail-ie.fr/short/2873/lagence-nationale-de-lutte-contre-les-manipulations-de-linformation-nouvelle-arme-anti-fake-news-du-gouvernement.

2 Intelligence Demands Linked to European Autonomy in Trade, Technology, and Security

BJÖRN FÄGERSTEN

The European Union (EU) has long had ambitions to achieve "strategic autonomy," often understood as freedom of action and the capacity to chart its own course in foreign and security policy.[1] In practice, the nub of the desired autonomy has been seen in relation to the United States and its desire for Europe's loyalty. In response to a lack of US commitment, especially during the Trump administration, the UK withdrawal from the EU, and the Russian invasion of Ukraine, EU member-states have stepped up their ambitions with regard to their security capacity and autonomy. The 2016 EU Global Strategy (EUGS) made this goal public, albeit without a clear definition. This level of ambition places high demands on the capacity to provide independent intelligence for member-states at the national level and for the EU at the institutional level. As China's power increases, the unipolar era is ending at the same time as great power rivalry is increasing in the economic sphere. In this geo-economic era, during which states are competing on trade, innovation, and data flows, the ambition for strategic autonomy or sovereignty has taken on a broader meaning than just traditional security policy. In light of all this, the present chapter seeks to identify the intelligence needs caused by the objective of strategic autonomy, examine how the EU currently meets these needs, and analyse the drivers of and obstacles to expanded intelligence capacity. The main argument presented here is that multipolarity and geo-economic rivalry have together encouraged greater European intelligence cooperation due to a recognized need for more strategic autonomy.

Power, Autonomy, and Intelligence

Knowledge is power, or at least a prerequisite for being able to exercise power effectively. Thus, states as well as organizations have always tried to inform themselves about the outside world and the interests of other states and organizations. This pursuit of knowledge has been of particular relevance in the

40   Björn Fägersten

field of security policy, where other actors are expected to hide their intentions, hinder others' search for knowledge, and be hostile to one another. Intelligence activities aim precisely to gather information and close knowledge gaps on issues related to security and vital interests. Such activities are closely linked to state sovereignty, in the sense of a state controlling its own territory and future.

Until the beginning of the twenty-first century, the EU operated without any real intelligence capacity. The EU was only indirectly involved in security policy, and it functioned primarily as a platform for cooperation, not as an actor aiming to project conventional power. Over time, however, ambitions have grown for the EU to become an actor in its own right – first in trade policy, later in foreign policy, and now in security policy.[2] When in the late 1990s the EU was given a role in international crisis management through the "Petersberg tasks," it was a question of activity without any real autonomy – a capacity that could be used when other entities, the EU member-states, and the United States could agree on its desirability. The limitations of this arrangement were clear. It was time-consuming, for unity had to be reached within the EU, and dependence on the United States and its capabilities made it difficult for Europe to take more responsibility for security in its own region. The wars in the Balkans illustrated the impotence of European countries. At the same time, the Gulf War exposed the EU's dependence on – and inferiority to – the United States when it came to intelligence machinery. The solution – a compromise between Atlanticists and champions of greater European autonomy, as represented by the United Kingdom and France, respectively – was formulated in the 1998 Saint-Malo Declaration. The goal, which was later followed up in formal EU documents, was for the EU to be vested with a certain capacity to carry out operations without assistance, that is, with a certain degree of autonomy. This turn-of-the-century ambition for Europe to have a role and responsibilities in regional crisis management, combined with increasingly ambitious foreign policy coordination under a new EU High Representative (HR) for the Common Foreign and Security Policy/Secretary General of the Council of the European Union, was the clearest elaboration of the need for improved intelligence within the EU. This limited autonomy and the intelligence requirements it generated must therefore be seen in relation to both the United States and the EU member-states. The EU could only become an actor with some autonomy if space were freed up in "both directions." (This is discussed in depth in the next section.)

The EU's security policy development since 2000 has largely been about achieving this limited form of autonomy, and it has had varying degrees of success in doing so. Questions about what kinds of initiatives the EU should be able to lead and with what material capacity they should be carried out have dominated the agenda. However, with a weak US commitment to Europe during the Trump years, a sceptical UK leaving the EU, and an increasingly aggressive Russia, the late 2010s saw a qualitatively higher level of ambition.

The EU started out striving for an autonomous capacity for smaller crisis management efforts; its goal now is strategic autonomy in a much broader sense. Note that it is in this context that politicians like French president Emmanuel Macron speak of "European sovereignty," a concept that includes many more policy areas than have traditionally been discussed under the heading of autonomy. This broader yet adjacent notion of European sovereignty has been picked up by Germany's Olaf Scholz as well as by European Commission (EC) president Ursula von der Leyen in her 2022 State of the Union address to the European Parliament.[3] Given how the relatively limited ambitions for autonomy have so far been driving and shaping the EU's intelligence capacity, there is every reason to assume that today's higher ambitions will entail significant intelligence needs in the future.

The next section examines the concept of strategic autonomy: the implications of the EU's new objectives, their basic elements and the intelligence needs they create, and whether the EU's current intelligence capabilities fill these needs and or leave gaps. The chapter then elaborates on some of the problems facing the EU in creating further cooperation in an era of growing great power competition.

The Anatomy of European Autonomy

Within the EU, the ambition for autonomy increased significantly throughout the 2010s. The EUGS notes that "an appropriate level of ambition and strategic autonomy is important for Europe's ability to promote peace and security within and beyond its borders."[4] The Russian invasion of Ukraine and the threat this poses for Europe's security order has further increased the need for European capacities. EC president Ursula von der Leyen promised to transform the EU into a "geopolitical" actor in which policies on trade, technology, and defence and security would all be interconnected. This clearly has placed new demands on the EU's capabilities and ambitions.

The debate over autonomy and Europe's ability to act independently in the global arena has been ongoing since the 1950s, but with the EUGS – and in the light of a US administration focusing elsewhere, Brexit, and the increasingly unstable geopolitical situation with a rising China and a resurgent Russia – that debate has hardly weakened. Yet despite this long political debate and the fact that the term appears in official documents with increasing frequency, there is still no clear and unambiguous definition of strategic autonomy.

What does strategic autonomy mean in an EU context? Autonomy is from the Greek *auto*, "self," and *nomos*, "rules, norms, or order." The self in this case is Europe as an actor, often in the form of the EU. However, Brexit has led more people – even within the EU – to refer to European strategic autonomy, as the UK's capacity is viewed as essential to Europe's ability to establish norms, rules, and order for Europeans.

The capacity to act, sometimes referred to as "actorness," is fundamental to autonomy. To achieve autonomy, however, freedom of action must be added to the capacity for action. The study of international relations has shown how this freedom of action is often limited by hierarchies and commitments to other parties, for example within military alliances[5] or in relation to a hegemon.[6] For most actors, there is some form of conflict between freedom and the capacity to act where, for example, collective action can strengthen capacity but also limit individual freedom. For both the EU and Europe as a whole, freedom of action is limited from two sides: partly by the EU member-states, which set limits on the EU's role through the level of delegation, and partly by the United States, which has long had a decisive influence on the capacity of the EU and the degree of freedom it has been able to strive for, and which has opposed a more independent military role for the EU. Today, it is also useful to discuss the extent to which other great powers, in particular China, are limiting Europe's autonomy by affecting its capacity and freedom.

In recent years, the EU has shifted the focus of its autonomy from a capacity to act to independence and self-sufficiency. The reasons can be found in the unmet promises of globalization: regime convergence toward liberal democracy did not take place, and links among societies – the connectivity that was believed to drive regime change – have now been weaponized in world politics. The facilitators of liberal globalization have thus become the vulnerabilities of the geo-economic era. In both China and the United States, policies of decoupling have been set in motion to manage these vulnerabilities, especially in areas of critical technology. Other actors find it difficult to defend themselves, and within the EU this tendency has been pushed by already existing protectionist currents. The result is a movement in which autonomy is defined less and less as self-empowerment and more and more as self-sufficiency. But independence is not the same as influence. For the EU, which has built much of its political influence on having economic, political, scientific, and even intelligence interactions with other systems, an autonomy defined predominantly as independence risks reducing the real potential for influence over both its own and others' destinies.

Lastly, under what conditions can European autonomy be called strategic? Strategy, from the Greek *stratiyeia*, is based on the Greek words for "army" and "command." Strategy is, in a figurative sense, basically about adapting goals and means in order to secure vital interests in relation to other actors. This in turn means that a strategic actor must know both its own interests and those of others and allow these insights to inform its choices. It is the interplay between knowledge of one's own preconditions and the conditions of the outside world, together with the extent to which this understanding affects one's goals and means, that makes an actor strategic.[7]

Intelligence Demands Linked to European Autonomy   43

All in all, the concept of strategic autonomy emphasizes an actor's ability first and foremost to define its own priorities and, based on these, to make its own choices and implement its own intentions in the global arena.

Strategic Autonomy as a Driver of European Intelligence in the Past

Over the last two decades, the quest for autonomy in the security field has been an important driver of European intelligence capacities and European intelligence cooperation.

The inability of Europeans to deal with the situation in the former Yugoslavia provided a tense background to the Franco-British security summit in Saint-Malo in 1998, which can clearly be seen as the start of the developments in defence and security policy that the EU initiated in the late 1990s.[8] The Saint-Malo Declaration emphasizes the need for the EU to achieve operational autonomy in the field of defence policy and explicitly links this to the need for the EU "to be provided with appropriate structures and capabilities for intelligence analysis and the ability of relevant strategic planning."[9] Subsequent EU meetings have rearticulated this, and the member-states have since formulated the capabilities to be created by the EU and the types of operations it could carry out on the basis of these capabilities.[10]

These ambitions for autonomous capacity in security and defence led to the establishment of two different units working on intelligence analysis: the EU Intelligence Analysis Centre (IntCen) and the EU Military Staff Intelligence Directorate (IntDir). Together they form the Single Intelligence Analysis Capacity (SIAC). These two entities have no mandate to carry out traditional intelligence gathering and instead rely primarily on the information provided by member-states' intelligence and security services. IntCen and IntDir also use the material produced by the EU's various delegations and bodies, satellite and geospatial intelligence from its satellite centre, open source material, and, to some extent also, observations made on-site during various types of EU activities.[11]

IntDir's military intelligence activities were established following the conclusions of the Cologne European Council in 1999. The unit provides strategic intelligence information and an early warning system for a higher degree of common awareness and assessment. This was in response to the EU's increasingly ambitious steps in foreign and security policy. IntCen, in turn, was launched informally in 1999 as a support to Javier Solana, the HR, whose position had been created by the Treaty of Amsterdam. As EU security policy competencies grew and the European Security and Defence Policy[12] approached operational status, a number of member-states chose to start sharing intelligence with the HR in the summer of 2001.

In 2002 and 2003, the United Kingdom, France, Germany, the Netherlands, and Sweden seconded intelligence analysts to the unit. These member-states were invited to do this by Javier Solana, based on their size, their intelligence capabilities, and their strong bilateral relations. IntCen (then known as SitCen) was declared

44 Björn Fägersten

operational by the EU in January 2003.[13] Both IntCen and IntDir have grown substantially since then. The establishment of intelligence capacity in the foreign and security policy realm clearly related to the demands generated by ambitions for a more potent and autonomous European foreign and security policy.

European intelligence cooperation in relation to counterterrorism has also been motivated by ambitions for autonomy. The EU Agency for Law Enforcement Cooperation (Europol) is the main body for intelligence cooperation related to serious international crime, but it also handles intelligence information related to terrorism. Its mission was strengthened following the terrorist attacks of 9/11, the Madrid bombings of 2004, and the London bombings of 2005.[14] The driving force behind the collaboration was the perceived increased threat levels, which could not be adequately handled unilaterally. Similarly, the asymmetry between US and European intelligence capabilities and political pressure emanating from the United States after September 2001 accelerated the push for enhanced cooperation within Europol.

A similar logic applies to counterterrorism intelligence cooperation outside of the EU. One format for that cooperation is the multilateral Counterterrorism Group (CTG), which was established after 9/11. This group has its background in the Club de Berne, which was founded in the 1970s as a closed forum for all the EU member-states', Norway's, and Switzerland's intelligence chiefs to meet and discuss issues related to European intelligence cooperation. Increased demands to strengthen this cooperation after September 2001 led the members of the Club de Berne to create the CTG, among other things to strengthen institutional ties with the EU. Some EU member-states at the time also proposed the creation of a "European CIA." However, such proposals were rejected by the vast majority of member-states, and instead the formal link between the CTG and IntCen was established by the CTG setting up a unit within IntCen. Representatives of the CTG often participate in various EU forums, such COREPER, when terrorism is on the agenda. Above all, this development was driven by the threats from international terrorism and the ambition to be good yet independent partners to the United States in the fight against terrorism.[15]

In sum, intelligence cooperation in support of European counterterrorism efforts was driven by a rising threat that needed to be managed at a joint level and with a level of autonomy. Europeans wanted to cooperate with the Americans but have access to their own threat analysis and avoid being too dependent on US capacity.

Intelligence Demands of Expanded European Autonomy: Economy, Technology, Operations, and Decisions

The previous sections discussed the concept of strategic autonomy and how the different ambitions for autonomy in the security sphere have been important in the development of current European intelligence capacities. The current debate on the need for increased levels of European autonomy covers several policy areas, capacities, and vulnerabilities.

Historically, the focus of a state's autonomy has been material military capacity. Today, types of power appear to be less interchangeable as, for example, military power cannot readily be converted into economic, political, or scientific influence.[16] This means that different kinds of capacity – as well as, for that matter, a degree of freedom of action – are required to achieve autonomy in different areas.

To understand the intelligence requirements created by the EU's quest for strategic autonomy, four subcategories are analysed below: decision autonomy, operational autonomy, economic autonomy, and technological autonomy. This division, or variants of it, reappears in the more general literature on strategic autonomy.[17] While it may be a little simplistic, one could say that decision-making autonomy requires more in terms of a degree of freedom, while operational, technological, and economic autonomy are more capacity-intensive.

Decision Autonomy

For decision-making autonomy to exist, an actor must have an opportunity to make politically sensitive decisions, and there must be freedom of action on the basis of those decisions. The ambition to achieve European decision-making autonomy is in many ways defining for intelligence needs. Historically, the desire to create more autonomy and thus the ability to make independent decisions, often in relation to various crises in Europe's immediate area, have been the driving forces behind the EU's attempts to build more joint intelligence capacity. Examples of this are the wars in Yugoslavia in the 1990s, 9/11, the terrorist attacks in Madrid and London in 2004 and 2005 respectively, and the wave of terrorism that hit Europe in 2015–17. European intelligence cooperation hence seeks the capability to position the EU independently.[18] But even with considerable capabilities, this is not without difficulties. The failure of European intelligence agencies to anticipate the Russian invasion of Ukraine in 2022 and thereby allow for timely and concerted action illustrates the problems that even well-resourced agencies can encounter.

A primary task for an actor seeking political autonomy is to be able to identify which vital interests are to be promoted and defended. This is mainly a task at the political level, but national intelligence and security services often have a role in identifying interests, activities worthy of protection, and critical dependencies. To this introspective intelligence task can be added managing the means of pressure used by external actors. In the case of Europe, Russian influence and hybrid operations, and the work of European intelligence services in counteracting these, can serve as examples of intelligence supporting decision autonomy. Another example is the explicit threat by the United States to limit the exchange of intelligence with European states that allow the Chinese entity Huawei to participate in the construction of 5G networks. Here, it is dependence on US information that constitutes an obstacle to decision-making capacity and thus a vulnerability to pressure.

Decision autonomy also requires external intelligence work to stay informed about the outside world – its trends, tendencies, and events – in accordance with one's own interests. This also includes other actors' preferences and possible courses of action in an overarching sector, in what is often referred to as strategic analysis of the surrounding world. Overall, the EU's political autonomy depends on a range of intelligence-related capabilities, both internal and external. These can be generated by exchanges between national actors or the building up of common resources.

Operational Autonomy

Operational autonomy is about the ability to plan and implement decisions without the support of an outside party. It is basically a matter of being able *de facto* to implement operational security policy in various forms and thus relies heavily on an actor's capacity to act. Just as in the case of decision autonomy, this form of autonomy requires an analysis of the surrounding world. However, it is often of a more specific and time-limited nature.

One recent European operation that raises issues linked to operational autonomy is the intervention in Libya in 2011, where Europe's autonomy was limited by its intelligence capabilities. Following the operation, the British government was criticized, among other things, for starting the operation without "reliable intelligence information" about the situation in Libya.[19]

The operation in Libya was also marked by the difficulty the various participating states had with sharing intelligence. Among other things, French pilots did not have access to US aerial photographs and situation reports prior to operations against Libyan targets. This led to rising frustration and mistrust among the various participants.[20]

Discussion of operational autonomy has traditionally concerned the EU's capacity for crisis management operations, but other forms of security policy operations are also captured by the concept. One example, which also has internal implications, is hybrid threats, where coordinated or joint intelligence is crucial not only in terms of warnings and threat analysis, but also in more operational events, regardless of whether it is physical or digital threats that need to be dealt with. Overall, operational autonomy requires access to high-quality intelligence material. Such information must often have a high degree of timeliness and must be quickly updatable, in contrast to the more strategic analyses, which are the basis for longer-term political decision-making.

Economic Autonomy

The geo-economic rivalries that characterize our times have made European politicians eager to achieve greater autonomy in the economic and trade domains as well. This could be about making the EU less vulnerable to risks along global supply chains, securing access to foreign goods and services, avoiding certain products being exported to third countries, or blocking others from trading with and/or accessing the European market through sanctions or by screening foreign direct investment (FDI). All of these ambitions place possible demands on intelligence. They can mean assisting with screening foreign direct investment, where China is currently the focus, and its possible political connections, or deciding which aspects of technology and innovation are particularly worthy of protection or unsuitable for export.

Another concrete example of an intelligence capacity linked to economic autonomy is the EU's ability to impose sanctions on various actors in the world, currently on display in relation to Russia. The EU Sanctions Tool falls under the Common Foreign and Security Policy (CFSP), where both EU member-states and the HR have an opportunity to propose sanctions. However, the European External Action Service (EEAS) plays a key role in identifying, among other things, the types of measures that might be appropriate and which actors would be affected by the sanctions. Clearly, the EEAS has a clear influence on the introduction of sanctions through its coordinating and proposing roles.[21] The EU's foreign service is thus dependent on its intelligence capacity, especially when the EU employs targeted sanctions, such as the freezing of assets or visa bans, against individuals.[22] The ability to withstand and deter others' sanctions is also a key aspect of economic autonomy, and this demands intelligence for attribution and targeted economic response.

Technological Autonomy

A final component of strategic autonomy involves an actor's control over critical digital and technological systems. As EU Commissioner Thierry Breton stated: "Our capacity to take our destiny in our own hands boils down essentially to the mastery of tomorrow's technologies."[23] The ability to develop, acquire, deploy, and protect critical infrastructure is part of European strategic autonomy, for the use of critical infrastructure to gather information and control other actors is an increasingly important factor in today's geo-economic era.[24] Like operational autonomy, this form of autonomy requires a lot of capacity. The goal of autonomy in the technical field is emphasized in the Global Strategy, where it is stated that "a sustainable, innovative and competitive European defence industry is necessary for Europe's strategic autonomy and for a credible common security and defence policy."[25] Josep Borrell, the EU High Representative of the Union for Foreign Affairs and Security Policy/Vice President of the European Commission (HR/VP), has also argued that trade and technology issues must now be seen as foreign policy issues in which the EU must take strong initiatives.[26] Similar points are being made by German and French politicians, often under the term European digital sovereignty, which alludes to the industrial capacity dimension.

What are the industrial and technological aspects of autonomy, and what do they require of intelligence capacity? In a broader interpretation of technological autonomy, where not just the defence industry but an actor's entire critical infrastructure is taken into account, intelligence services have a very important role to play. Protection of digital infrastructure and interests by defensive as well as offensive means, such as the ability to secure important information systems or to apply cyber sanctions, can also be included here.[27] The question of attribution in the cyber realm is here key and usually creates demand for intelligence support.

The EC sets out in the EU industrial strategy that the EU must establish "technical sovereignty" in areas of strategic importance such as defence, space, 5G and 6G networks, and quantum computing.[28] This is likely to have a major impact on intelligence work in Europe, in terms of both intelligence support to achieve this form of autonomy and what the technological developments will mean for intelligence work itself. Traditionally, since Turing and Welchman's Enigma decryption in the 1940s, intelligence services have benefited greatly from new technology and from computer technology in particular.[29] Technological development together with the increased use of different types of sensors – in both operational environments and everyday life – are therefore likely to increase the amount of useful information available to the intelligence services. Dealing with this fast-expanding flow of information is likely to overwhelm traditional manual intelligence processes.[30] New technologies, such as AI, have therefore been identified as an important new capacity in intelligence work in the future.[31]

The increasing use of misinformation through social media, among other things, by both state and non-state actors, such as Russia and the Islamic State (IS), has also received increased attention in recent years. The EU has strengthened its work against misinformation.[32] Here, developments in machine learning for the analysis of social media have been cited as an example of how new technology can reduce the burden of intelligence analysts.[33] An increase in such capabilities can also be linked back to the category of operational autonomy as this could accelerate the ability to detect various threats. This, together with an increased requirement for data security and a greater need to be able to carry out various forms of counterespionage, has increased the importance of new technology and the development of common resources at the EU level.[34]

Geo-economic and geopolitical factors have also been brought to the fore, among other things, through the development and expansion of the 5G network. The United States, Australia, New Zealand, and Japan, among others, have prevented Chinese companies from participating in the construction of their 5G networks.[35] This has contributed to a debate in Europe regarding how the EU should deal with these issues in the future. European intelligence services should be able to assist with screening the Chinese companies that want to participate in the expansion of 5G in Europe, on everything from the structure of their products to the ownership of the companies. The centrality of this technology is linked to the fact that it will be a key part of a number of services – from the Internet of Things to cloud data and AI – that will be vital to society's future critical functions.[36] Thus, the way in which our social systems are interconnected and digitized today could mean increased vulnerability to external influences in the future.

Taken together, this area affects an actor's ability to retain control over basic industrial and technological systems, partly to maintain the ability to act independently and partly to counteract enforced dependencies. From an intelligence perspective, opportunities will be needed to examine and detect societal vulnerabilities and negative dependencies as well as to enable attribution. Thus, in an increasingly digitized and technological world, intelligence services will play an increasingly important role, especially for those actors whose goal is "digital autonomy" or "technical sovereignty."

The EU's Current Intelligence Capabilities and their Contribution to Strategic Autonomy

When it comes to decision-making autonomy, operational autonomy, economic autonomy, and technological autonomy, the EU has come further in some aspects than in others. This is reflected in the existing and planned levels of resources for intelligence support.

Regarding decision-making autonomy, there is clear agreement on the need for European autonomy, but there have also been problems with agreeing on what the strategic objective should be. A common political will to act collectively and independently of external actors like the United States and China continues to elude member-states. As discussed earlier, decision-making autonomy depends on intelligence support to identify a state's interests as well as on broad external analyses of trends, threats, and patterns of action of other actors. Strategic analysis as well as analyses of the business environment are conducted by a number of actors, such as the EC's Situation Room and the European Strategy and Policy Analysis System (ESPAS), which does future-oriented analysis work. The intelligence services are relevant here, as much of the information required is not openly available.

50   Björn Fägersten

IntCen plays a key role in this work, and its intelligence capabilities have been strengthened in recent years. IntCen provides analyses and intelligence information for various time horizons. Its intelligence assessments and reports are more from a long-term strategic perspective for the EU as a whole, but it also contributes shorter-term intelligence analyses, especially after crises or acute events. IntCen also provides threat and risk assessments for EU personnel around the world – for example, prior to postings at EU delegations or in relation to EU military and civilian operations. Finally, the unit provides *ad hoc* information in various forms to EU decision-makers ranging from the HR/VP to EU Special Representatives, EC bodies, and the European Parliament.[37] IntCen is unique in that it contributes intelligence analyses directly to decision-makers and not to national authorities or bodies such as Europol.[38] IntCen's intelligence capacity is growing in part because it is able to further validate national data and subsequently put together the "broader puzzle that national intelligence services may have missed."[39]

Extensive intelligence work is underway in the field of counterterrorism to both strengthen the EU's decision-making capacity at the strategic level and provide more operational capacity for the EU and participating member-states. Europol plays an important role in European intelligence cooperation through its efforts to combat international crime and terrorism. Following the terrorist attack on Charlie Hebdo in January 2015, political demands increased to strengthen cooperation on counterterrorism within the EU. This led to the creation of the European Counter Terrorism Centre (ECTC) within Europol in January 2016.[40] The ECTC is now the central hub for counterterrorism in the EU and a single point of contact for all national law enforcement agencies, as well as third countries. Its task is to gather and analyse information from these agencies and countries.[41] As noted earlier, cooperation bodies with no direct or formal ties to the EU contribute to the EU's intelligence capabilities. For example, cooperation has been strengthened within the CTG in recent years, among other things through the establishment in 2016 of a common information database for exchanges of information among member-states' intelligence and security services. An operational database provides all thirty intelligence services with access to common information, which is updated in real time. Finally, the ties between the various EU bodies and the CTG have been strengthened, which means, among other things, that the CTG is now invited to EU meetings that have terrorism on the agenda. Europol, IntCen, the EU Counter-Terrorism Coordinator, and representatives of US intelligence services now also participate in the CTG's strategic meetings.[42]

In terms of operational autonomy, Europe is still dependent on US resources and capabilities when carrying out more demanding tasks, as illustrated earlier by the Libyan operation. This fact was on painful display during the evacuation from Kabul in 2021. Smaller-scale crisis management can be said to fall within the framework of operational autonomy, however, which is also the level of what is politically authorized. In addition to counterterrorism (see above), intelligence work in support of EU operational autonomy concerns precisely this form of small-scale crisis management capacity. Although the primary aim of IntCen is to strengthen the EU's decision-making capacity at the strategic level, the unit has gradually gained a role in operational support.[43] There have been promising new developments regarding operational support; the EU's new security doctrine – the strategic compass – highlights the need for more intelligence capabilities specifically in terms of advance planning and scenario analysis to enable EU operations.[44]

The EU Satellite Centre (SatCen) also contributes operational capacity – in particular through IMINT (Imagery Intelligence) and GEOINT (Geospatial Intelligence) – to the various EU bodies (the EEAS, the EU military staff, INTCEN, Frontex, and the EC), to EU member-states, and to the UN and the Organization for Security and Co-operation in Europe (OSCE). SatCen delivered more than 3,000 reports to various actors in 2019. For example, the centre contributed to the EU NAVFOR in Somalia, Operation Atalanta, among other things by monitoring known pirate bases, identifying where merchant ships were being hijacked, and monitoring and identifying human trafficking. EU training efforts (e.g. EUTM MALI) and monitoring missions (EUMM GEORGIA) also benefited from information provided by SATCEN during the year. These various forms of image analysis have increased the operational capability of the EU's various civilian and military operations and missions.[45]

In the area of economic autonomy, the role for intelligence support is still in its infancy. This is not a surprise, considering that the EU has long separated economic matters from security policy (and hence intelligence). The most obvious application relates to sanctions: intelligence from member-states has been channelled to joint decision-making bodies through IntCen. The EU screening mechanism for foreign investments has seen national decision-makers establish links to their intelligence and security services to receive intelligence support. It is still unclear whether similar links have been made at the EU level. What is not unclear, however, is that the EU is acquiring intelligence as it plays a coordinating role in the new mechanism. By investigating FDI and serving as a central node for information about it, the EU has taken on a panopticon role that has strengthened its hand as a geo-economic actor.[46] As the EU increases cooperation with other actors, this role as a central node will become even more important, which in turn will require more intelligence support from member-states and help relevant EU bodies become stronger in their own right. Regarding the newly established Trade and Technology Council for EU–US cooperation, Tyson Barker argues it will be increasingly important for US agencies like the Bureau of Industry and Security (BIS) and the Committee on Foreign Investment in the United States (CFIUS) to create channels for intelligence sharing with their European counterparts as

52   Björn Fägersten

EU member-states expand their screening and market access restriction capabilities.[47] Similar intelligence needs in the counterterrorism field, driven by the demand from US agencies, have expanded the role of joint EU bodies, and the same can be expected in the economic and trade areas. A market area with growing intelligence demands is competition policy: security interests and looming threats could justify the relaxation of merger restrictions within the EU's internal market. Such policies, motivated by economic autonomy, would need intelligence support to grasp the security interests affected.[48]

With regard to technological autonomy, intelligence support at the European level is still relatively undeveloped. That said, rapid development is easily foreseeable, especially as this kind of autonomy has become a priority for the newly geopolitical EC. The main challenge here is that much of the industrial policy that is supposed to serve as the basis for the development of greater autonomy runs counter to more traditional free trade policies, which still predominate many EU member-states. As noted earlier, the new objective of technological sovereignty/autonomy reflected in the EU's industrial strategy entails a new level of ambition. This should make for increased investment in European technology and digitization. Protecting this technological development will be a major task for Europe's intelligence services. The increasingly close cooperation with industry could entail a greater need for European intelligence cooperation. An example is the foreign takeover of critical technology firms and the intelligence work that is needed to support efficient screening mechanisms. One area that is not sufficiently developed to support technological autonomy is intelligence cooperation to fight industrial espionage. In this area, Western intelligence agencies seem to make little distinction between friendly and non-friendly countries, and this hampers intra-European cooperation. Finally, one area that has seen development is the hybrid area where strategic analysis on physical and digital threats to Europe's critical infrastructure is done jointly within the Hybrid fusion cell, located within the EU's IntCen.

In sum, it could be said that active work is underway in all dimensions of autonomy and that this will heighten the need for further intelligence within the EU. The EU's three-year overview of the Global Strategy emphasizes that cooperation between IntCen and IntDir has been strengthened in recent years through the joint Single Intelligence Analysis Capacity (SIAC) format. At the same time, the EEAS has emphasized that greater information exchange and intelligence cooperation will be required among member-states as well as among EU institutions in order to strengthen the EU as a foreign policy actor.[49] Important to remember, however, is that strategic autonomy remains a controversial objective that is not shared by all the member-states. Consequently, differences among member-states could affect the EU's ability to achieve autonomy, which in turn could reduce opportunities for greater cooperation in the intelligence field.

Uncertainties and Potential for Development

The analysis thus far has brought to light the significant intelligence needs that have been generated by the EU's ambition for autonomy in various areas. It has also shown how intelligence cooperation at the EU level currently meets these needs and where gaps exist. The work on establishing the necessary cooperation, as well as planning additional intelligence capacity for future needs, faces a number of challenges. There are inherent cooperation problems: the absence of a common intelligence culture and of cooperation beyond the EU framework.

International intelligence cooperation requires personal networks and contacts. This presupposes trust and a willingness to cooperate among the various intelligence services, which are built up primarily through past experiences of cooperation, as well as through sharing a common organizational and/or professional culture and sometimes common rules and regulations. At the same time, however, intelligence cooperation is tightly linked to national sovereignty, an area of "high politics" that states are reluctant to regulate jointly.[50] In addition, bureaucratic interests will affect how willing various organizations are to share information.[51] For example, organizational and professional differences between police and intelligence organizations can lead to cooperation problems.[52] As discussed earlier, police cooperation, especially in relation to terrorism, has been strengthened and institutionalized within the EU. However, the willingness of the intelligence services to share information has to a great extent remained limited due to the greater sensitivities of their work.[53]

The different professions and nationalities involved in multilateral intelligence cooperation mean that the lack of a common European intelligence culture is a major problem for cooperation.[54] French president Emmanuel Macron clearly emphasized this in his Sorbonne speech when he argued in favour of "creating a European intelligence academy ... to strengthen the ties between our countries through education and exchange."[55] This idea was later realized in March 2020 when the Intelligence College in Europe was established. The twenty-three participating member-states aim to promote and facilitate strategic dialogue among their intelligence services; they also hope to contribute to enhanced cooperation with academia and with national and European decision-makers.[56] Unlike in the United States, exchange and dialogue between intelligence services and academia have been neglected and are far less frequent.[57] The Intelligence College could contribute to the development of cooperation among decision-makers, intelligence services, and academia. It is also intended to increase understanding of the significance of and need for increased collaboration on intelligence analysis by decision-makers in, for example, the EC and the European Parliament.[58] In November 2018, a similar initiative was established by Greece and Cyprus in the field of permanent structured cooperation (PESCO) on defence, in the form of the Joint EU Intelligence School (JEIS).

54   Björn Fägersten

This project is intended to contribute training in intelligence disciplines for member-states' security and intelligence services.[59] Both the Intelligence College in Europe and the JEIS are somewhat new, so their significance for future European intelligence cooperation is still uncertain.

Another challenge to the development of intelligence support for the EU is that intelligence services operate largely outside its framework. This applies not only to older established networks, such as the Club de Berne, but also to newer creations, such as France's Intelligence College in Europe. Together with the strengthening of the CTG through the security services' cooperation platform, this illustrates that bilateral and "minilateral" cooperation among the traditional intelligence and security services continues to be the norm within Europe. Another cooperation body established outside the EU framework is the Paris Group, which was set up in 2016 as a discussion format for various European intelligence services. The Paris Group has representatives from Austria, Belgium, Denmark, France, Germany, Italy, Ireland, the Netherlands, Norway, Poland, Spain, the United Kingdom, and Sweden; it is also attended by the director of IntCen and the chairman of the CTG. The added value provided by the Paris Group is said to be that external intelligence services, such as the British MI6, can participate in the collaboration.[60] Since the UK has left the EU, cooperation outside the EU framework, such as in the CTG and the Paris Group, has benefited overall European intelligence cooperation. There is still a great deal of uncertainty about what future relations between the EU and the UK will be like. There is a risk that Brexit will have a strongly negative impact on European intelligence cooperation because, among other things, there are questions over British participation in intelligence cooperation with Europol as well as the Schengen Information System II (SIS II) and the EU Passenger Name Record (PNR). Cooperation within IntCen and IntDir, and the UK's ability to access information from Galileo and SatCen, are also likely to be affected.[61] The EU, for its part, risks losing one of Europe's most competent intelligence providers. Europol's former director Rob Wainwright has emphasized that "the UK's contribution to EU internal security decision-making is invaluable."[62]

Finally, the rapid development of technology has brought a number of legal, ethical, and military technological issues into focus with regard to the EU's future intelligence capabilities. New technology, AI, and quantum computing represent a major opportunity for those working with intelligence. Better developed technological and electronic espionage presents new challenges for the intelligence services, not least as the distinction between espionage and warfare becomes more difficult to draw. "New" societal vulnerabilities such as increasingly powerful technology also mean that non-military means of power will become increasingly important in the future.[63] Here, the intelligence services could play a significant role in exposing and addressing the various vulnerabilities that society might face.[64]

Conclusion

The EU has long been striving for greater autonomy. That has been a driving force behind the building of its current intelligence capacity. The ambition to achieve European strategic autonomy will certainly drive intelligence cooperation further. This will apply to all four of the sub-areas analysed earlier – decision autonomy, operational autonomy, economic autonomy, and technological autonomy – albeit to varying degrees.

What are the prospects for intelligence cooperation within Europe? The EU's legal structure places limits on how cooperation can be achieved. Without treaty change, a supranational intelligence service at the EU level is impossible. However, Article 73 of the Treaty on the Functioning of the European Union (TFEU) emphasizes the possibility of strengthening cooperation among member-states' intelligence services, as member-states may "organise between themselves and under their responsibility such forms of cooperation and coordination as they deem appropriate between the competent departments of their administrations responsible for safeguarding national security." Also, there are measures that could be taken within the prevailing legal framework. More joint training and education could be carried out under the auspices of IntCen, not only for the analysts stationed there but also for national intelligence analysts, who could then be seconded to multilateral work for short periods. This could prepare the foundations for more trusting collaboration and information sharing. The EU could also make better use of its network of delegations from an intelligence perspective by ensuring that relevant delegations are staffed with analysts with cutting-edge security expertise. This would also increase the value of the EU as an intelligence actor for member-states, which sometimes lack the necessary resources. Progress has already been made in increasing security expertise within delegations, but the new geo-economic era calls for the reverse trend as well. That is, the trade, infrastructure, and development experts who traditionally manned the delegations are increasingly in demand in intelligence work as these are key areas of great power rivalry.

Another area for investment would be new joint air and sea intelligence platforms, for example through the European Defence Fund (EDF). This would enhance decision-making autonomy and also strengthen the EU's role in asserting and protecting global goods such as the freedom to navigate international waters. Intelligence applications in high-tech areas such as quantum computing are also suitable for large-scale cooperation as such technologies often exceed the resources of individual member-states. The above proposals would greatly increase the EU's capacity for strategic autonomy when it comes to political decision-making and operations. Europe's intelligence cooperation in the area of technical autonomy is currently neglected. More focus on counterespionage – for example, within Europol – would do much to prevent industrial espionage and protect Europe's technological base. The question arises, however, whether

56   Björn Fägersten

intelligence can be strengthened in this area without introducing more democratic influence and control over the EU intelligence machinery.

Ultimately, the issues surrounding European strategic autonomy and its intelligence requirements will be determined by the member-states' own balance of autonomy. As noted earlier, the EU's capacity as an autonomous actor is limited by the national sovereignty of the member-states, on the one hand, and the role of the United States in European security, on the other. If Europe wants to develop greater strategic autonomy, it will require significant investment in several areas of intelligence. Some of these developments will involve cooperation so close that in practice they would erode aspects of national autonomy. The states that want to develop common strategic autonomy must therefore accept that this will to some extent be at the expense of their national autonomy. Here, it is conceivable that an acceptance of this fact is greater for certain areas, such as industry, than for the most demanding area of operational autonomy, which is close to the defence of national territory. So it is likely that Europe, to the extent that increased strategic autonomy is actually achieved, will move toward a variable autonomy with continuing strong powers for the member-states and dependence on the United States in certain areas, while a degree of autonomy vis-à-vis external parties is created in other areas that will require member-states to transfer some of their autonomy to the European level.

NOTES

1   Parts of this chapter expand and develop joint work with Calle Håkansson, published in Swedish as "Underrättelsebehov för strategisk autonomi," *Statsvetenskaplig tidsskrift*, vol. 122, Nr 3 (2020).
2   Gunnar Sjöstedt, *The External Role of the European Community* (Westmead: Saxon House, 1977); Maria Strömvik, *To Act as a Union: Explaining the Development of the EU's Collective Foreign Policy*, Department of Political Science, Lund University (2005); Jolyon Howorth, *Security and Defence Policy in the European Union* (New York: Red Globe Press, 2014).
3   See Speech by Federal Chancellor Olaf Scholz at the Charles University in Prague on Monday, 29 August 2022; and 2022 State of the Union Address by European Commission President Ursula von der Leyen, 14 September 2022.
4   European External Action Service, *Delade visioner, gemensamma åtgärder: Ett starkare Europa – En global strategi för Europeiska unionens utrikes- och säkerhetspolitik* (Brussels, 2016), https://eurooppatiedotus.fi/wp-content/uploads/sites/19/2017/04/global-strategi.pdf.
5   Glenn H. Snyder, *Alliance Politics* (Ithaca: Cornell University Press, 1997).
6   David Lake, *Hierarchy in International Relations* (Ithaca: Cornell University Press, 2011).

Intelligence Demands Linked to European Autonomy 57

7 Kjell Engelbrekt and Jan Hallenberg, *European Union and Strategy: An Emerging Actor* (Abingdon: Routledge, 2008).

8 Gunilla Herolf, *Europeiskt säkerhets- och försvarspolitiskt samarbete* (Stockholm: Sieps, 2018), 34, https://sieps.se/globalassets/publikationer/2018/sieps-2018_4 -web.pdf.

9 *Franco-British St. Malo Declaration*, 4 December 1998, https://www.cvce.eu/content /publication/2008/3/31/f3cd16fb-fc37-4d52-936f-c8e9bc80f24f/publishable_en.pdf.

10 See European Council, "Conclusion of the Presidency," Cologne, 3–4 June 1999, https://www.europarl.europa.eu/summits/kol1_en.htm; European Council, "Presidency Conclusions," Helsinki, 10–11 December 1999, https://www.europarl.europa.eu /summits/hel1_en.htm; and European Council, "Conclusions of the Presidency," Nice, 7–10 December 2000, https://www.europarl.europa.eu/summits/nice1_en.htm.

11 Maïa K. Davis Cross, "A European Transgovernmental Intelligence Network and the Role of IntCen," *Perspectives on European Politics and Society* 14, no. 3 (2013): 388–402; Björn Fägersten, "For EU Eyes Only? Intelligence and European Security," *European Union Institute for Security Studies* (EUISS) Brief no. 8, 2016, https://www.iss.europa.eu/content/eu-eyes-only-intelligence-and-european -security.

12 Since 1 December 2009, the Common Security and Defence Policy CSDP.

13 Björn Fägersten, "Sharing Secrets – Explaining International Intelligence Cooperation," *Lund Political Studies* 161 (2010): 171–3, https://www.lunduniversity .lu.se/lup/publication/c6072c5b-0a67-4361-898e-412ebb75c627.

14 Fägersten, "Sharing Secrets," 148–53.

15 Fägersten, "Sharing Secrets," 191–202.

16 Daniel W. Drezner, Ronald R. Krebs, and Randall Schweller, "The End of Grand Strategy: America Must Think Small," *Foreign Affairs*, May–June 2020, https:// www.foreignaffairs.com/articles/world/2020-04-13/end-grand-strategy.

17 See, for example, Daniel Fiott, "Strategic Autonomy: Towards 'European Sovereignty' in Defence?," *European Union Institute for Security Studies* Brief no. 12 (2018), https://www.iss.europa.eu/content/strategic-autonomy-towards-'european -sovereignty'-defence; and Barbara Lippert, Nicolai von Ondarza, and Volker Perthes, eds., "European Strategic Autonomy: Actors, Issues, Conflicts of Interests," *SWP Research Paper* 4 (2019), https://www.swp-berlin.org/publications/products /research_papers/2019RP04_lpt_orz_prt_web.pdf.

18 Fägersten, "For EU Eyes Only?"; Maïa K. Davis Cross, "Counter-Terrorism in the EU's External Relations," *Journal of European Integration* 39, no. 5 (2017): 609–24.

19 Foreign Affairs Committee, "Libya: Examination of Intervention and Collapse and the UK's Future Policy Options," United Kingdom House of Commons, Third Report of Session 2016–17, 16 September 2016, https://publications.parliament.uk /pa/cm201617/cmselect/cmfaff/119/119.pdf.

20 Stewart Webb, "Improvements Required for Operational and Tactical Intelligence Sharing in NATO," *Defence against Terrorism Review* 6, no. 1 (2014): 55.

58   Björn Fägersten

21 Francesco Giumelli, "How EU Sanctions Work: A New Narrative," European Union Institute for Security Studies, Chaillot Papers no. 129 (2013): 10–11, https://www.iss.europa.eu/content/how-eu-sanctions-work-new-narrative.

22 Martin Russel, "EU Sanctions: A Key Foreign and Security Policy Instrument," European Parliamentary Research Service, 2018, https://www.europarl.europa.eu/RegData/etudes/BRIE/2018/621870/EPRS_BRI(2018)621870_EN.pdf.

23 T. Breton, "Neither Autarchy nor Dependence: More European Autonomy", Linkedin, 25 August 2022, https://www.linkedin.com/pulse/neither-autarchy-nor-dependence-more-european-autonomy-thierry-breton/?trackingId=wxbd7iCwJ2cFQAokOkkhTw%3D%3D.

24 Daniela Schwarzer, "Weaponizing the Economy," *Berlin Policy Journal*, January 2020, https://berlinpolicyjournal.com/weaponizing-the-economy.

25 European External Action Service, *Delade visioner, gemensamma åtgärder*, 40, https://op.europa.eu/en/publication-detail/-/publication/3eaae2cf-9ac5-11e6-868c-01aa75ed71a1/language-sv.

26 Jacopo Barigazzi, "Borrell urges EU to be foreign policy 'player, not the playground,'" *Politico*, 9 December 2019, https://www.politico.eu/article/on-foreign-policy-josep-borrell-urges-eu-to-be-a-player-not-the-playground-balkans.

27 European Union Council, *Council Decision (CFSP) 2019/797 of 17 May 2019 concerning restrictive measures against cyber-attacks threatening the Union or its Member States*, 17 May 2019, https://eur-lex.europa.eu/legal-content/EN/TXT/?uri=uriserv:OJ.LI.2019.129.01.0013.01.ENG&toc=OJ:L:2019:129I:TOC.

28 European Commission, "A New Industrial Strategy for Europe," *Communication from the Commission* 102 final, 10 March 2020, https://eur-lex.europa.eu/legal-content/EN/TXT/?uri=CELEX%3A52020DC0102.

29 Daniel Fiott, "Digitalising Defence: Protecting Europe in the Age of Quantum Computing and the Cloud," European Union Institute for Security Studies, Brief no. 4 (2020), https://www.iss.europa.eu/content/digitalising-defence.

30 Tate Nurkin and Stephen Rodriguez, "A Candle in the Dark: US National Security Strategy for Artificial Intelligence," Atlantic Council Strategy Paper Series, 10 December 2019, 26, https://www.atlanticcouncil.org/uncategorized/a-candle-in-the-dark-us-national-security-strategy-for-artificial-intelligence.

31 See, for example, Daniel Fiott and Gustav Lindstrom, "Artificial Intelligence: What Implications for EU Security and Defence?," European Union Institute for Security Studies Brief no. 10 (2018), https://www.iss.europa.eu/content/artificial-intelligence---what-implications-eu-security-and-defence.

32 See, for example, Elsa Hedling, "Blending Politics and New Media: Mediatized Practices of EU Digital Diplomacy," PhD diss., Lund University, 2018.

33 Nurkin and Rodriguez, "A Candle in the Dark," 26–7.

34 Lippert, von Ondarza, and Perthes, "European Strategic Autonomy," 20–1.

35 Nigel Inkster, "The Huawei Affair and China's Technology Ambitions," *Survival* 61, no. 1 (2019): 105.

Intelligence Demands Linked to European Autonomy   59

36 European Political Strategy Centre, *Rethinking Strategic Autonomy in the Digital Age* (Brussels: European Commission, 2019), https://op.europa.eu/en/publication-detail/-/publication/889dd7b7-0cde-11ea-8c1f-01aa75ed71a1/language-en.

37 "Fact Sheet," European Union IntCen, 5 February 2015, https://www.statewatch.org/media/documents/news/2016/may/eu-intcen-factsheet.pdf.

38 Mai'a K. Davis Cross, "The Limits of Epistemic Communities: EU Security Agencies," *Politics and Governance* 3, no. 1 (2015): 96.

39 Simon Duke, *Will Brexit Damage Our Security and Defence? The Impact on the UK and EU* (New York: Palgrave Macmillan, 2019), 65.

40 "European Counter Terrorism Centre – ECTC," Europol, 25 February 2022, https://www.europol.europa.eu/about-europol/european-counter-terrorism-centre-ectc.

41 Europol, "European Union Terrorism Situation and Trend Report 2019," https://www.europol.europa.eu/cms/sites/default/files/documents/tesat_2019_final.pdf.

42 General Intelligence and Security Service (AVID) of the Netherlands, "Annual Report 2017," March 2018, https://english.aivd.nl/about-aivd/the-intelligence-and-security-services-act-2017/annual-report; Government of the Netherlands, "Increasing Cooperation between Europe's Security Services," 2016.

43 Björn Fägersten, "Intelligence and Decision-Making within the Common Foreign and Security Policy," *Swedish Institute for European Policy Studies* 22 (2015): 4, https://www.sieps.se/en/publications/2015/intelligence-and-decision-making-within-the-common-foreign-and-security-policy-201522epa/Sieps_2015_22epa.

44 European External Action Service, *A Strategic Compass for Security and Defence: For a European Union That Protects Its Citizens, Values, and Interests and Contributes to International Peace and Security* (Brussels, 2022).

45 European Union SatCen, "EU SatCen Annual Report 2019" (2020): 29–37, https://www.satcen.europa.eu/keydocuments/EU%20SatCen%20Annual%20Report%2020195ea979f2f9d71b083826a79a.pdf.

46 Loïc Carcy, "The new EU Screening Mechanism for Foreign Direct Investments When the EU Takes Back Control," *Bruges Political Research Papers* 84 (2021), http://aei.pitt.edu/103426.

47 Tyson Barker, "Biden's Plan to Cooperate with Europé on Tech," *Foreign Affairs*, 16 June 2021, https://foreignpolicy.com/2021/06/16/bidens-mission-to-defeat-digital-sovereignty.

48 Mark Leonard and Jeremy Shapiro, eds., *Strategic Sovereignty: How Europe Can Regain the Capacity to Act* (European Council on Foreign Relations, 2019), https://ecfr.eu/archive/page/-/ecfr_strategic_sovereignty.pdf.

49 European External Action Service, "The European Union's Global Strategy: Three Years On, Looking Forward" (Brussels, 2019): 10–11, https://eeas.europa.eu/sites/eeas/files/eu_global_strategy_2019.pdf.

50 Stanley Hoffmann, "Obstinate or Obsolete? The Fate of the Nation-State and the Case of Western Europe," *Daedalus* 95, no. 3 (1966): 862–915.

60　Björn Fägersten

51 For a discussion, see Björn Fägersten, "Bureaucratic Resistance to International Intelligence Cooperation – the Case of Europol," *Intelligence and National Security* 24, no. 4 (2010): 500–20.
52 Fägersten, "For EU Eyes Only?"
53 Hartmut Aden, "Information Sharing, Secrecy, and Trust among Law Enforcement and Secret Service Institutions in the European Union," *West European Politics* 41, no. 4 (2018): 990–1.
54 See, for example, Ruben Arcos and José-Miguel Palacios, "The Impact of Intelligence on Decision-Making: The EU and the Arab Spring," *Intelligence and National Security* 33, no. 5 (2018) 737–54.
55 Emmanuel Macron, "Initiative for Europe," *Présidence de la République* (26 September 2017): 5, https://www.diplomatie.gouv.fr/IMG/pdf/english_version _transcript_-_initiative_for_europe_-_speech_by_the_president_of_the_french _republic_cle8de628.pdf.
56 Intelligence College in Europe, "Letter of Intent," 1 March 2020, https://www .intelligence-college-europe.org/wp-content/uploads/2020/03/LoI-English.pdf.
57 José-Miguel Palacios, "Intelligence Analysis Training: A European Perspective," *International Journal of Intelligence, Security, and Public Affairs* 18, no. 1 (2016): 42.
58 Jacopo Barigazzi and Rym Momtaz, "European spies dare to share," *Politico*, 26 February 2020, https://www.politico.eu/article/european-spies-dare-to-share -intelligence-college-in-europe-ice.
59 Council of the European Union, "Permanent structured cooperation (PESCO) projects – Overview," 2018, https://www.consilium.europa.eu/media/39664/table -pesco-projects.pdf.
60 European Union Counter-Terrorism Coordinator, "Implementation of the counter-terrorism agenda set by the European Council," *Council of the European Union*, 4 November 2016, https://www.statewatch.org/media/documents/news/2016/nov /eu-council-implementaiton-anti-trrorismStrategy-13627-16.pdf; Heiner Busch and Matthias Monroy, "Analysis: Who Drives EU Counter-Terrorism? On the Legislation of the European Union," *Statewatch*, May 2017, http://statewatch.org /analyses/no-315-who-drives-eu-ct.pdf.
61 Nigel Inkster, "Brexit and Security," *Survival* 60, no. 6 (2018): 27–34; Anthony Glees, "What Brexit Means for British and European Intelligence Agencies," *Journal of Intelligence History* 16, no. 2 (2017): 70–5.
62 Cited in Claudia Hillebrand, "With or Without You? The UK and Information and Intelligence Sharing in the EU," *Journal of Intelligence History* 16, no. 2 (2017): 94.
63 Malin Severin, "Early warning and non-linear warfare – challenges for intelligence services," FOI-R--4577—SE (March 2018).
64 Björn Fägersten, "Forward Resilience in the Age of Hybrid Threats: The Role of European Intelligence," in *Forward Resilience: Protecting Society in an Interconnected World*, ed. Daniel Hamilton (Washington, D.C.: Center for Transatlantic Relations, 2016).

3 Transatlantic Intelligence Sharing and Cooperation: Existing Challenges and Opportunities

ADRIANA SEAGLE

As a form of international cooperation, intelligence sharing is difficult to capture in open sources due to the nature, size, quality, and frequency of information. The challenge with the transatlantic partnership is that intelligence sharing "can be presented everywhere."[1] Nevertheless, some recommend beginning the inquiry with the focus on the leading actor.[2]

The strength of the transatlantic partnership has been tested, whether it involves the United States' dependability to remain committed to European security or the European Union's barring of high-risk 5G vendors from its markets. This chapter examines the extent to which transatlantic intelligence sharing can move beyond counterterrorism and law enforcement cooperation to focus on pressing geopolitical challenges resulting from the rise of China and advances in technology. Historically, transatlantic intelligence cooperation has been impacted by a lack of trust, divergent perceptions of secrecy, privacy, and civil liberties, changes in US foreign and security interests, and different understandings of threats. The overreliance on US intelligence capabilities and NATO prompted the EU to re-examine the prospects for creating a joint European intelligence system. However, a European intelligence system wired by Huawei's technology raises serious security concerns when it comes to intelligence sharing and cooperation. An examination of practices in transatlantic intelligence sharing and cooperation reveals that prospects for strategic independence and self-reliance through decoupling from the previous framework are possible if "America First" and European strategic autonomy are considered. The opportunity to move beyond the existing sharing tradition also lies in the prospects for reinventing new spaces for cooperation and intelligence sharing in the new security system of trade, digitalization, technology, and geopolitics.

Applying in-depth analysis of existing narratives associated with the transatlantic partnership, I focus in this chapter on areas in which transatlantic decision-makers use a constant flow of information to optimize state security.[3] I

62   Adriana Seagle

review practices of transatlantic intelligence sharing and cooperation in trade, data sharing and privacy, technology, and geopolitics.

Intelligence Sharing and Cooperation in the International System of Trade

Available information on the transatlantic partnership suggests that the United States and the EU are re-evaluating the level of their interaction because the focus of the United States is increasingly on Asia, while the strategic position and role of the EU has changed. The Biden administration claims that the United States is "back" at the partnership table to rebalance disputes in trade, address burden sharing, and convey interest in and support for European security. The existing practices, however, indicate that while the United States is indeed "back," it is willing to work only with those who help themselves. The literature on intelligence sharing and cooperation in the trade sector is unevenly developed since most of the attention is directed toward the military, transnational crime, and terrorism. More research will benefit the field of economic transatlantic intelligence sharing, given that trade impacts health, prosperity, and standards of living, with spillover effects in agriculture, the environment, industry, intellectual property, technology, and goods and services.

Regarding intelligence-sharing arrangements, some have found that during the Cold War, when rules, regulations, and practices were being created, trade shaped the transatlantic partnership into a hierarchy with the United States as the dominant state.[4] Unlike the European powers, which retained political privileges and access to raw materials and resources, the United States relied on its strength, expertise, and leadership style to encourage Europeans to join in the building of an international system that would remain open and free.[5] Scholars who apply the theory of markets and hierarchies to explain intelligence sharing claim that a hierarchical position privileges the dominant state when the conditions for sharing are being created and interpreted, including as they relate to mechanisms of oversight, compliance, and punishment; as this overview will show, that arrangement has been perpetuated.[6] The Cold War era constituted the economic integration phase of the partnership during which rules, regulations, and practices for engagement were created and strengthened. The United States continued to dominate the transatlantic partnership after the Cold War, during the NATO expansion and the attempts to democratize Eastern Europe. That journey was not smooth: the defender of a *free and rules-based order* clashed several times with Europeans – for example, around the US withdrawal from the Kyoto Protocol and refusal to join the International Criminal Court (ICC). At the time, Europeans perceived US actions as acts of "unilateralism, sabotage, and irresponsibility."[7] The aftermath of 9/11 is described in the literature as the most prolific and transformational phase of the partnership, for that

Transatlantic Intelligence Sharing and Cooperation   63

is when both actors engaged in creating and consolidating intelligence-sharing institutions around common security interests. Assessments reveal that after 9/11 and the Madrid and London attacks, transatlantic intelligence cooperation intensified in terms of sharing information about drug trafficking, organized crime, border security, and money laundering.[8]

The transatlantic partnership in trade is also conceptualized as the "defining force of the global economy" due to the intensity, volume, and size of investment.[9] Despite this partnership's importance, the EU claims that achieving "mutually acceptable commitments" with the United States in trade is a challenge, for the EU's current interests and strategic priorities are not being acknowledged.[10] This situation has triggered in Europeans a desire to escape the hierarchical structure of security benefits and intelligence sharing established by the United States. In awe of "strategic awakening" and more aware of its power and interests in the international system, the EU is showing a willingness to decouple from the existing US-led structure in order to engage in geopolitical competition with the United States for security and influence in the Indo-Pacific region.[11] Some wonder whether the pan-European strategy of "inclusivity" and cooperation with China in that region will lead to tensions with strategic partners.[12]

The Office of the US Trade Representative lists prosperity, jobs, and decent standards of living as among the benefits of trade.[13] The EU is sometimes treated like a threat to US economic security rather than as a partner in the defence of the international system of rules-based trade; even so, the United States and the EU are each other's biggest source of foreign direct investment, and, despite tariffs, both are committed to reforming and upholding the rules-based multilateral trading system.[14] Africa, meanwhile, is becoming a strategic field for economic trade competition. The United States is Europe's second-largest trade partner and Africa's third-largest.[15] China and the EU, however, appear to be in a better position to shape trade and access to natural resources in Africa. China is Africa's largest creditor and the United States is its largest investor, but the EU is its preferred trading partner. Retaliatory tariffs and unequal trade agreements continue to shape these partnerships despite US trade initiatives with Africa and the EU. It appears that the United States and the EU are competing for benefits in the same areas of security interests and economic gains. The United States identifies strategies to regain influence in Africa; the EU enjoys preferential status in trade. This indicates that for the United States, Africa may require more engagement and support than diplomatic and policy leadership "to transition to a partnership model based on reciprocal trade."[16]

The EU does not expect great improvements, given that the United States' trade agenda includes items such as "boosting United States manufacturing, strengthening rules, forcing US federal agencies to buy United States goods, and imposing extra taxes on companies looking to take their supply chains

64   Adriana Seagle

offshore."[17] Instead, promising opportunities in the transatlantic partnership include addressing China's trading practices, strengthening coordination on foreign investment screening, and sharing intelligence about commercial threats. Modernizing trade rules and institutions of trade and e-commerce, as well as developing privacy- and human-rights-centred ways for companies to safely transfer data between the EU and the United States, are other potential areas for engagement. In addition to trade issues, the transatlantic partnership is confronted with diverging perspectives on domestic and foreign policy interests, different meanings attached to surveillance and privacy, unequal technological development, regional and global geopolitical challenges, and a dearth of mutual trust. "We need to reinvent useful forms of cooperation – coalitions of projects and players," French president Emmanuel Macron has stated, "and we need to modernize our structures and create a level playing field for everyone. To do that, we also need to reconsider the terms of the relationship: I believe the second way forward is a strong and political Europe."[18]

Transatlantic Cooperation: Data Sharing and Privacy Protection

Some argue that we are living in a universe of trillions of gigabytes and are basically "drowning in data." This data saturation comes from social media outlets, YouTube, Google searches, pictures, websites, biometrics, and everything we visit, read, talk, and listen to daily on the Internet.[19] In this context, an emerging approach to individual privacy and data protection influences the flow of intelligence sharing and constitutes an area in which the transatlantic community can work together toward common solutions. The disagreements over data sharing in the transatlantic partnership are reflected in the different conceptualizations of privacy and approaches to collection, protection, and dissemination of intelligence data. The EU argues that people should be in control of their own data, not corporations or governments. The EU is against exporting the data of its citizens or people residing within its borders without specific legal commitments from the United States that that data will be protected the same way it is in Europe.[20] Differences over what constitutes privacy, surveillance, data collection, and data protection affect the European digital economy, individual security, and international trade. Some argue that to remain in the European market, the United States will need to change its approach to surveillance. "Government surveillance of personal data is something the United States in its turn accuses China of doing through Huawei ... Data drive[s] much of the world's biggest companies like Facebook, Google, Alibaba, and Amazon and is also prized for national security to prevent extremist attacks. Mining large sets of people's data has become crucial to winning elections, such as the use of Facebook data."[21] In a data-driven economy, Europeans want control and sovereignty over their data. They have stringent privacy standards when transferring

Transatlantic Intelligence Sharing and Cooperation   65

information across borders. In July 2020 the European Court of Justice invalidated the "Privacy Shield agreement with the United States on grounds that the United States can demand access to European data for national security reasons."[22] This court injunction is one of the most important steps pursued by the EU to reassert its position in the transatlantic partnership. It amounts to an attempt by the EU to shape US practices of mass surveillance, to influence the digital future of Europe, and to improve the EU's bargaining position in the partnership.

In Europe, mass surveillance is illegal. Also, people have control over the sale of their data, including "the right to be forgotten." Americans do not have either. Anu Bradford writes that the EU leads in data protection and regulation because "the privacy right is a fundamental right in the European Union that cannot be contracted away."[23] The common belief that Americans control their own data and negotiate privacy with individual companies is incongruous with reality: in fact, individual bargaining is often weak, and people have no choice but to accept a company's policies. For example, deleting one's grandmother's hacked Facebook account can be difficult if not impossible to accomplish when the grandmother has forgotten her phone number, password, and email and is no longer using the account. Facebook does not seem to be concerned about the grandmother's situation or her psychological well-being when a hacker impersonates her on Facebook and Instagram.

Privacy challenges as they relate to intelligence sharing reflect different standards of collection and different uses of information. Compared to European standards for individual protection, US standards seem weaker, as does the regulation of private actors. The United States prioritizes free speech, perhaps above and beyond individual privacy.[24] Europeans hope to reach an agreement with the United States on data sharing that is rooted in human rights and democratic values. They are concerned about accountability, judicial review, existing frameworks, and adequate oversight of private actors. The EU has serious questions about US data collection methods and how data are used. For example, the transatlantic partnership on surveillance is affected by the different meanings attached to interference and collection. In the view of the EU, interference with an individual's privacy occurs at the inception of collection, when an individual is placed under surveillance, and at sharing, when that individual's data are shared with another party.[25] For Americans, by contrast, interference occurs at analysis, when data are being processed for further use. The data-sharing dilemma in the transatlantic relationship arises when the EU requires the consent of the European people to share their data with the United States. According to the EU Agency for Fundamental Rights (FRA), "surveillance measures constitute an interference with the right to private life, and European courts consider the collection of data by intelligence services to amount to an interference [with individual privacy]. Such interference needs to be justified

66 Adriana Seagle

to be human rights compliant."[26] A joint intelligence system is not fully developed in Europe, with the result that issues arise related to fragmented laws, levels of secrecy, oversight, accountability, and technical capacities. Thus, the United States prefers to engage in data sharing with Europeans at the bilateral rather than multilateral level.[27] In the US view, this approach is more secure and provides control over and assurances about concerns related to protection of sources and methods.

By controlling data, the EU hopes to shape Europe's sociopolitical, digital, and economic future. By putting "people first," Europeans hope to strengthen democracy as well as economic and environmental security.[28] Putting "people first" seems to contrast with the United States' perspective on economic development. According to the EC, "digital solutions that put people first will create new opportunities for businesses, will develop trustworthy technology, will foster an open and democratic society, will enable a vibrant and sustainable economy and will help fight climate change and achieve green transition."[29] From the EU's perspective, the creation of a "common standard framework" with the United States on data sharing has the potential to be extended to the global level so as to include Latin America, Asia, and Africa. Europeans reiterate that "genuine data protection" should not be perceived as "digital protectionism." It is only an opportunity to avert "digital oligarchy" of private companies that want to create rules for free speech. Angela Merkel, for example, objected to Twitter's and Facebook's decisions to bar the former US president from their media platforms.[30] Both Germany and France saw the complete dismissal of an elected president problematic, first because it was a corporate decision and not a citizens' decision, and second because online platforms within the United States are not regulated against hate speech. The regulation of a president's digital behaviour was perceived in Europe as a manifestation of "digital oligarchy" with the potential to become one of the greatest threats to digital democracy. America noticed this and began regulating the digital oligarchy through a lawsuit filed by the US Federal Trade Commission against Facebook and its attempt to form a social-networking monopoly. Europeans take immense pride in the Code of Conduct Countering Illegal Hate Speech model they have created, a model that has since been employed by the UN and in Canada, Japan, and the United States.[31]

The Geopolitics of Tech: Unequal Technological Development and the Huawei 5G Networks

The transatlantic intelligence-sharing partnership is also affected by new geopolitical challenges arising from great power competition, technological change, and Europe's delay in investing in digital infrastructure and technology. For a long time, Europe relied on the United States for technology and intelligence, and this led to subordination, dependency, complacency, disengagement, and underinvestment in models of intelligence sharing.[32] The asymmetric dependency on US technology left Europeans unprepared to develop just-in-time intelligence. This overreliance exposed them to security risks, delays in responses, and disinformation.

The Chinese-led digital belt initiative triggered in Europe a desire to build a modern digital infrastructure; in the United States, that same initiative was seen as an opportunity to shape the conversation about technology. Whose voice, technology, and initiative are prominent in the transatlantic partnership? At the European level, investments in the infrastructure of intelligence sharing have been modest; some have assessed them as patchy and outdated. Richard J. Aldrich argues, for example, that the existing infrastructure of transatlantic intelligence sharing was created during the Cold War and that its structure is not properly equipped to share information on issues beyond counter-intelligence. Aldrich notes that the relationship has also been impacted by process issues such as reluctance to share, problems with secrecy and source protection, constitutional sensitivities, privacy concerns, and the EU's data protection policies.[33] Moreover, the lack of a "European Union joint intelligence agency" has tilted the bilateral frameworks of sharing in favour of the United States. Some argue that the United States expected a multilateral "bold new intelligence sharing framework" from the Europeans. The EU, however, could not deliver that because of concerns over secrecy, privacy, and civil liberties.[34] France has launched efforts to resolve the structural problem of unequal technology. Macron, for example, argues that to be considered a serious actor in global politics, the EU will need to be first "a political power" and a technologically independent union:

> Europe needs to build its own solutions in order not to *depend on American or Chinese technologies*. If we are dependent on them, for example in telecommunications, *we cannot guarantee European citizens the secrecy of information and the security of their private data*, because we do not have this technology. As a political power, Europe must be able to provide solutions in terms of cloud technology, otherwise your data is stored in a space that does not come under its jurisdiction – which is the current situation. So, when we talk about such concrete issues as this, we are talking about politics and citizen's rights. If Europe is a political space, then we must build it so that our citizens have rights that we can politically guarantee.[35] (emphasis mine)

Attempts to protect European data have been made in security and defence policy through PESCO and the European Development Fund (EDF). Accordingly, Europeans prohibit foreign companies with third-party affiliations from gaining access to sensitive information, intellectual property, and data transfers outside of Europe. In the transatlantic partnership, the United States perceives the lack of access to information as excluding US companies from the European market, while the EU views it as a matter of reciprocity between the two powers. Europeans argue that the "American International Traffic in Arms Regulations (ITAR) also bans the export of defense-related data, technology, or knowledge from the United States without a licence, under penalty of fines or imprisonment."[36] The events of 9/11 intensified the need for transatlantic intelligence cooperation even though, decades after the end of the Cold War, some assessed that cooperation as "awkwardly challenged" because of hesitancy to share information, partial exchange of information, and different conceptualizations of threats and interests.[37] Transatlantic intelligence sharing and cooperation has been assessed as "superficial, selective, and problematic, affected by compartmentalization, source protection, different notions of privacy," and a reflection of the United States' security and intelligence interests.[38]

The technological divide between the United States and Europe has been driven by advances in technology and felt mostly in the European counterterrorism systems, which have a weak capacity to search fingerprint databases.[39] Turning to Huawei to build European digital infrastructure sounds appealing to Europeans but is a bone of contention for the United States. This issue divides the transatlantic partners and Europeans between those who believe the company will provide European data to the Chinese government and those who believe it will build affordable and competitive 5G networks that will help digitalize Europe's society and economy. For some in the EU, 5G technology is an opportunity for digitalization and development; for the United States, Huawei poses a national security and intelligence-sharing vulnerability, besides being a threat to transatlantic networking infrastructure and intelligence sharing. The United States believes that Huawei will be co-opted by the Chinese government to spy on its competitors; as such, "it is critical that European countries not give control of their critical infrastructure to Chinese giants like Huawei, or ZTE."[40] The United States has warned against Huawei while encouraging Europeans to invest in European companies.[41] Through various channels, the United States has warned Europe that a closer EU–Huawei business relationship would impact information sharing, intelligence cooperation, and interconnection between America and the EU: "America cannot have close security, intelligence and technology ties with Europe unless the European Union cuts ties with Chinese giant Huawei and embraces 'Western telecom industry.'"[42] Cutting their dependence on cheap Chinese fifth-generation digital infrastructure network was not easy for Europeans, who had achieved some major advances in the 5G network. Europe, as some suggested, "was stuck between the United States, the biggest problem, and China, the biggest fear."[43]

Investing in critical technology and reducing technological dependency of any kind is on the European agenda. Progress on transatlantic cooperation began at the G7 when members agreed to reform the international tax architecture and to subject Big Tech to a minimum 15 per cent tax.[44] Competition in the global digital race is fierce, and Europe stands against major investments made by China, the United States, and India. A new European strategy of investment focuses on funding EU-born digital start-ups in artificial intelligence and quantum computing.[45] As more of the economy is powered by online data, policymakers in the EU are questioning the US monopoly on digital infrastructure, fearing that US dominance in cloud computing through Amazon and Google will affect the EU's status as an e-commerce competitor.[46]

Strategic Geopolitical Challenges and the Transatlantic Bond

Internal and external geopolitical challenges also impact the transatlantic partnership. Internally, the level of European integration in security and foreign policy affects the partnership because, as Josep Borrell has stated, "geopolitics begins at home" since that is where Europeans struggle toward coherently integrating internal and external interests to create a common foreign policy. According to Borrell, Europe does not have a common voice in foreign policy because Europeans do not understand the world in the same way. China is developing rapidly, and this has pressured the transatlantic partnership to monitor access to resources, infrastructure, and markets. China's strategy for connecting people to people is intended to influence development of rail lines, highways, and the energy sector. Meanwhile, even while the United States has designated China (along with Russia) as a military threat that is "undermining the rule-based order," the EU views China as a potential "partner in climate change," "strategic rival in human rights," and "competitor and partner in economic development."[47] Americans view China and Russia as intending to weaken the transatlantic bond through economic coercion, asymmetric threats, and technology. China granted the EU access to its market via the EU–China Comprehensive Agreement on Investment (CAI), but that deal is currently on hold because of human rights violations and coordinated sanctions imposed by the United States, Canada, and the EU. In response to the sanctions, China has urged the EU to depoliticize access to economic markets and development. France and Germany have called for a policy of multilateralism with China, especially since the EU represents for China "open access to European markets, technology, and financial structures."[48] As some may speculate, a closer partnership between the EU and China stands to affect US interests in every domain, including economics, security, and technology.

China is the EU's biggest trading partner, including in energy, gas, and steel, as well as its biggest investor in port management and infrastructure.[49] Formulating a coordinated foreign policy for transacting with China is difficult because within the EU, intelligence is fragmented and national and foreign policy interests take precedence over the EU's foreign policy goals. Moreover, attitudes toward China are divided with regard to economic influence and sabotage. Some countries perceive China's efforts in Europe as a new source of investment and economic growth, others as a source of division and insecurity. France, for example, points to China's unfair trading practices and would like to see China involved in cooperation on climate change, intellectual property, and fair trade.[50] Both France and Germany would like to see more stringent screening measures for foreign investment.[51]

The United States would prefer a stronger European Union that is not at risk of high-tech espionage and sabotage or loss of sovereignty over data. As Mike Pompeo suggested, "sovereignty is not only about land, but it is also about information … The truth is that only nations able to protect their data will be sovereign."[52] Fear of foreign penetration and underdeveloped technological infrastructure is encouraging the United States to continue to pursue bilateral intelligence sharing with European countries; for mentoring purposes, it is trying to maintain a different relationship with the "new Europe."

Resurgent Russia and Nord Stream 2

Nord Stream 2 has been described as a "failed test for European Union unity and trans-Atlantic coordination because it discloses political and security divisions inside Europe with respect to Russia, casts doubt on trans-Atlantic security ties, and exacerbates mistrust on both sides of the Atlantic."[53] Threats to withdraw US security protection for Europe as well as US sanctions on European companies put Germany on notice to change its position. "European sovereignty must not be misunderstood or reinterpreted as a fortress Europe. Strong Europe, yes. Isolation from the USA, no," said Peter Bayer, the German transatlantic coordinator.[54] Austria, France, and Germany saw the isolation of Putin as counterproductive for European security, yet the United States believed it had the global support to pressure Russia to keep its promise to strengthen democracy, human rights, and the rule of law in its sphere of influence.

Within the EU, changing geopolitical currents are overheating the economic competition and threatening the survival of the union from various directions. Nord Stream 2 is a major foreign policy challenge for Germany as well as an issue that is dividing Europe over how to conceptualize common threats to domestic and foreign policy interests. Washington applied sanctions on companies involved in completing the pipeline and promoted narratives that drew attention to threats to the United States.[55] Germany applied the principle of sovereignty to question US motives for interfering in Nord Stream 2.[56] France reminded Europeans of the possibility of building up European strategic autonomy to prevent companies from being sanctioned by the United States as well as to create a stronger Europe. As President Macron argued:

How do we decide for ourselves? That is precisely what autonomy is: the idea that we choose our own rules for ourselves. This means revisiting policies that we had become accustomed to, technological, financial, and monetary policies, policies with which we, in Europe, are building solutions for ourselves, for our companies, for our fellow citizens, which enable us to cooperate with others, with those we choose, but not depend on others, which is still too often the case today.[57]

Russia's invasion of Ukraine concluded some aspects of the controversial chapter on Nord Stream 2; however, the debate continues with the dismantling of the pipeline infrastructure. In hindsight, Nord Stream 2 tested Germany's reliability and ability to unite Europeans against an imminent threat. Although viewed as "one of the leading physical powers in NATO," Germany could not convince Russia not to invade Ukraine, nor could it persuade NATO to refrain from sending lethal weapons to the conflict zone. As the German chancellor said: "The Russian invasion of Ukraine marks a turning point. It threatens our entire post-war order. In this situation, it is our duty to do our utmost to support Ukraine."[58]

In retrospect, a joint European intelligence system could have prevented the deepening of divisions and properly guided the EU toward pursuing short- and long-term energy security and economic interests. Perceptions that one country within the EU will get more than others on the periphery are not new in European politics, and mistrust creates divisions easily exploited. Poland, Ukraine, and Slovakia, for example, perceive Nord Stream 2 as deepening the political and energy security of Russia, while Hungary and Germany envision the project as an economic opportunity with spillover effects for European security and economic development.

Intelligence-Sharing and Transatlantic Strategic Trust

Trust ought to influence the transatlantic partnership at many levels, including US loyalty and leadership as well as the EU's capacity to remain a reliable partner for delivering results. Since its founding, the transatlantic partnership has been renewed, rescued, reinvented, transformed, and now modernized. Whether it was military relations, improvement in trade and economic cooperation, or contention over the euro, the transatlantic partners strove for closer political cooperation and consultation. In the 1940s, the United States desired and promoted European integration more than the Europeans themselves; by the 1960s, the United States feared growing European influence over trade. Some authors argue that US support was always conditional and based on the benefits of and changes to the international political scene. "In the early years of the European Economic Community (EEC) the United States saw the Europeans as somewhat inferior to the Americans in every realm whether it was economic progress, management techniques, education or technological innovation, they also believed that partnership with Europe was giving very little benefits to the United States."[59] The end of the Cold War deepened the transatlantic partnership to include a common agenda and a joint plan of action to strengthen democracy, human rights, and the rule of law. Some authors assess the transformation of this relationship in "revolutionary" terms because it set up an institutional framework, renewed transatlantic solidarity, recognized the interdependent character of globalization, and identified specific areas of cooperation.[60] I contend that the transatlantic partnership is in search of a relationship of equality, as well as a common strategy to solve socio-economic and political challenges related to global crime, terrorism, environmental destruction, poverty, and disease. Economic, educational, scientific, and cultural cooperation was supposed to transform transatlantic diplomatic relations from an alliance into a relationship of equal partners. Both partners promised to inform and consult each other on matters that affected common security interests.[61]

Historically, transatlantic intelligence sharing and cooperation has been initiated and coordinated by the United States in the military sector. More recently, it has evolved to include exchanges of information in the human security sector. Through NATO, the United States has provided Europe with expertise and technological means to collect, analyse, and disseminate information about the former Soviet Union. The rapid development of technology and the investment gap within the partnership has placed the EU in a subordinate position and at a great disadvantage. Recent reports reveal a gap of €2 billion per year in investment.[62] Furthermore, the EU's ineffective efforts to combat corruption and strengthen democracy have affected mutual trust with the United States. In its "emergence as a global regulatory power," the EU has been unable to achieve the concrete results the Americans expected, and this has affected the relationship.[63] Corruption, defined as "the abuse of power for private gain" is a "eurocrime" and a threat to European security and transatlantic intelligence sharing because it erodes trust in governments and the EU's capacity to address issues such as human trafficking, money laundering, counterfeiting, and border security.[64] Since the end of the Cold War, Europeans have expected to address global threats in partnership with the United States; the United States, however, has wanted Europe to first become secure at home while addressing weak institutions and corruption in transitioning democracies. The United States instrumentally used NATO's deterrence umbrella to guarantee security in Europe and to ensure that countries on the European periphery had opportunities to strengthen their democracies and build roads, bridges, hospitals, and schools. The United States wanted the EU to strengthen its economic integration and cohesion and to advance common goals of democracy, human rights, and the rule of law. Amid these challenges, the United States intends to modernize its alliances so as to transact with more "open and secure" partners. The Americans

Transatlantic Intelligence Sharing and Cooperation 73

continue to invest in socio-economic modernization through a military lens in the hope that while they improve their military capabilities and readiness, EU countries will reach a deeper understanding of one another's domestic security needs.[65]

Mutual trust drives intelligence sharing; a deficit in trust impedes it. From one perspective, it impacts the partnership when top-secret-cleared individuals are found passing secrets to Russia in exchange for money, or when, say, Bulgaria expels Russian diplomats for "activities incompatible with diplomatic work."[66] From another perspective, pursuing strategies such as the recent AUKUS plan or the withdrawal from Afghanistan without proper European consultation spreads disillusion and mistrust in the partnership.[67] When signing the Transatlantic Declaration at the end of the Cold War, both members agreed to closer consultations:

> To achieve their common goals, the European Community and its Member States and the United States of America *will inform and consult each other on important matters of common interest, both political and economic, with a view to bringing their positions as close as possible, without prejudice to their respective independence.*[68] (emphasis added)

Europeans are concerned about shifts in US loyalty and in their interests in Europe.[69] France, notably, insists on clarifying NATO's role in European security: "We are in a moment of clarification for NATO. We must clarify the new concepts and our new willingness. Who is the enemy? NATO was created to fight against the USSR. Now who is the enemy? Who [are] the terrorists and the main enemy now of our societies, obviously?"[70] Americans prefer not to think about allies in isolation; even so, the Biden administration refers to Europe in the context of both allies and partners. In his speech titled "Reaffirming and Reimagining America's Alliances," Antony Blinken stated:

> Now, America's allies and partners may be listening to my words and saying, "We need to know what we can expect from you." Because as I said, *trust has been shaken to some degree over the past few years.* So, let me be clear about what the United States can promise to our allies and partners. When our allies shoulder their fair share of the burden, they will reasonably expect to have a fair say in making decisions. We will honor that. That begins with consulting our friends early and often. This is a key part of the foreign policy in the Biden–Harris administration, and it is a change our allies already see and appreciate.[71] (emphasis added)

The transatlantic intelligence-sharing system has survived periods of high tension. "Snooping on allies" is a betrayal of trust, besides being a "waste of energy," according to past German chancellor Angela Merkel, who questioned

US intentions, reiterating that "security depends on trust between allies" and the prioritization of core problems.[72] Ursula von der Leyen has called for "a fresh start with each other."[73] After 9/11, transatlantic intelligence sharing and cooperation demonstrated a degree of success in counterterrorism; sharing intelligence in the socio-economic, business, and technology sectors will require more investment, stability, integration, and trust. Merkel believed that sharing intelligence on common threats could build more trust between allies and "more trust can mean more security."[74] The transatlantic relationship was impacted by Donald Trump's offensive rhetorical attacks to the extent that some have labelled the transatlantic challenges "the crisis of leadership in the United States and the crisis of democracy in Europe."[75]

Also relevant are disunity among alliance members and cultural differences in how Americans and Europeans understand intelligence sharing and integration. Since the end of the Cold War, Europeans have debated whether to create a joint European intelligence system wired by European technology; the idea has yet to bear fruit, because the word intelligence does not have a common meaning and collecting information too often triggers emotions related to state surveillance and communism.[76] Americans perceive intelligence sharing and integration at the European level as impossible. In their view, Europeans thrive in a climate of heavy regulation and institutional disorder; thus, any attempt to create a joint intelligence system that is functional and efficient is doomed to fail because Europeans lack a mutual understanding of threats and a solid history of trust among themselves. In the US vocabulary, intelligence is about developing a strategic advantage over a country or enemy by protecting secrets and sources and controlling information. In the European sense, intelligence is law enforcement information shared bilaterally or multilaterally to counter threats against the state. Lack of trust, the compromising of sources, and hoarding information as a means to acquire and preserve power are the most frequent obstacles to intelligence sharing and cooperation.[77] "Information is power and in intelligence, one has only enemies, no friends," said once a senior French intelligence official.[78]

European strategic autonomy is part of an attempt to decouple from Cold War era structures. Europeans perceive Russia as a greater threat than China. The question of how to approach China and Russia is a contentious one. Europeans would like to see a combination of military strength and civilian engagement. Regarding China, Europeans would like to combat China's state surveillance model through regulation, inclusion, and dialogue. They would welcome US leadership in creating global standards for digital surveillance.[79] Europeans view strategic autonomy in security and defence as a way of addressing European strategic interests and managing prospective conflicts. The military instrument can allow them to act based on European security interests in the Euro-Atlantic and Indo-Pacific regions. Since NATO's founding, the

United States has enjoyed the strongest influence in the transatlantic partnership; however, behind closed doors Europeans well understand that more US missiles in Europe could provoke Russia. In the event that the United States becomes more autonomous in decision-making or begins restricting access to intelligence and defence technology, they would like to have a European army to defend themselves.[80]

Following Russia's invasion of Ukraine, Europe is more aware of the need to invest in intelligence technology and share infrastructure to avoid strategic surprises. However, the Ukrainian case also demonstrates that Europe is insufficiently prepared to define and defend security interests on the continent in the absence of NATO and the United States. Moreover, the invasion of Ukraine has exposed Russia's fierce determination to use force against opponents in its spheres of influence. From the European perspective, the lack of progress in shaping intelligence sharing within the transatlantic partnership has been revealed by the failure to anticipate Russia's intentions and the neglect of intelligence on risks to Europe's energy security. Distrust in the information shared by the United States is also relevant to consider, given that, despite all the access it had to highly classified intelligence from reliable sources, including modern satellites, interceptions, and human sources, the United States struggled to convince Europeans that Putin planned to invade Ukraine.[81] This is another indicator that division and mistrust still exist in the transatlantic partnership. Some report that "Europeans are quietly working on building resilience and a European security infrastructure, including a European cloud, a semiconductor industry, energy networks, and a military-industrial capacity."[82] From the US perspective, Russia's invasion presented Washington with another great opportunity to assess the strength and will of the alliance, rebuild confidence in it, and project power worldwide by reassuring allies and partners.

In retrospect, transatlantic intelligence sharing and cooperation reveals that the two largest democratic blocs share a common history, substantive challenges, and opportunities in intelligence and security. The EU's influence within the transatlantic partnership is increasing, and the EU is becoming strategically more assertive. Aware of the international power dynamics and of geopolitical and technological realities, it is seeking a stronger partnership based on respect, equality, and fair competition. European strategic autonomy is a sign of maturity, decoupling, and a desire to exert more control over security and defence matters in Europe. The EU is willing to engage with the United States on strengthening multilateral action and institutions. In trade, transatlantic intelligence-sharing opportunities are possible when it comes to defending the international system of rules-based trade, addressing China's trading practices, and strengthening oversight of foreign investment.

At the same time, differences within the transatlantic partnership have become more stark. The EU is against exporting European data without specific legal commitments from the United States that data will be protected. Data-sharing issues have challenged both parties to negotiate a legal framework for collection and sharing that is rooted in human rights and democratic values. Unequal technological development is a structural problem that challenges the transatlantic partnership in at least two ways. First, the EU is behind the United States and China in industrial digitalization and is taking steps to more tightly regulate US companies. Second, turning to Chinese companies such as Huawei to build European digital infrastructure has the potential to create an irreparable transatlantic rift, given that the United States perceives that company as a threat to its strategic interests. Regional and global geopolitics also affect the transatlantic partnership as a result of differing perceptions of threats. The United States categorizes China and Russia as military threats, whereas the EU is still debating whether China is a source of investment and economic progress or a threat to European unity and security. Even so, transatlantic cooperation on Russia and China remains an area of convergence in which both parties can find opportunities to cooperate. Strengthening the transatlantic partnership is desirable, but to bring Europeans on board, the United States will need to find something more concrete and appealing than fighting Russia. Embracing Europeans' desire to engage in the Indo-Pacific region and waiving sanctions on the Russian pipeline are two great opportunities to start building community in transatlantic relations. As former Italian prime minister Silvio Berlusconi once said, "Europe needs America and America needs Europe."[83]

Mutual trust and respect are at the core of transatlantic intelligence sharing. Europeans hope to see in the United States a partner that is loyal to European security interests and that acknowledges the EU as an equal partner. They would like to see in the United States a partner they can trust to engage in regulating technology and global trade and with which to craft global standards to protect common values. The United States would prefer to see more cohesion and stability within the EU. It would like to engage with a stronger, more reliable, and more innovative partner. As an American political scholar once noted, "the future is not some place we are going, but one we are creating. The paths are not to be found but made."[84] As the EU becomes more assertive in its role and more interested in partnership, the United States can continue to provide leadership, knowledge, and support regarding how to reinvent and strengthen multilateral institutions. For example, improvements to transatlantic intelligence sharing and cooperation could begin in Europe through investment, innovation, and the development of green security institutions and frameworks for intelligence collection and sharing. Taking the initiative in building a twenty-first century intelligence-sharing infrastructure may prompt the United States to seek a stronger partnership with the EU in terms of developing standards for surveillance that will contain the digital authoritarian model.

NOTES

1 Maciej Osowski, "EU-US intelligence sharing post 9/11: predictions for the future," *E-International Relations*, 8 March 2011, 3, https://www.e-ir.info/2011/03/08/eu-us-intelligence-sharing-post-911-predictions-for-the-future; Adam D.M. Svendsen, "Connecting Intelligence and Theory: Intelligence Liaison and International Relations," *Intelligence and National Security* 24, no. 5 (2009): 700–29.
2 Svendsen, "Connecting Intelligence and Theory," 704.
3 Svendsen, "Connecting Intelligence and Theory," 713.
4 James Igoe Walsh, *The International Politics of Intelligence Sharing* (New York: Columbia University Press, 2010).
5 Tasneem Sultana, "A Survey of US–Europe Relations," *Pakistan Journal of European Studies* 30, no. 2 (2014): 56–75.
6 Walsh, *The International Politics of Intelligence Sharing*, 17.
7 Martin Phillipson, "The United States Withdrawal from the Kyoto Protocol," *Irish Jurist, New Series* 36 (2001): 288–304; "US renounces world court treaty," BBC News, 6 May 2002, http://news.bbc.co.uk/2/hi/americas/1970312.stm.
8 John M. Nomikos, "Transatlantic Intelligence Cooperation, the Global War on Terrorism, and International Order," in *International Order in a Globalizing World*, ed. Yiannis A. Stivachtis (London: Ashgate, 2007), 162.
9 European Commission, "Trading with the United States," https://ec.europa.eu/trade/policy/countries-and-regions/countries/united-states.
10 Council of the European Union, "Council Decision authorizing the opening of negotiations with the United States of America for an agreement on the elimination of tariffs for industrial goods," Brussels, 9 April 2019, https://www.consilium.europa.eu/media/39180/st06052-en19.pdf.
11 European Union External Action, "EU Strategy for Cooperation in the Indo-Pacific," 19 April 2021, https://eeas.europa.eu/headquarters/headquarters-homepage_en/96741/EU%20Strategy%20for%20Cooperation%20in%20the%20Indo-Pacific.
12 Frederic Grare and Manisha Reuter, "Moving closer: European views of the Indo-Pacific," European Council of Foreign Relations, 13 September 2021, https://ecfr.eu/special/moving-closer-european-views-of-the-indo-pacific/#conclusion.
13 Office of the United States Trade Representative, "Benefits of Trade," https://ustr.gov/about-us/benefits-trade.
14 Council of the European Union, "EU–US Summit statement: Towards a renewed Transatlantic partnership," 15 June 2021, https://ec.europa.eu/trade/policy/countries-and-regions/countries/united-states.
15 Witney Schneidman and Joel Wigert, "Competing in Africa: China, the European Union, and the United States," Brookings Institution, 16 April 2018, https://www.brookings.edu/blog/africa-in-focus/2018/04/16/competing-in-africa-china-the-european-union-and-the-united-states.

16 Schneidman and Wigert, "Competing in Africa."

17 Jim Brunsden and Aime Williams, "EU seeks to 'reboot' US trade relationship in post-Trump era," *Financial Times*, 9 November 2020, https://www.ft.com/content /eaef2ca9-b2b5-4cd3-82ed-09e52c21843e.

18 "Interview granted to *Le Grand Continent Magazine* by the French President Emmanuel Macron," 16 November 2020, https://www.elysee.fr/en/emmanuel -macron/2020/11/16/interview-granted-to-le-grand-continent-magazine-by-the -french-president-emmanuel-macron.

19 Sunil Soares, *Big Data Governance: An Emerging Imperative* (Boise: MC Press, 2012).

20 Stewart Baker, "Time to get serious about Europe's sabotage of US terror intelligence programs," *Washington Post*, 5 January 2016, https://www .washingtonpost.com/news/volokh-conspiracy/wp/2016/01/05/time-to-get -serious-about-europes-sabotage-of-us-terror-intelligence-programs.

21 "EU court cancels US data-sharing pact over snooping concerns," NBC News, 16 July 2020, https://www.nbcnews.com/tech/tech-news/eu-court-cancels-us-data -sharing-pact-snooping-concerns-rcna50.

22 Carlo Piovano, "EU court cancels US-data sharing pact over snooping concerns," *Washington Post*, 16 July 2020, https://www.washingtonpost.com/world/the _americas/eu-court-strikes-down-data-sharing-pact-with-us/2020/07/16/5afeae68 -c73b-11ea-a825-8722004e4150_story.html.

23 Anu Bradford, *The Brussels Effect: How the European Union Rules the World* (Oxford: Oxford University Press, 2020), 132.

24 Samuel W. Royston, "The Right to Be Forgotten: Comparing the US and European Approaches," *St. Mary's Law Journal* 48. no. 2 (2020): 253–75.

25 FRA European Union Agency for Fundamental Rights, "Surveillance by intelligence services: fundamental rights safeguards and remedies in the EU. Vol. II: field perspectives and legal update," 2016, 35, https://fra.europa.eu/sites/default /files/fra_uploads/fra-2017-surveillance-intelligence-services-vol-2_en.pdf.

26 FRA European Union Agency for Fundamental Rights, "Surveillance by intelligence services," 9.

27 Jan-Hendrick Dietrich and Satish Sule, eds., *Intelligence Law and Policies in Europe* (London: Hart, 2019).

28 European Commission, "Shaping Europe's digital future," https://ec.europa.eu /info/strategy/priorities-2019-2024/europe-fit-digital-age/shaping-europe-digital -future_en.

29 European Commission, "Shaping Europe's digital future."

30 Birgit Jennen and Ania Nussbaum, "Germany and France oppose Trump's Twitter exile," *Bloomberg*, 11 January 2021, https://www.bloombergquint.com/politics /merkel-sees-closing-trump-s-social-media-accounts-problematic.

31 "Speech by Commissioner Reynders at American Chamber of Commerce on the Digital Transatlantic Economy," European Commission, Brussels, 26 March 2021,

https://europa.eu/newsroom/content/speech-commissioner-reynders-american
-chamber-commerce-digital-transatlantic-economy_fr.

32 Walsh, *The International Politics of Intelligence Sharing*, 5.

33 Richard J. Aldrich 2004, "Transatlantic Intelligence and Security Cooperation,"
International Affairs 80, no. 4 (2004): 740.

34 Aldrich, "Transatlantic Intelligence and Security Cooperation," 740.

35 "Interview granted to *Le Grand Continent Magazine* by the French President
Emmanuel Macron."

36 Sophia Besch and Luigi Scazzieri, "European Strategic Autonomy and a New
Transatlantic Bargain," Centre for European Reform, Policy Brief, 11 December
2020, https://www.cer.eu/publications/archive/policy-brief/2020/european
-strategic-autonomy-and-new-transatlantic-bargain.

37 Aldrich, "Transatlantic Intelligence and Security Cooperation," 731–53.

38 Aldrich, "Transatlantic Intelligence and Security Cooperation," 732.

39 Robin Simcox, "Europe, Stop Trying to Make 'Intelligence Sharing' Happen,"
Foreign Policy, 14 April 2016, https://foreignpolicy.com/2016/04/14/europe-stop
-trying-to-mak-brussels-paris-bombings.

40 Ed Cropley, "Breakingviews – UK's Huawei call is anti-Trump parting gift to EU,"
Reuters, 28 January 2020, https://www.reuters.com/article/us-britain-usa-huawei
-breakingviews-idINKBN1ZR20Q.

41 Peter Newman, "How the US Buying Ericsson or Nokia Would Impact
Networking," *Business Insider*, 10 February 2020, https://www.businessinsider.com
/us-could-buy-ericsson-nokia-to-compete-against-huawei-report-2020-2.

42 Alexandra Brzozowski, "US ambassador: Europe should forget Huawei, embrace
Western tech," *Euractiv*, 1 January 2021, https://www.euractiv.com/section/global
-europe/interview/us-ambassador-europe-should-forget-huawei-embrace-western-tech.

43 Giannis Seferiadis, "EU hopes for 'tech alliance' with Biden after Trump Huawei
5G ban," *Nikkei Asia*, 12 January 2021, https://asia.nikkei.com/Spotlight/Asia
-Insight/EU-hopes-for-tech-alliance-with-Biden-after-Trump-Huawei-5G-ban.

44 Reuters, "The G7 has agreed to set a global minimum tax rate: What does it mean
and how will it work?," *Euronews*, 19 July 2021, https://www.euronews.com
/next/2021/06/05/the-g7-has-agreed-to-set-a-global-minimum-tax-rate-what
-does-it-mean-and-how-will-it-work; Mark Scott and Laurens Cerulus, "EU-US
'tech alliance' faces major obstacles on tax, digital rules," *Politico*, 2 December 2020,
https://www.politico.eu/article/eu-to-us-president-elect-joe-biden-lets-be-tech-allies.

45 Mark Scott, "What's driving Europe's new aggressive stance on tech," *Politico*, 27
October 2020, https://www.politico.com/news/2019/10/28/europe-technology
-silicon-valley-059988.

46 Scott, "What's driving Europe's new aggressive stance on tech."

47 Antony J. Blinken, "Reaffirming and Reimagining America's Alliances" (Speech),
NATO Headquarters Agora, Brussels, 24 March 2021, https://www.state.gov
/reaffirming-and-reimagining-americas-alliances.

48 Andrew Small, "European ideas about a new world political regime to tackle the issues of China," *JAPECO*, 10 March 2021, https://www.jef.or.jp/journal/pdf/236th_Cover_Story_06.pdf.

49 Alexandra Ma, "This is China's playbook to pit EU countries against each other," *Business Insider*, 24 March 2019, https://www.businessinsider.com/inside-china-playbook-to-pit-eu-countries-against-each-other-2019-3.

50 Dave Lawer, "How Emmanuel Macron sees the China challenge," *Axios*, 5 February 2021, https://www.axios.com/france-macron-china-strategy-europe-1e8d986c-5aa8-4a57-9ae0-85b130b1e914.html.

51 Ma, "This is China's playbook."

52 Anna Mikhailova and Ben Riley-Smith, "Britain's sovereignty at risk if it allows Huawei to access 5G network, US Secretary of State warns," *The Telegraph*, 26 January 2020, https://www.telegraph.co.uk/politics/2020/01/26/britains-sovereignty-risk-allows-huawei-access-5g-network-us.

53 Giovanna De Maio, "Nord Stream 2: A Failed Test for EU Unity and Transatlantic Coordination," *Order from Chaos*, 22 April 2019, https://www.brookings.edu/blog/order-from-chaos/2019/04/22/nord-stream-2-a-failed-test-for-eu-unity-and-trans-atlantic-coordination.

54 Max Haerder, "Transatlantic coordinator calls for a moratorium on Nord Stream 2," *WirtschaftsWoche*, 31 March 2021.

55 "US: Nord Stream raises intelligence concerns," *Euractiv*, 18 May 2018, https://www.euractiv.com/section/energy/news/us-nord-stream-raises-intelligence-concerns.

56 "Maas: Germany not planning to back down in US Nord Stream 2 dispute," *DPA International*, 28 December 2020, https://www.dpa-international.com/topic/maas-germany-planning-back-us-nord-stream-2-dispute-urn%3Anewsml%3Adpa.com%3A20090101%3A201228-99-829542.

57 "Interview granted to *Le Grand Continent Magazine* by the French President Emmanuel Macron."

58 David M. Herszenhorn, Lili Bayer, and Hans Von Der Burchard. 2022. "Germany to send Ukraine weapons in a historic shift on military aid." *Politico*. 26 February 2022. https://www.politico.eu/article/ukraine-war-russia-germany-still-blocking-arms-supplies.

59 Sultana, "A Survey of US–Europe Relations."

60 Alan Henrikson, "Atlantic Diplomacy Transformed: From the 'Transatlantic Declaration' (1990) to the 'New Transatlantic Agenda' (1995)," Fifth Biennial International Conference of the European Community Studies Association, 31 May 1997, http://aei.pitt.edu/2613.

61 "Transatlantic Declaration on EC-US Relations, 1990," European Parliament, https://www.europarl.europa.eu/cmsdata/124320/trans_declaration_90_en.pdf.

62 "EIB warns of 5G investment gap between EU and US," *EUObserver*, 24 February 2021, https://euobserver.com/tickers/151033.

63 Bradford, *The Brussels Effect*, 1.

64 Migration and Home Affairs, "Corruption," *European Commission,* accessed 29 March 2021, https://ec.europa.eu/home-affairs/what-we-do/policies/organized-crime-and-human-trafficking/corruption_en.

65 Blinken, "Reaffirming and Reimagining America's Alliances."

66 Mark Lowen, "Italian officer 'caught selling secrets to Russia," BBC, 31 March 2021, https://www.bbc.com/news/world-europe-56588506.

67 Atlantic Council, "Transcript: President Macron on His Vision for Europe and the Future of Transatlantic Relations," 5 February 2021, https://www.atlanticcouncil.org/news/transcripts/transcript-president-macron-on-his-vision-for-europe-and-the-future-of-transatlantic-relations; Michelle Nichols, "EU backs France in submarine dispute, asking: Is America back?" *Reuters*, 21 September 2021, https://www.reuters.com/world/europe/eu-foreign-ministers-discuss-submarine-dispute-monday-2021-09-20.

68 "Transatlantic Declaration on EC–US Relations, 1990."

69 Atlantic Council, "Transcript: President Macron on His Vision for Europe."

70 Atlantic Council, "Transcript: President Macron on His vision for Europe."

71 Blinken, "Reaffirming and Reimagining America's Alliances."

72 Frank Zeller, "Germany kicks out top US intelligence officer in spy row," *Agence France Presse*, 10 July 2014, https://news.yahoo.com/germany-expels-top-us-intelligence-officer-spy-row-142742446.html.

73 Zeller, "Germany kicks out top US intelligence officer in spy row."

74 Zeller, "Germany kicks out top US intelligence officer in spy row."

75 Nicholas Burns, "The Transatlantic Relationship in Crisis," Speech in Madrid, Spain, 6 July 2018, https://www.belfercenter.org/publication/transatlantic-relationship-crisis.

76 Dietrich and Sule, *Intelligence Law and Policies in Europe*, 32.

77 Simcox, "Europe, Stop Trying to Make 'Intelligence Sharing' Happen."

78 Simcox, "Europe, Stop Trying to Make 'Intelligence Sharing' Happen."

79 Erik Brattberg, "Reinventing Transatlantic Relations on Climate, Democracy, and Technology," Carnegie Endowment for International Peace, 23 December 2020, https://carnegieendowment.org/2020/12/23/reinventing-transatlantic-relations-on-climate-democracy-and-technology-pub-83527.

80 Alexandra Brzozowski, "Can reform and refocus save 'brain dead' NATO?" *Euractiv*, 4 December 2020, https://www.euractiv.com/section/politics/news/can-reform-and-refocus-save-brain-dead-nato.

81 Shane Harris, Karen De Young, Isabelle Khurshudyan, Ashley Parker, and Liz Sly, "Road to war: the US struggled to convince allies, and Zelensky, of risk of invasion," *Washington Post*, 16 August 2022, https://www.washingtonpost.com/national-security/interactive/2022/ukraine-road-to-war.

82 Tom McTague, "Putin has made America great again," *The Atlantic*, 19 February 2022, https://www.theatlantic.com/international/archive/2022/02/russia-ukraine-invasion-american-role/622864.

82   Adriana Seagle

83 Daniel Fried, "The US–European Relationship: Opportunities and Challenges,"
    US Department of State, 8 March 2006, https://2001-2009.state.gov/p/eur/rls
    /rm/62740.htm.
84 John H. Schaar quote, in *Goodreads,* accessed 4 November 2021, https://www
    .goodreads.com/author/show/343198.John_H_Schaar.

4 Don't Hold Back: Canadianize

THOMAS JUNEAU AND STEPHANIE CARVIN

Should Canada have a foreign human intelligence service? The United States has the Central Intelligence Agency, the United Kingdom has the Secret Intelligence Service, and Australia has its Australian Secret Intelligence Service; Canada has not had an equivalent since the end of the Second World War. The government has access to some foreign intelligence through several agencies with the appropriate mandates and collection capabilities, but overall, Canada is a net recipient of foreign intelligence thanks to its many intelligence cooperation partnerships, especially the Five Eyes. But given the threats that are emerging in the twenty-first century, including rising great power competition, cyber, foreign interference, and transnational violent extremism, in a less stable global environment, is it time to rethink this state of affairs?

On the one hand, Canada can compensate for its weaker foreign intelligence collection capabilities through a range of cooperation partnerships. At a limited cost, Canada has access to an immense pool of raw and finished foreign intelligence, much of it collected by some of the world's most important intelligence powers. However, this situation comes with downsides. One of these, which is the focus of this chapter, is that the large amount of foreign intelligence that Canada receives usually reflects the priorities and interests of others and not necessarily those of Canada. It also makes Canada vulnerable if some of those allies and partners choose to reduce this cooperation.

To be sure, so far this has been a "happy problem": Canada is lucky to be in a position where it receives large amounts of foreign intelligence – more than it can consume – from allies and partners. Many countries suffer, to varying degrees, from the opposite problem – the difficulty in getting good amounts of reliable foreign intelligence – while facing more threats than Canada. Nevertheless, it is useful, especially in the context of Canada's deteriorating threat environment and its growing anxiety with regard to the future reliability of the United States as a close ally, to think about the implications of this paradox and about what Canada has done, and could do, to improve the situation.

The (admittedly limited) debate in Canada has long focused on whether the country should establish its own foreign human intelligence service. This is an important question, and there are valid arguments for and against. Yet whatever the merits of the arguments on either side, it remains that Canada is simply unlikely to implement such a major reform to its national security architecture for the foreseeable future, for a range of economic, political, cultural, and institutional reasons.

To mitigate the challenges posed by its heavy reliance on foreign intelligence, and with little prospect that a foreign human intelligence service will be established, Canada's national security and intelligence community has in recent years taken steps to "Canadianize" its foreign intelligence collection and analysis. The use of foreign intelligence and its input into broader decision-making processes has increasingly come to be viewed through a prism more focused on specifically Canadian interests. In this chapter, we present the context that has led to the emergence of this trend and explain why it is, all things considered, a positive development.

After an overview of our methodology, we explain how Canada became over the decades a major beneficiary of various intelligence cooperation partnerships. We then analyse the costs and benefits of the status quo. After that, we debate the two main alternatives to this status quo: the creation of a foreign intelligence service, which we argue is unlikely, and then the notion of Canadianization. We then explain how the Canadianization of foreign intelligence has already begun. Finally, we analyse the consequences by focusing on how it benefits Canadian national security directly while also positioning Canada to diversify and intensify its intelligence partnerships in an increasingly multipolar world.

Methods

The research for this chapter stems from a larger project examining the relationship between intelligence analysis and policy-making in Canada. We conducted sixty-eight interviews with serving and retired national security practitioners, mostly from Canada but approximately 15 per cent from allied countries. Within Canada, interviewees were individuals with experience on either the analytical side (as analysts and managers) or the consumer side (as policy-makers using intelligence analysis), and sometimes both. Interviewees ranged from desk officers and analysts all the way up to deputy ministers and agency heads. We also interviewed senior political advisers to serving and past ministers and prime ministers. In addition, we interviewed serving and retired practitioners in the United States, which allowed us to better understand the Canada–US intelligence relationship, on which Canada is so dependent, and to draw limited comparisons between the Canadian and American experiences. Interviewees thus represented a broad sample, regarding both the nature of their work and their level in the hierarchy. In addition to these interviews, we relied on primary documents, media reports, conversations held under the Chatham House rule, and the limited academic literature on Canadian national security.

The majority of our interviewees agreed to speak only on the basis of strict anonymity. So we do not identify them, either by name or by place of work. Even when interviewees (most of them retired individuals) agreed to speak on record, we have chosen to keep their comments anonymous, for the sake of consistency and on the grounds that the Canadian intelligence and national security community is so small that the identification of one person might accidentally lead to the identification of another, if only by a process of elimination.

Canada's Limited Foreign Intelligence Collection Capability

Canada's lack of a foreign human intelligence agency does not prevent it from collecting foreign intelligence. Several departments and agencies have a mandate to do so.[1]

The Communications Security Establishment (CSE) is Canada's national cryptologic agency. It is responsible for collecting foreign intelligence through the global information infrastructure, defined under section 2 of the *CSE Act* as "information or intelligence about the capabilities, intentions or activities of a foreign individual, state, organization or terrorist group as they relate to international affairs, defence or security." Importantly, CSE cannot knowingly collect information on any Canadian citizen. However, it may provide technical assistance to intelligence and law enforcement agencies on a range of tasks, including monitoring communications, with the proper legal authorization, in most cases a warrant.[2]

The Canadian Security Intelligence Service (CSIS) collects security (rather than foreign) intelligence. It may operate outside of Canada so long as the threat it investigates relates to the security of Canada as defined in the *CSIS Act*. In addition, this act stipulates that the service can collect foreign intelligence but only "within" Canada and on matters requested by the Minister of Foreign Affairs or the Minister of National Defence. In practice, this means the collection of "non-threat related intelligence" that pertains, for example, to Canada's international competitiveness.[3]

The Department of National Defence and the Canadian Armed Forces (DND/CAF) collect and analyse the widest variety of intelligence to support their mandate, including geospatial, signals, and human intelligence, among a wide range of capabilities. The main unit that does so is the Canadian Forces Intelligence Command, or CFINTCOM. However, intelligence gathering is limited to the Department's and the Forces' core responsibilities, which include "research and development, capability development and defence procurement, and capability development and force generation activities," as well as the planning and execution of routine and contingency operations. CFINTCOM can also respond to lawful requests for intelligence support from external stakeholders, and it provides intelligence products to other government departments and agencies in line with Canada's national security objectives.[4]

Within Global Affairs Canada (GAC), Canada's foreign affairs ministry, the Global Security Reporting Program (GSRP) has a dedicated staff that collects "political reporting" based on missions in critical countries around the world. GSRP officers do not operate covertly; they are declared diplomats whose work is in full compliance with the Vienna Convention on Diplomatic Relations and who simply spend most of their time meeting a range of interesting individuals who hold potentially relevant information. They then circulate reports back to headquarters. It is, in this sense, traditional diplomatic reporting. That said, GSRP reporting is also widely distributed among Canadian intelligence agencies and shared with allies.[5]

Finally, it is worth mentioning two analytical units that do not collect intelligence but use intelligence from both Canadian and foreign intelligence agencies to build analytical products in support of national security policy and operations. The Intelligence Assessment Secretariat within the Privy Council Office (PCO/IAS) provides high-level strategic analysis to the prime minister, Cabinet, and the rest of the public service.[6] Additionally, the Integrated Terrorism Assessment Centre (ITAC) produces threat and risk assessments generally, and specifically for special events. It is also responsible for setting the National Terrorism Threat Level.[7]

Canada as a Major Beneficiary of Intelligence Cooperation Arrangements

Canada does not have a dedicated foreign human intelligence agency, but it does collect and analyse foreign intelligence through a variety of means. The amount it collects itself is still relatively limited compared to many of its key allies; the bulk of the raw and finished intelligence it has access to instead flows from a range of cooperation arrangements.

Of these arrangements, the most important is the Five Eyes, an intelligence-sharing partnership between Australia, Canada, New Zealand, the United Kingdom, and the United States with its origins in the Second World War. Within the Five Eyes, the most active partners are the United States, the United Kingdom, and, to a lesser extent, Australia, all of which have foreign human intelligence agencies and similar views on key geostrategic issues, such as Indo-Pacific security. The announcement of an Australia/UK/US security/nuclear submarine agreement dubbed "AUKUS" in 2021 is a notable example of this.[8] While Canada remains a key partner, many of our interviewees described it as less active or present than these three countries at Five Eyes meetings.[9] Nevertheless, it is through these relationships that Canada obtains the vast majority of its foreign intelligence, whether signals, human, or other forms. The result is that Canada gets the information, but, as one interviewee framed it, "How much are we helping shape the information?"[10] Essentially, Canada gets the information but often accepts it as a passive recipient.

Within the Five Eyes, Canada works most closely with the United States, through both formal agreements and less formal relationships on a range of issues such as border security and law enforcement. While a largely shared world view is important, the foundation upon which this close relationship rests is Canada's geographic proximity to the United States, including the long undefended border between them. It is common, then, for those working in the Canadian intelligence and national security community to frequently have direct contacts with their US counterparts. At the same time, this situation perpetuates free-riding behaviour: the Canadian government does not have to work hard to maintain a relationship since it is something of a necessity for both countries. There is no burden for Canada to bring something to the table in meetings or to maintain the relationship. Instead, bilateral engagements between analysts tend to be strategic, or opportunities for the Canadian government to learn what interests the United States, rather than tactical intelligence exchanges on key issues. According to one interviewee, however, this means that the US side often tends to bring their "B-Team" to meetings and not their top analysts.

Canada also has a range of cooperation agreements with other countries. For example, CSIS alone has more than 300 foreign relationships in 150 countries and territories. These are authorized by the Minister of Public Safety and supported by the Minister of Foreign Affairs. Such partnerships are made in accordance with section 17 of the *CSIS Act*. Each relationship is based on an assessment of Canada's security requirements, human rights considerations, and the reliability of the foreign partner.[11] While these relationships are not as important to Canada as the Five Eyes, they do offer important information and assistance when events of international importance occur or if a threat to the security of Canada emerges abroad. At the same time, these relations can pose problems, as many intelligence agencies around the world engage in torture or hold individuals in conditions that amount to torture in Canadian law (see the chapter by Reg Whitaker). As such, the sharing of information that may be the result of or cause mistreatment is subject to laws set out in the *Avoiding Complicity in Mistreatment by Foreign Entities Act*.[12]

In summary, Canada's status as a net importer of intelligence is based largely on structural factors, especially its geographic position that provides it with safety, as well as on its proximity to the United States, whose security guarantee largely shields Canada from traditional security threats. This is supported by the ability of successive governments to forge alliances with like-minded

Costs and Benefits of the Status Quo

The benefits of Canada's foreign intelligence arrangements are many. In the first and most obvious instance, Canada gains access to substantial amounts of intelligence collected by some of the world's most advanced intelligence powers. It also saves money by depending on others to collect information. The cost of establishing a separate foreign human intelligence agency would be considerable – even the costs associated with merely enhancing the capabilities of existing agencies would not be negligible.

It is also true that Canada's limited foreign intelligence footprint means that it avoids or minimizes certain risks. Human intelligence collection requires clandestine activity that can break the laws of target countries. When caught or discovered, it can lead to international embarrassment and/or scandal. In worst-case scenarios, intelligence officers can be taken hostage, jailed, or killed. As Daniel Livermore argues, it is not clear that Canada would benefit from taking such risks when it already receives so much information and can typically get the rest of what it needs from open sources.[13] Relatedly, others claim that there is a certain reputational benefit: Canada can stand aloof from other countries that engage in spying, while still benefiting from the efforts of those that do. This, according to such a view, protects its international reputation as well as its diplomats.[14]

Because Canada relies on allies and partners to provide it with large amounts of raw and finished foreign intelligence, its policy-makers do not suffer from a lack of access. Indeed, senior Canadian policy-makers often suffer from the opposite problem: they have access to *too much* information that they do not have time to consume. In this sense, it is not even clear that there is an audience for the vast amounts of new information a foreign intelligence service would collect.[15]

However, while Canada has thus far incurred few costs for its approach to national security, this is unlikely to remain the case going forward. As Canada's security environment deteriorates, notably as a result of intensified great power competition and as the United States continues to be politically unpredictable, the costs of inaction are likely to increase. Events in early 2022 illustrated these risks. First, in late January and early February, thousands of truckers and other protesters in a "Freedom Convoy," many of whom adhered to a range of extremist right-wing views, occupied the streets in the parliamentary precinct in Ottawa, the national capital, and blocked key border crossings with the United States. Part of the challenge for Canada at the time was that conservative American politicians and media such as Fox News encouraged the protests. Add to that, right-wing extremists in the two countries have been steadily building

Don't Hold Back: Canadianize   89

closer ties. The crisis thus raised difficult questions for the Canadian national security community: looking ahead, how can it monitor a complex threat that is emerging in part from the same country that is also the most important source of its intelligence?

Second, while the government was still dealing with the ramifications of the convoy, the international situation took a dramatic turn with the Russian invasion of Ukraine on 24 February 2022. Western allies quickly rallied in support of Ukraine. However, in the months leading up to the conflict there had been serious division among NATO allies regarding what the intelligence about Russian intentions revealed. The Americans and British were very clear that Russia intended to invade Ukraine, and they declassified intelligence assessments in an attempt to deter President Vladimir Putin from going through with his plans. At the same time, others countries, including France and Germany, downplayed the threat, dismissing US and UK intelligence assessments.[16] Publicly, Canada kept quiet about its understanding of the situation, although at the time of writing it is unknown whether it took a position in conversations with its allies. In this context, a challenge could emerge in coming years if there is similar division among Canada's Western or NATO allies over a complex international issue, such as China's intentions toward Taiwan. If, as discussed earlier, the United States becomes a less dependable ally, what information will intelligence analysts and Canadian policy-makers rely upon to make their respective judgments and actions?

Even with the current status quo, Canada's own interests and perspectives can become lost. It is impossible to quantify exactly how much intelligence Canada receives from the United States and other allies and partners, but it is far more than it collects itself. This means that the bulk of the raw and finished intelligence that Canadian policy-makers consume largely reflects the world through an US (or, to a lesser extent, other national) prism. Moreover, given that Washington determines what information Canada receives, this prism is shaped by US interests. As one interviewee in our research argued, it is legitimate for Canada to ask whether "we are developing our own resources enough or are ... relying too much on essentially second-hand information that we learn from others."

It is also true that at times the United States (and other intelligence partners) look at certain intelligence issues differently than Canada. An obvious example is the 2003 Iraq War: Canadian intelligence assessed that based on the information available at the time, it could not conclude that Iraq had stockpiles of weapons of mass destruction. Such a dramatic and eventually public break with Canada's most important intelligence allies, the US and UK, caused consternation among some policy-makers and members of the intelligence community, who worried about the consequences for Canada's intelligence-sharing partnerships.[17]

Of course, Canada is firmly a "Western" country likely to share similar views to its allies when it comes to geostrategic challenges posed by, for example, a rising China or revanchist Russia. At the same time, Canada depends on others' intelligence when shaping its views. While it is unlikely that Canada would have a dramatically divergent view on most issues (the 2003 invasion of Iraq aside), it is true that it has few alternative sources of foreign intelligence to rely on. So it may be more predisposed to share or absorb allied positions, even where it could or should have a different perspective, such as on the Arctic or engagement in the Indo-Pacific.

One interviewee asked, "When we look at issues, are we doing it through the Canadian lens?" Indeed, multiple interviewees raised the idea that "the Americans think differently about things and we have to always watch out for this." Another said that Canadian policy-makers make decisions "based on someone else's read. Information may not reflect relevance to our needs." In other words, Canadian officials at times read foreign intelligence obtained from allies and partners and, because of the limited sophistication of the national security culture at the highest levels of the Canadian government, they often fail to appreciate that the information they receive reflects the priorities of other countries. As a result, government officials may not be critically assessing what Canada's interests in a given situation are. Gathering more foreign intelligence itself would not magically solve these puzzles, but it would help Canadian policy-makers build a more properly Canadian picture of the challenges they face.

The risk here is that as a net recipient, Canada may be too deferential to allies' assessments. Some interviewees argued that even when there are disagreements with allies, including the Americans, there remains a tendency within Canadian political and policy leadership, as well as in some elements of the national security and intelligence community, to "go along to get along." In other words, Canadians are hesitant to develop an independent view and share it with allies, and also sometimes tend to take foreign intelligence at face value and resist challenging it internally.[18]

Importantly, it is not just differing priorities that Canadian officials need to be aware of, but also the reality that the United States' greater capabilities can influence its collection and analysis in ways that may steer it away from Canadian interests and priorities. For example, because the United States can leverage its diplomatic, economic, and military power to encourage or pressure other countries to behave in certain ways, it produces assessments that reflect these capabilities (or perhaps a misplaced faith in those capabilities). Canadians, assessing the same data but lacking the same ability to pressure or incentivize other states, often come to different conclusions about what is possible or likely.[19] As a hypothetical example, the United States may view the consequences of an event between Iran and Saudi Arabia in certain ways because of its military capacity in the Middle East, or because its diplomatic ties with the latter mean that it may have a certain amount of leverage. Canada, by contrast, may come to different conclusions about what is possible or likely to happen given that it is a marginal player with limited capacity in that area of the world. Collecting and analysing more of its own foreign intelligence would certainly not give Canada more than marginal leverage in its relations with regional powers such as Iran and Saudi Arabia. It would, however, help it develop and implement more optimal policies, based on information gathered on the basis of its own interests and capabilities.

Additionally, our research suggests that Canada does not use foreign intelligence in an optimal way that allows it to generate independent assessments. Many interviewees indicated that Canada does not assert itself as much as it could in international meetings with intelligence partners to make its views known. Even on issues that Canada views differently, interviewees reported that compared to American, Australian, and British representatives, Canadians tend to be less proactive. One interviewee noted that in cases where the Australians disagree with US assessments, they "bring it to the table." Canadians tend to do so less. Importantly, this is to Canada's detriment: "The more we talk, the better for us and the better for Canada."

Finally, Canada's reliance on its allies and partners, and especially on its southern neighbour, may become a greater vulnerability in the future. In this particular regard, the Trump era raised important questions about Canada's reliance on a benevolent US neighbour that may no longer exist.[20] Importantly, most interviewees noted that the working relationship between Canadian and US national security agencies during the Trump administration remained strong. This, however, is not guaranteed to continue. Trumpism is not dead – it remains a powerful movement in American politics and now arguably dominates the Republican Party.[21] Should Trump be re-elected in 2024, or should a similarly Trumpist or populist candidate win in 2024 or beyond, the country would likely take an even more nationalist and unpredictable turn and pull further away from its past approaches to international cooperation and multilateralism.

Two Options to Change the Status Quo

Moving forward, Canada is unlikely to maintain the status quo; as we discuss below, the trend toward the greater Canadianization of foreign intelligence has already begun, albeit somewhat timidly in some sectors. The question, rather, is the extent to which Canada will accelerate this trend. At its most extreme, this would imply the creation of a foreign human intelligence service.

Creation of a Foreign Human Intelligence Service

Over the years, there has been a muted debate on the margins of Canadian foreign and defence policy studies over whether Canada should consider establishing a foreign human intelligence service. This could take more than one form: a more modest option would be to provide CSIS with an enhanced mandate to collect intelligence abroad; the most ambitious option would see the establishment of a new organization.[22]

There is no consensus among scholars of Canadian national security on this issue. Many observers believe that foreign intelligence is important for policy-making at a general level, but there is also much scepticism about whether Canada genuinely needs, or if it would truly be able to leverage, such a capability. During our research, some interviewees referred to the often cited traditional arguments against a foreign human intelligence service: it could be a resource drain for the overstretched intelligence community, especially CSIS and CSE (which already face human resources challenges); the cost would be too high (especially since the federal government will likely face post-pandemic fiscal challenges throughout much of the 2020s); there is no obvious department that could house such a new agency; and Canada does not have the culture to support such an institution.[23]

Yet there are also compelling arguments in favour of such a new agency. Some of our interviewees argued that a foreign human intelligence service would provide more and better information and would, ultimately, improve policy-making. Other proponents view enhanced foreign intelligence collection not only as a key input into policy-making but also as a tool to better position Canada in its efforts to manage crucial alliances and partnerships. In particular, having in hand original and distinctive foreign intelligence – as opposed to the same material that the more powerful US side collects – would increase, even if only slightly, the limited leverage of Canadian officials when they engage with their US counterparts.

Canada has long been sheltered from foreign threats; as a result, there is limited interest among the country's political class and the general population in foreign affairs and national security generally. Canada's deteriorating threat environment has opened more avenues for considerations of national security and foreign policy, a trend that will likely continue for the foreseeable future. It is unlikely, however, that sufficient momentum will emerge to overcome the obstacles faced by proponents of a new foreign human intelligence agency.

Canadianization

Establishing a foreign human intelligence service arguably represents the most comprehensive step that Canada could take to mitigate its heavy reliance on foreign intelligence provided by allies and partners. However, since this is unlikely to happen in the short to mid-term, we focus on a second alternative: the Canadianization of foreign intelligence.

It is important to clarify here whether we are referring to the Canadianization of foreign intelligence in prescriptive or descriptive terms: are we offering normative analysis laying out a development that we suggest should happen, or are we describing an existing trend? The answer is both: the case can be made that Canadianization has, tentatively, already started; scattered developments in recent years have begun an embryonic shift in this direction. However, these are the result of a series of more or less connected initiatives, not of a conscious and proactive strategy by the government and the intelligence community. Only a few officials, moreover, use the label to describe this nascent trend. We also argue that this is a positive trend that should continue and intensify.

The first step is to define the concept. The "Canadianization" of foreign intelligence refers to a constellation of initiatives that aim to shift collection and analysis efforts toward the pursuit of more properly Canadian interests. The underlying idea is that in the absence of a foreign intelligence service and given Canada's heavy reliance on imported foreign intelligence, it is important for collection and analysis units in the Canadian intelligence community to further develop their own lens through which to view the world, define their own priorities, plan and execute operations and activities, and prepare analyses and assessments in ways that more strongly reflect Canada's interests.

There are at least three key drivers of Canadianization. First, there is the deterioration of Canada's international security situation, primarily due to the rise in non-geographically based challenges, such as malicious cyberactivity, economic security threats, foreign interference, and transnational ideologically motivated violent extremist movements. These have resulted in a number of shocks to the system, forcing more departments and agencies to play a role in national security and creating demand for intelligence products that had not previously existed. In this way, a second driver is better integration of the intelligence community with its non-traditional partners to deal with these emerging threats. Third, there is a growing realization that the traditional security alliances on which Canada has long depended are fragile. In particular, continuing political turmoil in the United States suggests that US retrenchment and distraction may undercut the viability, or at least the efficacy, of many of the arrangements of which Canada is part, especially the Five Eyes and NATO.

What does Canadianization look like in practice? There are many examples of recent or ongoing developments that, taken together, are responsible for the emergence of a nascent trend toward the Canadianization of foreign intelligence. In the first instance, there is the increasing collaboration between the traditional national security community and its non-traditional partners. For example, CSIS now works closely with Innovation, Science, and Economic Development (ISED) Canada in relation to security concerns surrounding foreign investments. CSE has partnered with Elections Canada to address concerns surrounding the integrity of elections and the risk of foreign influence. This cooperation between intelligence agencies and these non-traditional partners has been amplified by the COVID-19 pandemic, with intelligence agencies now working with the Public Health Agency of Canada and the private and public research sectors to defend against a range of emerging threats, including trade in counterfeit goods, intellectual property theft, and a surge in malicious cyberthreats.[24] The nature of these evolving threats and the requirements of new clients together suggest a growing salience of foreign intelligence – or, more specifically, of complex policy-making processes that incorporate foreign intelligence.

Of course, developing these relationships is not easy. Non-traditional national security partners often lack the resources that would simplify the automatic integration of intelligence into their day-to-day operations. This includes staff with high-level security clearance, secure electronic networks, and places to receive and store sensitive or classified information. An even greater challenge can be to overcome the differences among departments and agencies, each with its own mandate, goals, and internal culture. For example, media reports suggest that in 2019, CSE and CSIS disagreed over whether Canada should ban Huawei.[25] This dispute can be explained by the fact that CSE's mandate is to manage technical risk to the government of Canada whereas CSIS's mandate is to consider threats to the security of Canada in a much broader geostrategic environment. Bringing in departments and agencies that have mandates to increase foreign trade and investment creates further challenges in developing whole-of-government policies, given competing priorities. As these relationships develop over time, these conversations are likely to become easier.

A second example is the expansion of existing units with foreign intelligence mandates, or the development of new units entirely. For example, with GSRP, Global Affairs now has a cadre of about thirty diplomats abroad focused almost exclusively on meeting interesting contacts and gathering political reporting related to Canada's security interests. In 2018, this was complemented by the creation of a small intelligence assessment unit within Global Affairs, which the foreign ministry did not have until then. This unit now offers in-house analytical support tailored to the specific needs of senior departmental policy-makers.

Third, in a limited number of cases, the government has granted new powers to certain departments and agencies within the Canadian intelligence community. Perhaps the best example of this is that CSE has been granted new "active" (offensive) cyber powers since 2019 under the new *CSE Act*. This has transformed the organization from an intelligence collection agency into an agency also involved in offensive cyber operations. In December 2021, the agency confirmed for the first time that it was using these powers to target ransomware hackers.[26] This increased capacity, while not uncontroversial,[27] is important for assessing and defending Canadian interests.

Finally, since the spring of 2022, the Canadian Armed Forces have been producing weekly open-source assessments about the Kremlin's disinformation activities for public consumption.[28] These efforts reflect British and US approaches to declassifying information about the conflict to counter Russia's narratives about its intentions and the conflict generally – albeit in a much more modest way. Even if it is only focused on a specific aspect of the conflict, it represents the first attempt to offer ongoing intelligence assessments from a Canadian perspective to a domestic and international audience.

The trend toward the Canadianization of foreign intelligence is still nascent. Given the ongoing changes in Canada's threat environment, it is likely that the need to continue evolving in this direction will not abate. In this context, we suggest additional initiatives that could contribute to entrenching and intensifying it.

The first, necessary but far from sufficient condition for Canadianization would be a clearer definition of Canada's national security and foreign policy priorities. Indeed, one of the main complaints raised by intelligence practitioners in Canada is that it is difficult to focus collection and analysis on the basis of Canadian priorities if those priorities are often vaguely defined. Of course, better defining Canada's foreign policy priorities is easier said than done. For decades, experts (including retired diplomats and practitioners) have lamented successive Canadian governments' inability to clearly articulate coherent foreign policy and national security goals.[29] This is a major obstacle that will be difficult to overcome. That said, the emergence of more recent threats such as foreign electoral interference and concerns with certain foreign investments, notably from China, as well as worrying trends in the United States, have led to the emergence of more actionable priorities, if only to a limited extent.

Next, the consolidation of more mature institutions for the governance of intelligence matters is a precondition for the further Canadianization of foreign intelligence. While there is still scope for considerable improvement, since 2001 there have been significant improvements in the governance of the national security and intelligence community: there is now more coordination, within the community and in terms of its integration with broader government decision-making, notably through the establishment and steady professionalization of deputy-minister-level committees. This has led to better information sharing and more focused discussions at the highest levels of the bureaucracy.[30]

Moreover, Canada's intelligence culture has matured in recent years. This is partly due to growing cooperation with non-traditional partners driven by new and emerging threats, as discussed earlier. In addition, the COVID-19 pandemic has produced a greater need for senior officials throughout the government – not only in the national security realm – to consume intelligence, including foreign intelligence.[31] As such, while many government departments and agencies in the past mostly ignored intelligence, it is now increasingly common for them to "pull" intelligence products to inform their decision-making.

Yet despite this recent progress, Canada's national security and intelligence culture remains immature: in particular, intelligence literacy in policy circles remains low, even if it has improved. We assess that there is scope for

96   Thomas Juneau and Stephanie Carvin

improvement in several key areas, particularly training. Intelligence analysts need to better understand the policy context they are supporting, who their clients are, and how they consume information. While analysts are hired because they are smart and often have subject matter expertise, they need to learn to write in policy-friendly formats and to distinguish between "nice-to-know" and "need-to-know" in order to produce products that more optimally support the pursuit of Canadian interests.[32] Equally important, there is a need for more training on intelligence, particularly what it can and cannot do, for the policy side: to "Canadianize" intelligence, policy-makers need more familiarity with the intelligence community, its capabilities, and its functions.

At present, training in the intelligence and national security community is uneven. While some departments and agencies (such as CFINTCOM, FINTRAC, and CSIS) have their own bespoke programs, there are no community-wide standards. A few bodies in the public service provide courses, such as the Intelligence Analyst Learning Program (IALP), housed in PCO/IAS, and the Canada School of Public Service. Of note, the latter has increased its national security course offerings to meet the growing demand for training in this area. We believe that this growth in training opportunities should continue and that the community should develop flexible guidance for training.[33] In addition, the community should do more to encourage secondments and exchanges between policy and intelligence bodies in government.

Another important and relatively affordable step the government could take is to speed up the adoption of open-source intelligence (OSINT)[34] in the intelligence and national security community. As one interviewee noted, we "badly need better skills at exploiting OS[INT] ... There are so many answers to our questions that are available in OS and are more available than through classified means."[35] In our research, we generally found that there is a perception in the intelligence community that information that is not classified is less worthy. Yet in fast-moving situations, intelligence will often not keep up with the pace of events. As many interviewees emphasized, senior clients have access to multiple sources of information. This is an important point often misunderstood in the intelligence community. As one interviewee explained, policy-makers are willing to consume intelligence to keep abreast of important developments, but "we (also) have our own information channels," such as social and traditional media, other government analyses, and other stakeholders. Moreover, from the clients' perspective, "OS is much faster."[36]

As a part of developing OSINT capabilities, the community could do more to incorporate outreach programs that harness the expertise of those outside of government. Academics, journalists, and non-governmental organization workers, for example, have access to people who would not normally speak frankly with intelligence officers, and businesspeople can bring a different perspective and access to different data sets. These outside experts may not have access to classified information, but they can still provide novel information and insights, as well as a useful challenge function.

Additionally, GAC could revive its voluntary interview program, which drew upon the experience and knowledge of Canadians and others who had unique insights into developments abroad and who had specific knowledge of interest to Canada and its close allies. Locating such a program within GAC and not CSIS – which has its own programs to access comparable information – might make some Canadians less reluctant to meet with, and open up to, foreign ministry officials. Should this program be revived, it would of course need to be deconflicted with similar programs at CSIS and elsewhere within GAC (as diplomats and GSRP officers, in particular, regularly hold such meetings abroad).[37]

Although the perception among interviewees is that Canada is behind its allies in developing OSINT capabilities, there are signs that things are changing due to the constraints of the COVID-19 pandemic. As analysts have been forced to work from home without access to classified systems, they have been forced to increase their use of OSINT and to develop new OSINT products for the community, with many being well received.[38] However, it is not yet clear whether this will continue in a post-pandemic environment.

Consequences of Canadianization

The trend toward the Canadianization of foreign intelligence has been positive: it has brought gains at a manageable cost. First and most importantly, it has positioned the intelligence community to provide its customers – policy-makers in the national security and foreign policy realms, and beyond – with collection and analysis more closely tailored to Canadian interests, especially in a context where these interests are changing as Canada's security environment deteriorates. This should, with time, lead to better policy-making. Of course, the link between providing intelligence more adapted to Canadian needs and developing and then implementing more optimal foreign and national security policy is not automatic: to succeed, it presumes that policy-makers are able to develop better tools and, more broadly, foster a more mature national security culture. This is, at best, a process that must be measured in years and decades.

Continuing this trend toward greater Canadianization of foreign intelligence should not be viewed as being in opposition to Canada's major commitments to multiple intelligence cooperation partnerships. Nor does it imply that Canada will neglect its many intelligence partnerships. To the contrary, it will better position Canada to leverage these partnerships more optimally by contributing a more specifically Canadian perspective, so as to thereby gain more out of them. In such partnerships, where Canada is perceived – often rightly – as a free rider, good intelligence, raw or finished, is a currency that can be traded: by positioning itself to give more, Canada could also receive more.

More Canadianized intelligence would provide a different perspective; it would "tell the Americans something they don't already know" and better position Canadian officials to perform a challenge function.

Conclusion

In some ways, this chapter goes against the main theme of this edited volume, which is, with the return of great power competition and rising uncertainty about the future reliability of the United States, Western countries are rethinking their security relationships and seeking to diversify their patterns of intelligence cooperation. We certainly agree that it would be in Canada's interest to walk this same path. But we also make the parallel argument in favour of enhancing Canadian capabilities, of "Canadianizing" foreign intelligence in ways that would provide a more independent view that better reflects Canadian interests. Canadianization is a response to managing a less certain world in which Canada's dependence on its traditional security relationships is increasingly precarious. But paradoxically, it could also make Canada a better ally and partner by allowing it to contribute its own sources and world view to multilateral discussions.

We believe that Canadianization is an important idea to consider looking forward. Initiatives such as enhanced overseas collection or the creation of a foreign human intelligence service would require major legislative changes and should be the subject of robust debate among policy-makers, the media, academia, civil society, and the public. Such initiatives would necessitate new legal authorities for intelligence and national security agencies, if not new legal mandates entirely – something that could take years to achieve. But as the rest of this volume shows, Canada needs to move beyond the status quo quickly and develop its own independent views on how to manage great power competition: information that is generated through the prism of US power, or the geographic position of the UK and Australia, will not always align with Canadian interests and perspectives. Canadianization, while imperfect, will provide policy-makers with more immediate assistance as they confront some of the key challenges they now face.

NOTES

1 For more on these departments and agencies, and on the national security and intelligence community as a whole, see Stephanie Carvin, Thomas Juneau, and Craig Forcese, eds., *Top Secret Canada: Understanding the Canadian National Security and Intelligence Community* [hereafter *TSC*] (Toronto: University of Toronto Press, 2021).
2 Bill Robinson, "The Communications Security Establishment," in *TSC*, 77.

3 Craig Forcese and Leah West, *National Security Law*, 2nd ed. (Toronto: Irwin Law, 2020), 102.
4 Thomas Juneau, "Department of National Defence and Canadian Armed Forces," in *TSC*, 207.
5 Michael Nesbitt, "Global Affairs Canada (GAC)," in *TSC*.
6 Greg Fyffe, "The Privy Council Office (PCO)," in *TSC*.
7 Stephanie Carvin, "The Integrated Terrorism Assessment Centre (ITAC)," in *TSC*.
8 Stephanie Carvin and Thomas Juneau, "Canada's exclusion from 'Three Eyes' only confirms what was already the case," *Globe and Mail*, 17 September 2021, https://www.theglobeandmail.com/opinion/article-canadas-exclusion-from-three-eyes-only-confirms-what-was-already-the.
9 Thomas Juneau and Stephanie Carvin, *Intelligence Analysis and Policy Making: The Canadian Experience* (Stanford: Stanford University Press, 2021), 31–2, 176–7.
10 Juneau and Carvin, *Intelligence Analysis and Policy Making*, 31–2.
11 Canadian Security Intelligence Service, *Public Report 2020*, (2021): 44, https://www.canada.ca/en/security-intelligence-service/corporate/publications/2020-public-report.html.
12 Forcese and West, *National Security Law*, 406–9, 487–96.
13 Daniel Livermore, "Does Canada Need a Foreign Intelligence Agency," Centre for International Policy Studies, Policy Brief no. 3 (2009).
14 On this debate, see Alistair Hensler, "Creating a Canadian Foreign Intelligence Service: Revisited 25 Years Later," *Canadian Foreign Policy Journal* 26, no. 3 (2020): 360–5.
15 Juneau and Carvin, *Intelligence Analysis and Policy Making*, 29–32.
16 Stephanie Carvin, "Deterrence, Disruption and Declassification: Intelligence in the Ukraine Conflict," *CIGI Online*, 2 May 2022, https://www.cigionline.org/articles/deterrence-disruption-and-declassification-intelligence-in-the-ukraine-conflict.
17 Alan Barnes, "Getting It Right: Canadian Intelligence Assessments on Iraq, 2002–2003," *Intelligence and National Security* 35, no. 7 (2020): 925–53.
18 Barnes, "Getting It Right,"
19 Juneau and Carvin, *Intelligence Analysis and Policy Making*.
20 Aaron Ettinger, "Rumors of Restoration: Joe Biden's Policy and What It Means for Canada," *Canadian Foreign Policy* 27, no. 2 (2021): 157–74.
21 Tom Nichols, *Our Own Worst Enemy: The Assault from Within on Modern Democracy* (Oxford: Oxford University Press, 2021).
22 David Collins, "Spies Like Them: The Canadian Security Intelligence Service and Its Place in World Intelligence," *Sydney Law Review* 24, no. 4 (2002): 505–28; Stuart Farson and Nancy Teeple, "Increasing Canada's Foreign Intelligence Capability: Is It a Dead Issue?," *Intelligence and National Security* 30, no. 1 (2015): 47–76; Daniel Livermore, "Does Canada Need a Foreign Intelligence Agency;" Richard G. St. John, "Should Canada Have a Foreign Espionage Service," *Canadian Military Journal* 17, no. 4 (2017): 56–66; Michael Tierney, "Past, Present, and Future: The Evolution of

Canadian Foreign Intelligence in a Globalized World," *Canadian Military Journal* 15, no. 2 (2015): 44–54. For a more recent media intervention, see Peter Jones, Alan R. Jones, and Laurie Storsater, "I, spy: Does Canada need a foreign intelligence service?," *Globe and Mail*, 11 June 2021, https://www.theglobeandmail.com /opinion/article-i-spy-does-canada-need-a-foreign-intelligence-service.

23 Juneau and Carvin, *Intelligence Analysis and Policy Making*, 29–32.

24 Stephanie Carvin, "National Security and Intelligence Operations during the COVID-19 Pandemic," in *Stress Tested: The COVID-19 Pandemic and Canadian National Security*, ed. Leah West, Thomas Juneau ,and Amarnath Amarasingam (Calgary: University of Calgary Press, 2021).

25 Robert Fife and Steven Chase, "Canadian intelligence agencies at odds over whether to ban Huawei from 5G networks: official," *Globe and Mail*, 12 November 2019, https://www.theglobeandmail.com/politics/article-canadian-intelligence -agencies-disagree-on-whether-to-ban-huawei-from.

26 Alex Boutilier, "Canadian spy agency targeted foreign hackers to 'impose a cost' for cybercrime," *Global News*, 6 December 2021, https://globalnews.ca/news/8429008 /canadian-spy-agency-targets-cybercrime.

27 See Bill Robinson, "CSE to get foreign cyber operations mandate," *Lux Ex Umbra*, 24 June 2017, https://luxexumbra.blogspot.com/2017/06/cse-to-get-foreign-cyber -operations.html.

28 See for example, Canadian Armed Forces (@CanadianForces), 7 April 2022, https://twitter.com/CanadianForces/status/1512079898692620300?s=20&t=1PTYu Adadr93fukb-MMDOw.

29 Thomas Juneau, "Canada will pay the price for neglecting our foreign policy," *Globe and Mail*, 7 June 2020, https://www.theglobeandmail.com/opinion/article -canada-will-pay-the-price-for-neglecting-our-foreign-policy.

30 Juneau and Carvin, *Intelligence Analysis and Policy Making*, ch. 1.

31 West, Juneau, and Amarasingam, *Stress Tested*.

32 Juneau and Carvin, *Intelligence Analysis and Policy Making*, 59–67.

33 Juneau and Carvin, *Intelligence Analysis and Policy Making*, 152.

34 OSINT includes a wide range of sources of information: media (including social media), public data (published by governments), and professional and academic publications. OSINT, importantly, is not gathered through clandestine means, but it still needs to be collected, processed, and analysed.

35 Juneau and Carvin, *Intelligence Analysis and Policy Making*, 126.

36 Juneau and Carvin, *Intelligence Analysis and Policy Making*, 126.

37 Juneau and Carvin, *Intelligence Analysis and Policy Making*, 163–4.

38 Carvin, "National Security and Intelligence Operations during the COVID-19 Pandemic."

5 Intelligence Cooperation in Historical Perspective: From Cold War Bipolarity to the Multipolar Present

REG WHITAKER

Canada's intelligence cooperation and exchanges with its close allies have a history stretching back to the nineteenth century, but the modern era can be dated to the latter half of the twentieth. Intelligence arrangements arising out of the Second World War were recast in the late 1940s with the onset of the Cold War, which itself represented a partial breakdown of the wartime alliance against the Axis powers. Cold War intelligence cooperation was characterized by a certain asymmetry, with Canada's junior partner status confirmed by its decision not to establish its own central human intelligence collection agency. This chapter will examine the implications of this asymmetry, both positive and negative, for Canadian foreign and domestic policy.

The Cold War persisted for four decades, but long before the fall of the Berlin Wall and the implosion of the Soviet Union, challenges emerged for Canadian intelligence that were beyond the scope of the Cold War, including from violent non-state actors both domestic and international. This chapter examines some of the continuities and discontinuities in Canada's intelligence cooperation with its allies as bipolarity has given way to a multipolar international stage.

At the Birth of the Cold War

Day Zero for Canadian intelligence cooperation arrangements in the bipolar Cold War world was 7 September 1945. On that day, Igor Gouzenko, a cipher clerk in the Soviet embassy in Ottawa and GRU (Soviet military intelligence) operative, became perhaps the most significant walk-in in espionage history, delivering to Canadian authorities a sheaf of secret documents outlining an extensive Soviet spying operation in Canada employing public servants ideologically sympathetic enough to another country to betray the trust that Canada had placed in them by revealing state secrets.

From the moment it was accepted that Gouzenko was a genuine defector, the question of how to handle the explosive story of how one wartime ally was spying on another was embedded firmly in the nexus of Canadian relations with its two oldest and closest allies, Britain and the United States. An international resolution of the Gouzenko Affair was achieved when Canada's Prime Minister William Lyon Mackenzie King, British Prime Minister Clement Attlee, and US President Harry Truman agreed on a common course of action. Close interagency cooperation between the British and US intelligence and security communities and the Royal Canadian Mounted Police, augmented in Canada by a secret Royal Commission of Inquiry armed with extraordinary powers carried over from wartime, revealed to the public in Canada and abroad the workings of a Soviet espionage network in a friendly country that had been a wartime ally. Gouzenko also hinted at the outlines of Soviet espionage in the West: the NKVD (the predecessor to the KGB) ran a parallel Canadian network known to the GRU as the "Cousins" whose operations and sources were kept sealed from the GRU; more alarming were leads pointing to Soviet penetration at high levels of the US and British governments.[1]

The handling of the Gouzenko Affair established the form the Cold War would take in Canada domestically as well as the role that Canadian security and intelligence would play as the Western bloc began to confront the Soviets on a global scale. That the first shot in the Cold War was fired in Canada was striking, given Canada's peripheral role in great power politics up to 1945. It had the effect of spurring the development of Canada's place in intelligence cooperation within the North Atlantic Anglosphere.

The Cold War Intelligence Exchange Arrangement

In 1945, Canada was still largely dependent on British intelligence. After Gouzenko's defection, MI6 and MI5 in London were quickly contacted, and MI5 in particular took a close, hands-on role, sending one of its officers to Ottawa to liaise closely with the RCMP (MI6 had been elbowed out, which was fortunate, since MI6's point man on Gouzenko was none other than Kim Philby, the most infamous of the Kremlin's British moles). Suspects were detained and interrogated without counsel and without benefit of habeas corpus by the RCMP, armed with the draconian powers of the *War Measures Act*, which was still in effect at war's end; subsequently, suspects were brought under duress before the secret proceedings of the Royal Commission. British intelligence acted throughout as adviser and mentor to the RCMP. This was hardly surprising, for Canadian intelligence had been developing under British tutelage for a century, beginning in the nineteenth and early twentieth centuries, when Irish Fenian and Sikh dissidents – both active in Canada – fought against British Imperial rule in their colonized homelands. This brought about an exchange template under the terms of which the Canadians offered information on security risks and threats in Canada while the imperial centre offered intelligence on the Empire and the wider world.[2]

Intelligence Cooperation in Historical Perspective   103

By war's end, steps had been taken to expand and institutionalize RCMP liaison with the US Federal Bureau of Investigation (FBI), but those ties were not yet as strong as the ones with the British. Moreover, at the time of the Gouzenko Affair, the United States had yet to create the Central Intelligence Agency (CIA), while its predecessor, the wartime Office of Strategic Services (OSS), was already winding down. British intelligence, coming off its wartime triumphs – the decryption of Germany's Enigma code at Bletchley Park and the Double Cross system of turned Nazi agents – was of more help on the international intelligence dimension. Of course, as the Cold War took shape in the late 1940s, the United States would surpass Great Britain as the hegemonic power in the West. The important point is that the exchange template already established at the time of the Gouzenko Affair – Canada offering intelligence on Canadians and foreign actors in Canada, Britain offering wider foreign intelligence – was simply rolled over into the paradigmatic Cold War relationship between Ottawa and the US security and intelligence regime.

Another significant emerging feature within the intelligence community was the strengthening of horizontal bureaucratic linkages below the political level. This was dramatically highlighted when Mackenzie King surprisingly, and inexplicably, decided upon his own made-in-Canada initiative to resolve the still secret Gouzenko Affair. Had his path been followed, it would have ruptured the broad outlines of the previous agreement between himself and the British and American leaders. Mackenzie King proposed that the outgoing Soviet ambassador be informed that Canada knew about the spy ring; at the same time, the implicated Canadian public servants would be dealt with administratively and behind closed doors. When the British High Commissioner in Ottawa informed MI5 of this initiative, London was aghast and immediately contacted the RCMP, urging the Mounties to try to deter Mackenzie King and even volunteering MI5's professional authority to persuade the prime minister of the folly of his proposed action. The RCMP Commissioner went through the Minister of Justice to get a direct meeting with Mackenzie King, with officials from the justice and external affairs ministries present. At that meeting, the commissioner invoked not MI5 but instead the authority of J. Edgar Hoover and the FBI, asserting that Hoover was pursuing leads on grave penetration of the US government, leads that would be fatally undermined if the Soviets were notified of the Gouzenko investigation. It is unclear why the commissioner invoked Hoover rather than MI5, and it is not even certain that Hoover was ever actually consulted. But, suitably chastened by the spectre of the famous American bureaucratic empire builder, the prime minister withdrew his proposal, and the Gouzenko investigation returned to its original track, leading to the detentions and Royal Commission in February 1946.[3]

This entire episode, played out at the time behind closed doors, is both significant and ambiguous. Mackenzie King's initiative was, not to put too fine a

104   Reg Whitaker

point on it, harebrained, apparently predicated on the naive notion that Stalin knew nothing about Soviet spying and would put a stop to it after being informed by his ambassador. MI5 was quite right to point out that all the counter-intelligence advantages that could be wrung out of the Gouzenko defection would be lost if Mackenzie King were to go ahead. Even so, this was a *Canadian* spy affair and the head of the democratically elected Canadian government had invoked Canadian national sovereignty in setting out to handle it on his own. That his political initiative, however flawed, was shot down not by the persuasion of fellow political leaders Truman and Attlee but by bureaucrats in London and Ottawa colluding together and invoking their fellow bureaucrat in Washington speaks volumes about the relative autonomy from political interference that the intelligence bureaucracies of the three countries could exercise when acting in concert. This relatively autonomous cross-border horizontal network would remain at the heart of Cold War intelligence sharing.

The Royal Commission's report, all 733 pages of bureaucratic prose, was an international bestseller, providing a firm foundation for the domestic anti-Communist Cold War in Canada. It also served as a dramatic warning for Western states about the threat of Soviet espionage.[4] The impact of Gouzenko (and that of defecting spy Elizabeth Bentley in the United States around the same time) was quite devastating. We now know that at Stalin and the Politburo's command, almost all North American espionage networks were dismantled. They were rebuilt only in the early 1950s.[5]

With the Truman Doctrine, the Marshall Plan, NATO, and the Korean War, the Cold War under US leadership was firmly in place by the early 1950s. So were the parameters of human intelligence exchange. Under the UK/USA Agreements – the predecessors to what we now call the Five Eyes – terms were negotiated for signals intelligence, with the geography of listening posts the basis for division of responsibility. Even here, however, Canada's junior partner status was made clear from the outset. The decision not to create a Canadian foreign intelligence service – or perhaps more accurately the non-decision on creation of a foreign intelligence agency – cemented the post-Gouzenko intelligence exchange relationship at the heart of Canadian intelligence, which has in some form, however attenuated and complicated, persisted down to today.

The first comment on this is to note that generations of Canadian policymakers have stressed the value and significance of the foreign intelligence this relationship has provided. Proof of its worth is that whenever the relationship has been threatened, Canadian officials have gathered with alacrity to protect its continuation. Over the years, however, critical voices have pointed to the downsides of this arrangement. Without questioning the undoubted value of intelligence received over the decades that Canada would never have gained on its own, it is worth reflecting on those downsides.[6]

Downsides of Intelligence Cooperation during the Cold War

Context is important. For the several decades after Gouzenko, there was a broad Cold War consensus in the West, especially among the political and administrative elites. Canadians had little reason to question US and British governments' interpretations of the intelligence they had collected. But as the Cold War consensus grew more tenuous in the 1960s, especially as doubts grew about US leadership (tensions arose, for instance, over the Vietnam War), so too did doubts about whether intelligence received in the form of other countries' finished products was always appropriate from the point of view of Canada's national interests.

Doubts along these lines, even if they did not rise to the level of doubts about the ultimate value of the arrangements and certainly not about the alliance itself, could cause hesitation about the value of received intelligence for particular areas of Canadian foreign policy. This was especially the case when tensions arose with allies rather than with the Cold War antagonist. A strong example here was the tension between Canada and France over Quebec independence in the de Gaulle era. In 1967 de Gaulle on a state visit delivered his notorious "Vive le Québec libre!" speech, which earned him a sudden exit from Canada and *persona non grata* status from the federal government. This was embarrassingly public. Even before then, however, behind the scenes, Canadian officials had begun to worry that the French were quietly stirring discontent among Quebec separatists as well as francophone groups outside Quebec: one French diplomat had been ordered out for improper interference in Canadian affairs. Canada lacked good intelligence regarding the goals and strategic scope of surreptitious French activities on Canadian soil. A senior official in the RCMP Security Service told me a cautionary tale about the limits of intelligence cooperation when there are conflicting interests among allies. Faced with uncertainty about French motives, the Security Service sought input from its US ally: did they have intelligence on French international activities that would shed light on what they were doing in Canada? This request was politely rebuffed, on the grounds that France was an ally of the United States and it would be inappropriate for the Americans to spy on one ally on behalf of another. The Mounties then went to the British, and received essentially the same answer: no, sorry, we cannot help you even if we would like to.[7] Canada's relative lack of independent foreign intelligence capacity was particularly damaging because the apparent threat was being posed by an ally rather than by Cold War antagonists.

Inadequate intelligence on French activities drew the Security Service into muddy waters in Quebec. Among the scandals that led to the McDonald Commission was evidence of RCMP spying on the separatist Parti Québécois (PQ), which included stealing membership lists, bugging the bedrooms of PQ officials, and enlisting the number two man in the René Lévesque government as a

106 Reg Whitaker

sometimes-paid informant.[8] The politically disastrous optics of a federal security agency spying on a legitimate political party hastened the forced departure of the Security Service from the RCMP in 1984. Yet it had been genuine concern about potential French clandestine efforts to promote Quebec independence that helped draw them into this quagmire, although no smoking gun of French involvement in the PQ was ever found. One could call this an intelligence failure on many levels.

Another negative impact of the intelligence exchange arrangement became embarrassingly apparent while the Cold War consensus was still in place. If Canada was offering intelligence on Canadians to its allies, there was a danger that allied states could abuse that information to the detriment of individual Canadians and their rights. This danger was compounded by the emergence, as already noted at the time of the Gouzenko investigation, of cross-border working relationships between agencies below the level of political control. When the Canadian ambassador to Egypt, Herbert Norman, committed suicide in Cairo in 1957 following persistent charges of pro-Communist espionage by a witch-hunting US congressional committee, shock waves at the senior levels of the Canadian government brought tentative threats to end the intelligence exchange relationship with Washington. That outcome was averted, but reverberations from the affair have continued over the decades.[9]

The Norman tragedy had three key implications. First, the intelligence implicating Norman in espionage came to the FBI directly from the RCMP in the form of a "very inaccurate and damaging" report in October 1950.[10] When Canada's external affairs minister, Lester Pearson, realized that this flawed document had been passed to Washington, he insisted that a corrected version be sent. This was an object lesson in the potential negative impact of close cross-border liaison between agencies when the reputation of Canadian citizens is at issue. Second, FBI director J. Edgar Hoover made it a practice to feed witch-hunting congressional investigators information carefully selected from FBI files on subversives, using the politicians essentially as tools to advance his own political agenda. In this case the RCMP's flawed report about Norman was transferred immediately to the Senate Internal Security Subcommittee, which already had Norman in its sights. Although the corrected version went into the FBI files, the Senate subcommittee preferred the incendiary uncorrected version and based its renewed accusations on it in 1957. The Norman affair thus demonstrates that Canada could not count on the US intelligence authorities to protect the privacy and security of Canadians. Third, as was understood by the principals in the affair at the time – but as became known publicly only years later – the main target of the FBI and the Senate witch-hunters was not Norman, but Pearson himself, who later became Prime Minister of Canada, and on whom Hoover kept a thick file labelled "Espionage R[ussian]."[11] Norman was collateral damage in a game played by Hoover that tried and eventually failed

Intelligence Cooperation in Historical Perspective   107

to catch a much bigger trophy so as to do serious damage to Canada. That the RCMP, wittingly or not, had taken part in this travesty of US–Canadian relations was a highly negative comment on the shape that Cold War intelligence sharing had taken. Yet at the end of the day, the tragedy of Norman's death took second place to the value that Canada saw in the continuation of the intelligence-sharing arrangements that had claimed Norman as collateral damage.[12]

The most serious challenge to the Cold War consensus came from within Canada. In the 1960s, Quebec separatist groups began planting bombs as part of a terrorist campaign to achieve Quebec independence. At first, the Security Service viewed groups like the Front de libération du Québec (FLQ) within a Cold War framework as tools of Moscow. To its credit, given the lack of a smoking gun, the RCMP eventually gave up on the Moscow connection and focused on the rise of made-in-Canada terrorism. As already noted, there was more attention to a possible *French* connection, although this too was eventually abandoned for want of evidence. The main point is that to combat domestic terrorism in Quebec, the Canadian government was compelled to rely largely on its own intelligence, which was in fact more useful than the Security Service has generally been given credit for. The October 1970 Crisis was characterized by the Liberal government as resulting from an intelligence failure, although that failure was at least as much Cabinet's fault, for it had not heeded earlier warnings.[13] Operational excesses adopted under government pressure postcrisis led to scandal, public inquiries, and institutional reform. The entire saga of national security intelligence with regard to violent Quebec separatist movements was largely a made-in-Canada affair; international cooperation played only a minor role.[14]

Globalization of Canadian Intelligence Cooperation

In the 1970s, while Quebec separatist terrorism continued to loom on the radar, international terrorist threats also impacted Canada. In 1976, Montreal hosted the Summer Olympic Games. With memories of the massacre of Israeli athletes by Palestinian terrorists at the previous Olympics at Munich in 1972 still fresh, and with international terrorist activities by groups like the Baader-Meinhof Gang in Germany and the Japanese Red Army grabbing headlines around the world, the need for intelligence on international terrorist threats to Canadian security was obvious. A Cabinet directive in 1975 listed counterterrorism as a "core mandate" for the Security Service, which began setting up specialized counterterrorist desks on a regional basis. The intelligence challenge posed by the Olympics required moving beyond the traditional dependence on British and US cooperation and reaching out to other countries that were willing to share intelligence. The RCMP was the lead agency in what turned out to be the largest single post-war security operation up to that time, but it had no

108   Reg Whitaker

experience collecting the necessary counterterrorist intelligence abroad, nor had it a mandate to do so.[15] To an extent, the RCMP could draw upon diplomatic intelligence gathered through External Affairs, but that was limited with regard to emerging terrorist threats. An Overseas Liaison program extended Canada's international intelligence reach and developed fruitful cooperation with foreign police and security agencies on a much wider scale than in the pre-1976 era. In its own final assessment of Montreal, the Security Service indicated that "efforts on behalf of the Olympic security [in] the past two years have introduced us to new contacts and agencies not previously aware of our role. We have also developed closer relationships with some of the established contacts who now have better appreciation of our interests and capabilities."[16] Since the Montreal games were free of violent incidents, this excursion into greater integration with international counterterrorist networks was deemed a success and a template for the future.

Enhanced intelligence cooperation on terrorism has undoubtedly yielded benefits for Canada, which continue down to today. But as had been the case with Cold War cooperation, there have been inevitable downsides. In the 1980s, two parallel international developments may have affected Canadian policy in arguably negative ways. The election of President Ronald Reagan in the United States in 1980 led to a renewed emphasis on confronting the Soviet Union on a global scale. At the same time, terrorist activities by non-state actors were growing increasingly troublesome on several continents. There was a tendency in Reagan's Washington to meld these two trends and to conceptualize international terrorism as another arm of Moscow's pernicious global reach. This was unfortunate as it was based on flimsy evidence and had the effect of directing counterterrorist analysis away from those distinctive national and regional features that helped explain why nationalist, ethnic, and religious movements turned to violence. It is unclear just how extensive an influence this renewed Cold War framework had in shaping counterterrorism analysis in Western capitals, but to the extent that it did, it was not helpful. By the last few years of his presidency, however, Reagan had begun to seek a winding down of the Cold War; at that point, the first signs of intelligence cooperation between old Cold War adversaries, the KGB and the CIA, became visible. It turned out that Moscow was as concerned as Washington about the threat of unruly and violent non-state actors.

In 1985, Canada experienced its worst act of terrorism (and to this day the worst act in the history of air terrorism) when bombs originating in Canada planted on two Air India flights brought down an aircraft off the coast of Ireland. In all, 329 passengers and crew were killed, most of them Canadian citizens. The same day, two baggage handlers were killed in a separate explosion at Tokyo's Narita airport. As is well known, criminal investigations in Canada to achieve legal closure failed (except for one peripheral conviction). That failure

Intelligence Cooperation in Historical Perspective 109

led to a Royal Commission of Inquiry twenty years later and universal acknowledgment of a massive intelligence failure. If Montreal in 1976 was a success for fledgling intelligence cooperation against terrorism, Air India a decade later was a catastrophic failure. An uglier aspect of this failure was the destructive turf war that poisoned relations between the RCMP and the fledgling civilian security service, the Canadian Security Intelligence Service (CSIS), just a year into its life as a separate agency from the RCMP. There would be no point here in stirring up details of that conflict (which carried on into the post-bombing investigative phase, to the same bad effect) were it not for a weakness that it pointed to in the international intelligence-sharing framework.

Prior to the tragedy, there had been warnings of possible threats to Air India from Sikh separatist extremists. Those warnings had come from foreign sources through previously established intelligence channels. Most of them were from the Indian government and were directed, somewhat haphazardly, to the Mounties, either directly or through External Affairs. Some warnings, however, went to a CSIS liaison officer in Delhi. The two Canadian agencies, not always working with the same intelligence, arrived at different interpretations of what they were hearing. The RCMP tended to take the Indian warnings at face value. Some CSIS officers, by contrast, were suspicious of the Indian government's motives, especially of the activities of its intelligence service (the Research and Analysis Wing) in Canada, where it had been tracking Sikh and other threats to the Indian state without a great deal of liaison with their Canadian hosts. Two and a half weeks before the bombing, CSIS suggested to the RCMP that some of the threat warnings passed on by India *might* be misinformation designed to discredit Sikh opponents of the Indian state. The gap between the two agencies was apparent in terms of the credence they gave to foreign intelligence. I was chair of a panel reporting on aviation security issues to the Air India inquiry in 2007. We concluded in our Report to the Commissioner that while we took no view on the validity of concerns about the Indian government's behaviour, "CSIS would have been appropriately exercising judgment in attempting to assess critically the possibly mixed motivations of a foreign state with a crucial stake in a political conflict afflicting it."[17]

The latter point suggests a caution for all intelligence sharing about terrorism. International terrorism tends to emerge out of regional conflicts in which violent non-state actors challenge the integrity of states. When these conflicts are exported, the third-party states on whose diaspora territory the conflicts are played out typically look to the originating states for intelligence on the non-state actors. These states, however, are themselves partisan combatants in the conflict they are being asked to report on. This does not mean that intelligence from such sources is without value; it may in fact be very useful. But it must always be evaluated in light of the particular interests, national and otherwise, that have framed its interpretation. For recipient country analysts, the issue is

110   Reg Whitaker

not whether the originating country is a friendly ally; more salient is that, ally or not, that country's interpretive framework will reflect its own national interests first, not those of the recipient country. In 1981 the McDonald Commission examined exchanges of information with foreign agencies and highlighted the vulnerability of Canadians when intelligence on them is shared with foreign agencies without appropriate controls, as well as the core issue of conflicting national interests. It warned against Canadian authorities "in a position of dependence ... entering into relationships without giving adequate weight to possible conflicting foreign policy considerations" and the almost inevitable "friction" this will create "with those responsible for directing Canada's external relations."[18] Perhaps Palmerston's famous dictum for foreign policy – "We have no eternal allies, and we have no perpetual enemies. Our interests are eternal and perpetual, and those interests it is our duty to follow"[19] – might also be applied to intelligence cooperation.

Intelligence Cooperation in the Post–Cold War Era

Unfortunately, the lessons of the Norman affair seem to have been imperfectly learned. Almost a half century later, with the Cold War consigned to the history books and a new "global war on terror" declared as the focus of the Western intelligence community after 9/11, another Canadian fell victim to the reckless sharing of inaccurate intelligence with the FBI. Maher Arar, a young computer engineer of Syrian Canadian background transiting in 2002 at a New York airport en route home after a trip abroad, was kidnapped by US authorities and taken to Syria, where he was imprisoned and tortured under the notorious US "extraordinary rendition" program. After Arar's release and return to Canada, it emerged that his experience was the result of an egregious abuse of intelligence sharing with the United States. As part of joint counterterrorist operation A-O CANADA, itself set up under intense pressure from Washington following 9/11, the RCMP had provided an unauthorized "data dump" of all its project files to the FBI regardless of caveats against transfers out of the country. In these files, there were references to Arar as a peripheral "person of interest" on the basis that he had allegedly associated with persons who were suspected of terrorist links. But he was identified by the RCMP falsely as a "Muslim extremist," which was enough to trigger his kidnapping and torture. A commission of inquiry found evidence of extensive Canadian complicity in Arar's abuse at the hands of the Americans and Syrians;[20] as a result, the RCMP Commissioner resigned and Arar was paid more than $10 million in compensation for his mistreatment.

Norman and Arar are only the most prominent victims of Canada–US intelligence exchanges gone wrong. Over the decades, many Canadians have encountered difficulties travelling to the United States that are traceable to adverse Canadian information on them passed to the US (some as visible as future prime minister Pierre Trudeau and the author Farley Mowat, who wrote a book about it – many others have suffered in anonymity). Of course, one cannot automatically attribute innocence to such cases. The point here is that a lack of accountability has been an enduring feature of this policy.

There is some reason to believe that this lesson has indeed had resonance in the multipolar world that has succeeded the era of Cold War bipolarity. After 9/11 the Bush administration tried to re-establish hegemonic US leadership of the Western alliance with the declaration of a "global war on terror." Canada joined the military mission against the Taliban regime in Afghanistan, but it declined to join the 2003 invasion of Iraq. We now know that the Iraq war was ill-planned in its conception and a fiasco in its execution, with negative consequences reverberating down to this day. We also know that the public rationale for the invasion – Saddam Hussein's "weapons of mass destruction" – was based on intelligence that was at best deeply flawed and at worst fabricated. What we did not know publicly at the time was that the decision of the Chrétien government to stay out, interpreted widely then as a political decision with regard to domestic opinion (the Iraq refusal turned out to be the single most popular act of the three Chrétien Liberal governments), was in part based on diplomatic considerations, but also on Canadian intelligence that discounted the credibility of the heavily politicized US and British alarms about weapons of mass destruction. While it is unlikely that the Canadian decision to stay out was strictly based on Canadian intelligence, the latter did have a validation effect on a decision that Prime Minister Chrétien had already made.[21]

Conclusion

To return to where this chapter began in 1945 with the Gouzenko defection and the initiation of close intelligence cooperation with Canada's two closest allies, Great Britain and the United States, we can see that in some sense Canada has travelled full circle. In 1945, the British–US alliance was the overriding consideration in handling the espionage affair. In 2003, Canada refused to join those same allies in a bloody military adventure that Canada, based partly on its own sources, believed correctly had been misrepresented in allied intelligence assessments. The Conservative opposition in Parliament was scandalized that Canada was not "ready, aye ready" to fall into place behind its twin traditional allies. Others might see this decision rather as a glimmer of Palmerstonian realism about allies.

With the bizarre and unsettling Trump administration now barely into the history books, and with Britain going down the Brexit path, our traditional allies may appear less reliable sources of intelligence. The Five Eyes will continue to be a crucial intelligence partnership; Anglosphere cooperation will hardly disappear, nor would any Canadian government wish for that outcome. But at the very least, greater emphasis in future should be placed on Canadian interpretation based on Canadian sources, as well as on what can be gained in exchange. CSIS is playing a greater role in intelligence gathering abroad (although its legal position in regard to its mandate needs clarification), which could be a positive step, especially in relation to regions of the world where Canada must be extremely careful not to take any players at face value.

The shock Russian invasion of Ukraine in February 2022 has posed a severe challenge to the entire liberal international order, and also a more specific challenge to Canadian intelligence capacity. Canada has hastened to offer armaments and other forms of military assistance to Ukraine, in addition to joining in the robust array of Western sanctions against Russia, the new international pariah state, albeit one with a nuclear arsenal. On the one hand, the war in Ukraine reaffirms Canada's advantageous position with regard to its access to US intelligence, which in the lead-up to the invasion showed a surer grasp of Russian intentions than some other Western states (the head of French military intelligence had to resign over his agency's failures on the Ukraine file). At the same time, the presence of a very large and politically significant Ukrainian Canadian community (1.4 million in 2016, the world's third largest Ukrainian population, behind only Ukraine itself and Russia) with a long history of close involvement with the Canadian government over political conflict in the Ukrainian homeland[22] suggests incentives for specifically Canadian intelligence gathering on events in Ukraine. The high volume of Ukrainian refugee applicants to Canada will require enhanced security clearance capacity. The provision of military assistance requires enhanced intelligence on the military situation in the war and appreciation of the specific needs of the Ukrainian forces. While US intelligence will be of considerable assistance, clearly the relative weight of the Ukrainian community in Canada does call for interpretation specifically for Canadian eyes.

Today's international tensions have placed Canadian intelligence on relatively familiar ground. Tensions with China have risen precipitously in recent years, raising the spectre of another anti-Western Russian–Chinese alliance. While this might seem to imply a renewed Cold War, with little or no sharing of intelligence with competitive adversaries, twenty-first-century realities point to a more complex set of challenges.

Global security challenges – pandemics and climate change in particular – are pushing intelligence toward closer cooperation with countries and nongovernmental actors in ways that transcend ties with familiar allies alone. The lack of early warning of the outbreak of COVID-19 in China's Wuhan province had catastrophic consequences for the world. Ongoing distrust between China and the West impeded a concerted global response to the pandemic. The existential threat of climate change presents all countries, whatever their political and economic persuasion, with the same set of grave challenges. It is not possible to envisage successful mitigation of the worst effects of climate change without the cooperation of China, the world's second-largest economy, one that may be on a trajectory to surpass the United States in the near future. Such cooperation must include intelligence sharing of pertinent data across otherwise antagonistic national boundaries.

Even as a renewed Cold War is being proclaimed, negotiating intelligence sharing in this more complex multipolar world will be very different and more challenging than in the past.

NOTES

1 The most extensive recent account of the entire Gouzenko affair is Amy Knight, *How the Cold War Began: The Gouzenko Affair and the Hunt for Soviet Spies* (Toronto: McClelland and Stewart, 2005). MI5 records were also used to good effect in Dennis Molinaro, "How the Cold War Began ... with British Help: The Gouzenko Affair Revisited," *Labour/le Travail* 79 (Spring 2017): 143–55. See also my "The Gouzenko Affair: From Star Chamber to Court Room," in *Canadian State Trials*, vol. 5, ed. Susan Binnie, Eric Tucker, and Barry Wright (Toronto: University of Toronto Press, 2022), and the earlier account in Reg Whitaker and Gary Marcuse, *Cold War Canada: The Making of a National Insecurity State, 1945–1957* (Toronto: University of Toronto Press,1994), 27–112. See also J.L. Black and Martin Rudner, *The Gouzenko Affair: Canada and the Beginnings of Cold War Counter-Espionage* (Newcastle: Penumbra Press, 2006).

2 Reg Whitaker, Gregory S. Kealey, and Andrew Parnaby, *Secret Service: Political Policing in Canada from the Fenians to Fortress North America* (Toronto: University of Toronto Press, 2012), 19–59.

3 Whitaker and Marcuse, *Cold War Canada*, 50–4; Knight, *How the Cold War Began*, 94–7.

4 Privy Council Office, *Report of the Royal Commission to Investigate the Facts Relating to and the Circumstances Surrounding the Communication, by Public Officials and Other Persons in Positions of Trust of Secret and Confidential Information to Agents of a Foreign Power* (Ottawa: King's Printer, 1946).

5 Vladislav Zubok and Constantine Pleshakov, *Inside the Kremlin's Cold War: From Stalin to Khrushchev* (Cambridge, MA: Harvard University Press, 1996); Allen Weinstein and Alexander Vassiliev, *The Haunted Wood: Soviet Espionage in America – the Stalin Era* (New York: Random House, 1999). Gouzenko had another long-term impact on Western counterespionage, with very mixed results: he suggested that the motive for Westerners to spy for the Soviets was ideological to the exclusion of mercenary or more personal reasons, a focus that encouraged later self-destructive ideological mole hunts in the United States, Britain, and

Canada: Reg Whitaker, "Cold War Alchemy: How America, Britain and Canada Transformed Espionage into Subversion," *Intelligence and National Security* 15, no. 2 (Summer 2000): 177–210.

6 For more on this, see the chapter by Carvin and Juneau in this volume.

7 Confidential interview, February 1988.

8 Privy Council Office, *Commission of Inquiry Concerning Certain Activities of the RCMP* [McDonald], Second Report, – vol. 1: Freedom and Security under the Law (Ottawa: Minister of Supply and Services, 1981): 93–358. The McDonald Commission did not make reference to the remarkable case of the PQ Minister of Intergovernmental Relations, Claude Morin, acting as an RCMP informant: see Whitaker, Kealey, and Parnaby, *Secret Service*, 313–17; and see Morin's own defence, *L'affaire Morin: Légendes, sottises et calomnies* (Montréal: Les Éditions du Boréal, 2006).

9 Ongoing academic and political controversy sparked by two sharply contrasting accounts of the Norman affair – Roger Bowen, *Innocence Is Not Enough: The Life and Death of Herbert Norman* (Vancouver: Douglas and McIntyre, 1988), and James Barros, *No Sense of Evil: Espionage, the Case of Herbert Norman* (Toronto: Deneau Publishers, 1986) – led to an officially commissioned study, with full access to classified files, of "the loyalties of E. Herbert Norman" by retired External Affairs diplomat Peyton Lyon, in *Labour/le Travail* 28 (Fall 1991): 219–59. Lyon found no evidence that Norman had ever been a Soviet spy or agent of influence.

10 After the American allegations first surfaced, Norman had been questioned at length by the RCMP and External Affairs officials in 1950 and 1952 regarding his alleged left-wing politics. After being cleared as a security risk, Norman as ambassador in Egypt played an important role in brokering peace during the Suez Crisis. It was at this point that the American witch-hunting allegations were raised yet again, leading to Norman's suicide.

11 Whitaker, Kealey, and Parnaby, *Secret Service*, 215.

12 Whitaker, Kealey, and Parnaby, *Secret Service*, 211–17.

13 Six months before the FLQ set off the October Crisis by kidnapping a British diplomat and a Quebec cabinet minister, the RCMP Security Service was preparing contingency plans for political kidnapping threats, informing the solicitor general that the most likely targets would be foreign diplomats and Quebec political and governmental leaders, yet neither James Cross nor Pierre Laporte had any federal or provincial protection when they were seized by the FLQ; in Laporte's case, after the Cross kidnapping: Whitaker, Kealey, and Parnaby, *Secret Service*, 283.

14 Whitaker, Kealey, and Parnaby, *Secret Service*, 271–323.

15 Dominique Clément, "Canada's Integration into Global Intelligence-Sharing Networks: From Gouzenko to the Montreal Olympics," *Intelligence and National Security* 33, no. 7 (2018): 1053–69. See also Steve Hewitt, "Cold War Counter-Terrorism: The Evolution of International Counter-Terrorism in the RCMP Security Service, 1972–1984," *Intelligence and National Security* 32 (2017): 1–18.

Intelligence Cooperation in Historical Perspective 115

16 Quoted in Clément, "Canada's Integration," 1062.
17 Transport Canada, *Air India Flight 182: Aviation Security Issues* (Ottawa: CATSA Act Review Secretariat, February 2007). Redacted copies are among the documents of the Commission of Inquiry into the Investigation of the Bombing of Air India Flight 182. Two journalists published a book in 1989 claiming they had evidence of Indian intelligence's manipulation of the Air India attack to discredit Sikhs, a considerable stretch in my view, but they relied heavily on two sources within CSIS. See Zuhair Kashmieri and Brian McAndrew, *Soft Target: How the Indian Intelligence Service Penetrated Canada* (Toronto: James Lorimer, 1989); see also the second edition, *Soft Target: The Real Story behind the Air India Disaster* (Toronto: James Lorimer, 2005).
18 Privy Council Office, *McDonald Commission*, 635.
19 "Lord Palmerston, 1784–1865, British statesman; Prime Minister, 1855–8, 1859–65," *Oxford Essential Quotations* (4th ed.), https://www.oxfordreference.com /view/10.1093/acref/9780191826719.001.0001/q-oro-ed4-00008130.
20 Commission of Inquiry into the Actions of Canadian Officials in Relation to Maher Arar, *Report of the Events Relating to Maher Arar* (Ottawa: Public Works and Government Services, 2006).
21 Alan Barnes, "Getting It Right: Canadian Intelligence Assessments on Iraq, 2002–2003," *Intelligence and National Security* 35, no. 7 (2020): 925–53. To be clear, Barnes does not suggest that Canada had a single clear intelligence position on Iraqi weapons of mass destruction and other aspects of the case for invading Iraq. In the absence of an office of national intelligence, there was no focal point for arriving at a unified position. He does suggest that scepticism about American and British claims did arise and was sustained in the face of American and British pressure to toe the official line. The capacity of Canadian analysts to draw a more accurate picture reflected, Barnes argues, a lack of the kind of politicized direction from the top that characterized American and British intelligence on Iraq. On the Iraq decision, see also Carvin and Juneau in this volume.
22 During the First World War, 5,000 Ukrainian immigrants who had not yet been naturalized as British subjects were declared to be "enemy aliens" on the basis of their ethnicity alone and consigned to internment camps. During the Second World War, at the time of the Nazi–Soviet Pact prior to the German invasion of the Soviet Union, left-wing pro-Soviet Ukrainians were interned. Tensions between left and right Ukrainians rose during the war and especially during the Cold War, with the Canadian government officially favouring the anti-Communist Ukrainian Canadian majority.

6 Australia's National Intelligence Community: Challenges and Opportunities in a Multipolar World

PATRICK F. WALSH

This chapter examines how key capability reform recommendations related to academic outreach and research articulated in the 2017 Independent Intelligence Review (IIR) of Australia's National Intelligence Community (NIC) represent opportunities for improving Australian international intelligence cooperation. Intelligence cooperation for Australia's NIC has always been important to meeting the enduring intelligence collection and assessment priorities of successive governments. The long-standing networks, particularly via the Five Eyes, made up of regular person-to-person and virtual exchanges on strategic, operational, and tactical intelligence issues underscore the critical importance of intelligence cooperation. These networks have stood the test of time, but are they still sufficiently useful and resilient as the security environment becomes increasingly complex and uncertain? Also, given that Australia's NIC and Five Eyes partners have limited resources and are confronted with the difficulty of integrating new technologies and adapting their workforces, it seems even more critical for Canberra to review cooperation processes and initiatives regularly, strategically, and explicitly. Using two key themes as a foundation for analysis (academic outreach and research and regional stability), this chapter assesses areas where Australia's NIC has additional opportunities to build on existing cooperation arrangements, both within the Five Eyes and in other less traditional intelligence-sharing networks such as with Japan and India. In addition to exploring the opportunities presented in the 2017 IIR for enhanced intelligence cooperation, this chapter assesses what challenges exist in fostering enhanced intelligence relationships with the Five Eyes and non-traditional partners and identifies how these can be managed in the immediate future.

The 2017 IIR and Australia's NIC Reform Agenda

Before outlining areas of the 2017 IIR that can provide a useful foundation for additional intelligence cooperation between Five Eyes countries and key strategic partners (Japan and India), it is necessary to provide a brief overview on the 2017 IIR. The origins of the IIR were in November 2016, when then Australian prime minister Malcom Turnbull announced the commissioning of a third independent intelligence review – the other two having been in 2004 (Flood Report) and 2011 (Cornall and Black Report). Two respected senior bureaucrats, Michael L'Estrange and Stephen Merchant, were appointed as reviewers. Unlike with the Flood Report, there was no pressing intelligence failure needing investigation, and the 2017 IIR proved to be more comprehensive in reaching out to Australia's NIC agencies, political leaders, and other NIC customers for consultation. The reviewers identified various coordination, funding, IT, legislative, and accountability matters that could be strengthened. Limited space does not permit a full analysis of all twenty-three recommendations in the 2017 IIR report; further detailed analysis can be found in another article published by this author.[1] Instead, the rest of this chapter will focus on recommendations 1, 5, 7, and 14, for those are the ones that most relate to areas where further intelligence cooperation measures could be developed with international partners.

To be clear, the final published unclassified version of the 2017 IIR Report did not make any specific recommendations on how Australia's NIC could improve intelligence cooperation with the Five Eyes or other strategic partners such as Japan and India. The government's terms of reference (TORs) for the 2017 IIR did not specifically include an examination of Australia's NIC cooperation arrangements, and the reviewers did not explicitly take on intelligence cooperation as something that needed addressing. In the report's introductory remarks there was only an oblique reference to intelligence cooperation, with the authors indicating that "the development path of overseas intelligence partners and lessons for Australia was important."[2] This lack of a formal focus on the state of Australia's cooperation arrangements, while not surprising, represented a lost opportunity to reflect on how important international intelligence alliances and networks could be strengthened. However, as noted earlier, the report does underscore significant restructuring of Australia's NIC, and the current implementation of several recommendations provides additional opportunities for improving intelligence cooperation measures as the global security environment for Australia and its partners becomes ever more complex.

Rather than providing detailed analysis of recommendations 1, 5, 7, and 14 and how each could facilitate greater opportunities for intelligence cooperation, the following section discusses them thematically. Recommendations 1 and 5 relate to implementing major architectural change to Australia's NIC, and 7 and 14 focus broadly on several capability-building and funding initiatives (see appendix A). The next two sections provide an analysis of how the current implementation of recommendations from the 2017 IIR may provide a useful catalyst to further enhance intelligence cooperation opportunities for Australia's NIC, the Five Eyes, and strategic partners such as Japan and India.

Opportunities for Intelligence Cooperation with Five Eyes Partners

Recommendations 1 and 5, as noted earlier, relate to the establishment of new architectural arrangements within Australia's NIC, including the creation of a new Office of National Intelligence (ONI) and, within that, a mandate to improve coordination, integration, and enterprise management across all ten NIC agencies. Recommendation 5 suggested that an ONI Assessment Consultation Board be established, chaired by the Director-General ONI and consisting of senior leaders from ONI, other intelligence agencies, and relevant policy departments as well as individuals from business, non-government organizations, universities, and think tanks, who could add relevant perspectives to intelligence assessment matters. The intent of recommendation 5 was for ONI to develop a more intensive and substantive program of interaction with experts outside of government to inform assessments.[3] It is not clear whether ONI has yet implemented the assessment consultation board, but arguably a more important step would be for it to develop a multifaceted academic outreach program of the kind that the Canadian Security Intelligence Service (CSIS) has developed over the past decade.[4] The ONI's approach to academic outreach since its establishment in 2018 has been piecemeal rather than strategic. For example, it has established a National Intelligence Science Advisory Board. The board is chaired by senior ONI officials and includes senior executives from other NIC agencies, as well as selected senior researchers from key universities in Australia. Although the board has met a few times, it is not clear whether in its current configuration it can provide the necessary advice on research or other capability issues the NIC will face in the future.[5] The academics appointed to it largely have a science, technology, engineering, and mathematics (STEM) background, which is not enough for them to provide sufficient advice on how external academic researchers can best help address intelligence assessment or broader capability matters for Australia's NIC.[6] In short, at the time of writing, a new NIC enterprise-wide approach to academic outreach is still largely developmental, although some progress has been made.

The Australian NIC, and particularly ONI's enterprise management officials, can learn a lot from other Five Eyes partners that have more established and elaborate academic outreach arrangements in place, such as the US Office of the Director of National Intelligence (ODNI) and CSIS. For example, as mentioned, CSIS's academic outreach program regularly publishes open-source proceedings of workshops on a range of threat/risk topics that have been attended by external academics. Additionally, the CSIS academic outreach program has in the past sponsored or co-sponsored several intelligence conferences internationally, sometimes with the assistance of other Five Eyes partners, to gather trusted academics and intelligence personnel together in closed environments to discuss threat, risk, and capability issues. CSIS has

120   Patrick F. Walsh

also regularly welcomed academics, including this author, to its headquarters in Ottawa to meet with analysts and management to discuss security and capability issues. Jean-Louis Tiernan, the former director general of CSIS's academic outreach program, has written a useful chapter on the program for readers seeking further detail.[7]

In summary, a strategically focused and well developed NIC academic outreach program would not only improve intelligence assessments and capability issues in Australia but also offer an excellent way to improve in more coordinated ways academic outreach among Australia's other Five Eyes partners. What might be possible in an expanded Five Eyes academic outreach program? Several initiatives would likely be helpful in improving intelligence cooperation in the area of academic outreach. Two initiatives are worth considering in an expanded Five Eyes academic outreach program, from which all partners would benefit. First, there would be value in establishing a Five Eyes research grant program that encourages researchers and academics to collaborate across Five Eyes countries on emerging threat and capability issues that are priorities for the five countries, but in areas where no country necessarily has the broad spectrum of expertise to embark on the research on their own. There are several ongoing and emerging priority areas for the Five Eyes. These include, but are not limited to, covert collection challenges, space, identity management, emerging biological and material sciences, cyber, human behaviour/influence, and artificial intelligence (AI). A Five Eyes collaborative research grant could help address complex areas like these. This initiative would not take the place of long-standing research grant schemes in individual Five Eyes countries, or, in the case of the United States, more institutionalized research responses operated by Intelligence Advanced Research Projects Activity (IARPA) or the Defence Advanced Research Projects Agency (DARPA). Rather, the Five Eyes intelligence collaborative research scheme would seek to build the capacity of at least five research institutions (universities) across the Five Eyes as opposed to a single funded institution. The five collaborating research institutions would ideally also be funded for an extended period of time – five to seven years rather than the usual one to three years seen in a lot of research grant schemes across Five Eyes countries. Another important benefit of a Five Eyes intelligence collaborative research scheme would be the development of the next generation of researchers on intelligence issues – whether these be on threat, technological, or other non-technological capability areas relevant to Five Eyes agencies. The grant scheme could include, as part of its funding rules, allocations for postdoctoral and higher-degree research (HDR) students, whom universities successful in grants across the Five Eyes could co-supervise. This additional focus on doctoral and postdoctoral students would help build the equivalent of centres of excellence in particular areas across the five universities involved in the funding.

A second initiative worth considering to further promote academic outreach and collaboration across the Five Eyes is the establishment of a visiting fellow or scholar-in-residence program across Five Eyes agencies. Versions of this already exist to some extent, although the focus is usually on an agency like the CIA employing an US citizen, who thus becomes an official employee. We have seen this in the employment of official historians for the CIA, MI5, and ASIO.[8] What I have in mind is something bolder that would allow security-vetted and funded academics/researchers from each Five Eyes country to work for six to twenty-four months as non-nationals within the Intelligence Community (IC) of another Five Eyes intelligence agency. The appointed fellows could work on capability projects or as subject matter experts working with analysts to better understand particular threats/risks. For example, a British academic could work in Australia's NIC, and likewise an Australian could be a fellow in a British intelligence agency. Depending on the candidate and the security vetting process, they could gain more intimate access to classified information and produce reports and assessments that improve the understanding of complex threats/risks or provide advice of a technical nature about capability development. Given the sensitivities involved, fellowship applications and recruitment would likely not be a public process, but rather one closely held and organized by the Five Eyes intelligence network. Arguably, there is great value in having an academic/researcher from one Five Eyes country (e.g., Australia) working in another (e.g., the United States), providing expertise that may not be readily available in the host country's agency. Moreover, these fellows could help challenge bureaucratic cultural factors and groupthink within each Five Eyes intelligence community.

Recommendations 7 to 14 in the 2017 IIR, as noted earlier, relate to improving capability and funding. In particular, recommendation 7 suggested the establishment of a National Intelligence Science and Advisory Board (NISAB) to provide a more strategic and structural approach to technological change and its impact on the Australian NIC. While the NISAB has been established and the board has met remotely a few times, it has arguably, at time of writing, yet to find a raison d'être or a focus. Still, it can be hoped that as the NISAB develops an active advisory role for the NIC on technology, science, and even research, it will be able to provide additional opportunities for cooperation with other Five Eyes partners by leveraging similar institutional arrangements in other partner countries. Each country must identify, plan, and prioritize technological, scientific, and research knowledge and capabilities that allow their ICs to adapt to an increasingly more complex and uncertain security environment. However, at the same time, there needs to be a more strategic and coordinated approach across the Five Eyes ICs in the planning for technological and scientific change. A coordinated and, in some cases, more integrated planning approach would allow each Five Eyes country to better leverage each other's efforts. Each country could focus on areas where it can bring the most expertise and contribute in a coordinated and resource-efficient manner to the capacities of other partners. For example, the NISAB and its equivalents in other Five Eyes could develop a common Science and Technical Advisory Board to help identify technological and scientific challenges and opportunities that Five Eyes countries need to adapt to in the future, whether in AI, quantum computing, biotechnology engineering, nanotechnology, or human augmentation technologies.

Two final suggestions listed under recommendation 14 included an Australian NIC innovation fund to support the development of prototypes for transitioning research outcomes to operational systems and a NIC innovation hub to "facilitate ways in which government, industry and academia could come together to address capability needs and solutions and create new linkages."[9] At this point it is less clear whether ONI has made significant headway on either of these suggestions, though there may be progress over the next few years via the NISAB agenda.

Australia's NIC Cooperation with Non–Five Eyes Partners

The 2017 IIR recommendations discussed above that provide additional opportunities for promoting deeper intelligence collaboration among the Five Eyes partners are also relevant to enhancing intelligence cooperation between Australia, Five Eyes countries, and other strategic partners such as Japan and India. Australia and other Five Eyes partners have long had working relationships with the intelligence services in these countries. This section focuses on additional opportunities for Australia's NIC to expand on these with both Japan and India in ways that promote the mutual strategic and security interests of all three countries. Given the space constraints, the focus here will be on Australia's specific approaches to intelligence cooperation with Japan and India. If Australia's NIC promotes some of the initiatives discussed below, other Five Eyes countries may consider supporting them so as to strengthen cooperation efforts across the Five Eyes partnership.

Before identifying specific intelligence cooperation opportunities for the Australian NIC, India, and Japan, we might ask a fundamental question: why focus on these two countries? Australia's NIC has elaborate liaison and intelligence cooperation initiatives with a number of non–Five Eyes countries, so why India and Japan? Stated plainly, since 9/11 the strategic environment in the Asia-Pacific, now frequently referred to as the Indo-Pacific, has become increasingly volatile and uncertain, particularly with the rise of a more aggressive China. In response, while continuing to bolster Australia's bedrock alliance with the United States, including via the AUKUS[10] security partnership, Canberra has sought to engage more deeply with other democracies across the Indo-Pacific whose security policies also demonstrate growing concerns about a more malignant Chinese influence in their region. Japan and India increasingly represent for Canberra dependable partners also interested in upholding the existing open liberal principles governing the strategic environment in the Indo-Pacific.

Over the past fifteen years in particular, several bilateral and multilateral initiatives have brought Australia, Japan, and India together, although arguably the most significant has been the creation of the quadrilateral initiative (Quad) in 2004 among the United States, Australia, Japan, and India. The Quad initiative was largely a creation of former Japanese prime minister Shinzo Abe and was designed to balance power and manage issues such as transnational security, terrorism, and sea piracy in the Asia-Pacific region.[11] The original version of the Quad was put to one side in 2007–8 following a unilateral withdrawal by Australia early in Labour prime minister Kevin Rudd's first term of office "following Beijing's protests that it had been specifically designed to encircle it."[12] The Quad was revitalized in 2017 at a meeting of senior diplomats from the four nations on the sidelines of the ASEAN summit in Manila.[13] Further consolidation of the Quad has occurred since 2018 at various international forums.[14] China's more aggressive stance in the Indo-Pacific in recent years has only seen the Quad grow in strength and importance for its partners. This was reinforced in May 2022, when, within twenty-four hours of winning office, Australia's new prime minister, the Labour Party's Anthony Albanese, attended the Quad meeting in Tokyo.

For Shinzo Abe's government (he served two terms) and those of his successors, Yoshihide Suga and Fumio Kishida, the Quad has signalled a significant evolution in Japan, away from its post-war pacifist constitution and toward more assertive and militarized defence, national security, and foreign policies.[15] For example, Japan has removed its long-standing, self-imposed defence spending cap of 1 per cent of GDP and reversed previous trends by increasing the defence budget on a yearly basis.[16] The Quad, although Tokyo has not declared as much, also underscores a growing focus on a values-based approach to diplomacy, which holds that Japan as a democracy "should unite with countries of similar liberal and democratic values to urge other nations, most notably China, to follow a rules-based international regime."[17] India, at one time a non-aligned country, has joined the Quad and similarly aligned itself to principles of values-based diplomacy and a "free and open Indo-Pacific [FOIP] rooted in democracy, the rule of law, and respect for human rights," just as is advocated by the other member-states (the United States, Australia, and Japan).[18]

As Medcalf describes, "India has become increasingly pragmatic, creative and ecumenical in its security diplomacy. It has simultaneously deepened ties with Israel, Iran, the United Arab Emirates, France, Australia, Singapore and Vietnam, while maintaining a long-standing defence partnership with Russia."[19] New Delhi's involvement in the Quad reflects deepening security, military, and

124   Patrick F. Walsh

diplomatic ties with Australia, Japan, and the United States as it seeks to "hedge against Chinese influence in South Asia and beyond."[20] In particular, for New Delhi, the military aspects of the Quad relationship have grown more intense, with Australia and other Quad members participating in India's major naval exercise, named Malabar.[21] The other three Quad members' participation in Malabar has strengthened India's capacity for joint operations with more skilled and advanced naval forces besides enhancing its operational skills in the event of conflict with other regional navies, including those of China and Pakistan.[22]

Opportunities for Intelligence Cooperation

The growing strategic alignment of Australia and the other Quad member-states for a peaceful liberal order in the Indo-Pacific has been dominated so far by joint military activities, but it also signals opportunities for greater civilian intelligence cooperation. Australia already has in place intelligence cooperation initiatives with Japan and India that include regular intelligence liaison visits to Canberra by military and civilian intelligence officers from those countries on a range of matters such as counterterrorism, transnational organized crime, and maritime piracy. The establishment of the relatively new ONI with its enterprise management mandate has established a foundation for additional cooperation measures with India and Japan.

The growing mutual strategic interests of India, Japan, Australia, and the United States in the Indo-Pacific have brought forward several additional opportunities to step up confidence-building intelligence initiatives beyond those related to defence. One confidence-building intelligence cooperation measure – an easier one – would be for Australia's NIC to promote opportunities for collaboration on joint intelligence assessments that are of mutual priority, such as climate change, transnational crime, terrorism, and Asia-Pacific security issues such as China's grab for the South China Sea. As with all intelligence cooperation among non–Five Eyes partners, there are security and classification issues that require risk management when joint products are being drafted, particularly with regard to what SIGINT or HUMINT sources can be shared with non–Five Eyes countries. Yet such risks are manageable. Australia and its Five Eyes partners are quite experienced at sanitizing sources and methods as required when working with friendly countries outside the partnership. Moreover, facilitating opportunities to draft joint intelligence assessments with Japan and India (beyond the usual partners of the Five Eyes) would bring different perspectives and challenge groupthink within the Australian NIC on some issues.

Joint intelligence assessments could be facilitated via ONI, which could consider drawing on its joint capability fund to invest in regional intelligence workshops on security threats/risks and capability issues. Such workshops, convened in Canberra, New Delhi, and Tokyo, would provide intelligence officials from all these countries with an opportunity to discuss joint intelligence products and improve mutual understanding of complex threats/risks and capability issues. Australian and other Five Eyes intelligence local liaison staff in the workshop of the host country could also attend. The sessions could be run at a lower security classification (For Official Use Only or Restricted) rather than TOP SECRET, thus ensuring a wider opportunity for intelligence staff to participate.

Two other areas are worth considering to improve intelligence cooperation between Australia, Japan, and India. One would involve promoting visiting academic fellowships among these countries; these fellows would work on research that is of mutual priority to Australia's NIC and the other countries. Australian academics could be funded for six-month fellowships at universities or think tanks in Japan and India, and vice versa. Of course, such government-funded visiting fellowship arrangements already exist. However, the focus here would be on promoting intelligence studies scholarship, and applicants would be required to work on mutually agreed national security and intelligence priorities set by Canberra, Tokyo, and New Delhi.

A final area that Australia's NIC should consider investing in from its joint capability fund is the sponsoring of intensive strategic intelligence courses, in which intelligence officials from Australia, Japan, India, and other Five Eyes countries could participate. Across the Five Eyes countries, internal strategic intelligence analytical training is becoming more available. Less is known about similar training in Japan and India; clearly, though, the intelligence capabilities of both those countries demonstrate key weaknesses (see the following section). Hence, developing a greater strategic analytical capability across all Quad partners may be a tangible benefit, particularly to those countries' intelligence communities. The author has been involved for almost two decades in strategic intelligence analytical training courses for Australian federal security and law enforcement. One such course, the National Strategic Intelligence Course (NSIC), originally stood up in 1999, has offered national and state-based agencies the opportunity to work on strategic priority threat areas for two weeks in Canberra and in syndicates producing joint intelligence assessments.[23] Versions of the NSIC course have also been delivered in Washington, Wellington, and Leicester (UK) with the participation of analysts from key Five Eyes agencies. The course is co-delivered by Charles Sturt University (CSU), the Australian Federal Police, and the Australian Criminal Intelligence Commission and articulates with CSU's Masters of Intelligence Analysis. ONI could sponsor similar courses in Canberra or in other capitals (Tokyo and New Delhi) to promote strategic intelligence capabilities and expand trust and relationship building among analysts. While recognizing these opportunities for enhanced intelligence cooperation, this following section assesses some of the challenges and constraints in their implementation as well as ways to overcome them.

Intelligence Cooperation Challenges

Challenges for Future Five Eyes Cooperation

As noted earlier, ONI was only recently established (in 2018), and many of its enterprise management functions are still being developed, including its academic outreach and capability development programs. Additionally, ONI's National Intelligence Science and Advisory Board (NISAB) is still setting its agenda. Added to these internal bureaucratic constraints is whether capability funding sources will be maintained in the short to medium term given the budgetary pressures facing the Australian government in the wake of the COVID pandemic, which will have an impact on ONI's aspirations for future intelligence cooperation. ONI will require a consistent and strategic approach to ensure quicker progress on its academic agenda, and this could be partly assisted by learning from other intelligence communities' academic outreach programs, particularly those run by CSIS in Canada and ODNI in the United States. While in the short term ONI may not be quite ready to lead or participate in a Five Eyes collaborative research scheme as described earlier, this is an initiative it could undertake in the medium to longer term due to the benefits it would have for the development of knowledge and technology for Australia's NIC and other Five Eyes partners. Given that ONI is still evaluating its academic outreach priorities, sponsoring a fellowship program for other Five Eyes citizen researchers in the NIC may be premature. As indicated earlier, ONI could achieve easier wins in intelligence cooperation by sponsoring regular workshops on complex emerging threats that bring together IC staff, researchers, and academics. Regarding the initiatives discussed earlier for further enhancing Five Eyes intelligence cooperation, an expansion of current academic outreach initiatives would make sense. However, academic outreach programs will continue to be challenged by resource limitations, the changing priorities of intelligence community leaders, and the requirement to balance the need to facilitate greater external participation in managing threats and capability issues against maintaining security.

Challenges for Future Non–Five Eyes Cooperation

As discussed earlier, I suggest that there are four intelligence cooperation initiatives that Australia's NIC could promote to further collaboration with India and Japan: joint intelligence assessments, regional intelligence workshops, visiting academic fellowships, and strategic intelligence training. Each of these initiatives faces its own challenges. Regarding joint intelligence assessments with India and Japan, choices of topics for products would obviously need careful consideration regardless of whether these were bilateral assessments (Australia and India, Australia and Japan) or multilateral (Australia, Japan, and India, or other Five Eyes partners). Initially it may be more prudent to focus on issues where interests intersect in less controversial ways, such as climate change and terrorism, rather than, for example, India's relations with Pakistan. Regional intelligence workshops, which would promote face-to-face contacts among intelligence staffs from Australia, India, Japan, and other Five Eyes countries, would be a step up from writing products collaboratively but (usually) virtually. Intelligence production is a technological function, especially at the collection stage, but it also relies on building effective interpersonal relations within agencies and across ICs in different countries. Regional intelligence workshops could allow intelligence analysts from the Quad member-states and other Five Eyes countries to build trusting, effective networks at both operational and strategic levels across their ICs. However, leaving aside the barriers raised at the time of writing by the ongoing COVID-19 pandemic, tighter post-COVID IC budgets in all Quad countries may preclude investment in this initiative. Similarly, in the short to medium term, until COVID-19 vaccination coverage is sufficient and the pandemic transitions to an endemic global disease, any investment in visiting academic fellowships and strategic intelligence training is likely to be on hold at least for the next two years. If Australia's NIC did support an academic fellowship program on intelligence studies in India and Japan, it might despite its merits be further constrained by the sensitivities of national security and intelligence officials in Tokyo and New Delhi.

In addition to the short- to medium-term COVID-19 and post COVID-19 treasury challenges that Australia and other Quad members may face, there are institutional constraints in India and Japan that might hinder the pace and extent of such initiatives. Turning to India first, since 9/11 and the Mumbai terrorist attacks, there have been several review and reform programs of India's intelligence community, yet its current eight security agencies are still reluctant to share intelligence horizontally and vertically up to the higher echelons of government. Publicly available data on India's intelligence capabilities are understandably limited; that said, evidence suggests that despite some reform attempts post-Mumbai, it still suffers from a dearth of staffing, expertise, and depth.[24] This raises concerns over whether specific Indian intelligence agencies have the proper mix of skills and expertise to work on joint intelligence assessments and participate in regional workshops and strategic intelligence training.

Added to these internal constraints is the culture in India, where senior executives tasked with overseeing defence and security policy are, according to Medcalf, "typically generalists without relevant training, education or prior experience as security practitioners."[25] Medcalf further suggests that "strategic or security studies is rarely encountered in Indian universities, and few officials come to institutions such as the Ministry of External Affairs from such backgrounds, or even from such disciplines as international relations."[26] Moreover,

128   Patrick F. Walsh

as Kanwal has observed, there has been a disconnect in India between academic research and the making of security policy.[27] A combination of generalist leaders (i.e., not necessarily intelligence-agency trained) and lack of academic focus on intelligence and security studies may constrain intelligence community leaders' understanding of the benefits of the four cooperation initiatives discussed earlier. In particular, in Australia, the United States, and other Five Eyes countries there are strong and growing links among universities in international relations, security, and intelligence studies; the opposite is the case in India, and this may limit opportunities for Australian, Japanese, and other Five Eyes scholars to visit Indian research institutions and work on intelligence-related topics.

In contrast, the potential for Australia's NIC to make progress with Japan on the four cooperation initiatives discussed earlier may gain quicker and easier traction, for the defence and security relationships between Canberra and Tokyo are older and deeper than those between Canberra and New Delhi. However, as with India, there is scant evidence available regarding Japan's capabilities. Scholarship on contemporary Japanese intelligence reform, however, does show that since the early 2000s the Government of Japan has undertaken several initiatives to reform its intelligence community in order to respond more effectively to the changing security environment – particularly the rise of China, North Korea's nuclear program, and terrorism. Kobayashi suggests that the two major objectives of reform measures have been "(1) establishing an effective institutional mechanism connecting policymakers and the IC and (2) improving intelligence collection capabilities."[28]

The key central coordinating body is the Cabinet Intelligence and Research Office (CIRO), which has undergone reforms in recent years that have resulted in better connectivity between the intelligence community and policy-makers. Yet the strength of CIRO's mandate and that of its head (the Director of Cabinet Intelligence) vis-à-vis Japan's other intelligence agencies seems weak. This has resulted in less effective integration and cooperation, including information sharing, despite recent efforts.[29] Kobayashi's study of Japan's reforms summarizes a number of sources from political parties, policy think tanks, and academic scholars; all of them have identified common problems. These problems include insufficient mechanisms to properly deliver intelligence requirements from policy-makers to the intelligence community, partly due to the lack of community integration, as well as the weak leadership authority given to the CIRO and the DCI. There are also problems of intelligence collection in all areas (HUMINT, SIGINT, IMINT) and in intelligence analysis.[30] In 2015, there was also no evidence of an all-sourced strategic intelligence product like the national intelligence estimate (NIE) in the United States. Although it is possible that progress has been made since then, it is likely that the strategic analytical capability of Japan's IC requires further development.[31] Several other problems

Australia's National Intelligence Community   129

have emerged as well, including the lack of a fully developed counter-intelligence mechanism that includes a reliable security clearance system and laws to protect secret information. In 2013, however, under the Abe administration, progress was made to strengthen security laws. Abe enacted a controversial secrecy law, the Designated State Secrets Law, to prevent leaks of confidential information in order to protect information and intelligence sharing between the United States and Japan as per the alliance treaty.[32] There is another precedent for formal intelligence sharing between Australia and Japan: augmenting its long-running collaboration with the United States, Japan signed an Information Security Agreement with Australia in 2012. Furthermore, at the end of 2016, the United States, Japan, and Australia signed a similar trilateral agreement that deepened the extent of covert security cooperation.[33]

In the past decade, Japan has revamped its intelligence services, including placing them under the firmer central direction of its National Security Council. This has demonstrated to Australia and to the United States that it is improving its protection of intelligence and information sharing with those allies. Nonetheless, it is likely that Washington and Canberra will be looking for sustained improvement in many areas of intelligence capability to ensure that new cooperation initiatives among these three countries can be deepened and broadened. Still, in contrast to India, the extent of security and defence cooperation between Australia, Japan, and the United States is wide-ranging, which makes the four intelligence cooperation initiatives mentioned earlier possible despite institutional barriers in Japan. Moving beyond the challenges identified between Five Eyes countries, Australia, Japan, and India, the final section examines what areas of cooperation discussed earlier may be possible over the next three to five years.

The Outlook

I turn first to the key cooperation measures Australia can orchestrate with other Five Eyes partners. Domestically, ONI still needs a few more years to achieve all of its key enterprise management objectives, which have progressively been implemented since its establishment in 2018. However, although this new agency remains in the "formation" stage, ONI can still influence the broader academic outreach agendas of other Five Eyes partners to mutual benefit without in the short term requiring excessive financing for such initiatives (e.g., analysts' seminars, or inputs on emerging threats from academics). Additionally, through ONI's joint capability fund and its NISAB, Australia's NIC can identify research issues and capability priorities that it can work on in a more coordinated and integrated way with Five Eyes partners, with the intent of moving toward the implementation of a formal Five Eyes research collaboration program. There are several emerging areas that could be addressed more efficiently and effectively if all Five Eyes ICs' research and capability efforts were more strategic and collaborative: AI, nanotechnology, biotechnology, quantum computing, and a better understanding of human intent to exploit technology malignantly via the socio-behavioural sciences. The visiting fellowship idea described earlier, while of benefit to all Five Eyes, may raise security concerns in some Five Eyes countries and would likely take longer than three to five years to be implemented (if adopted at all). There are other areas where cooperation could be fostered among the Five Eyes that do not come from the 2017 IIR, such as health security and intelligence education; these would also help strengthen academic outreach, as well as other research and capability development areas this chapter has discussed. At the time of writing, the COVID-19 pandemic appears to be moving slowly out of its acute phase, which means that now is an ideal time for all Five Eyes ICs to collaborate closely on developing better health security intelligence early warning systems, given that climate change, globalization, and population growth will likely mean that COVID-19 will not be the last pandemic the world will have to manage in the years to come.[34] The Biden administration has shown some encouraging refocusing efforts on health security issues, but initiatives need to be coordinated, and collaboration with other Five Eyes partners would produce better results. Without the implementation of some of the suggested cooperation initiatives mentioned earlier, intelligence education is another area where a lot more work could be done in the Five Eyes. For example, a Five Eyes Masters Program could be established, delivered jointly by two or three universities, to improve standards in training and collaboration across the partnership.

Let us turn now to the outlook for intelligence cooperation between Australia and its two strategic partners, Japan and India. What are the prospects for greater cooperation despite the constraints? Regarding India, Australia's strategic and military ties with that country are deepening, although much of this is aligned to and leveraged on the back of greater Indo-US cooperation. India's membership in the Quad has allowed it access to high-tech US defence equipment to extend its regional power. There is also the possibility of growing Indo-US cooperation in intelligence sharing and real-time imagery under more recent joint agreements between Washington and New Delhi. These include the Basic Exchange and Cooperation Agreement (BECA) signed in October 2020, which gives India access to US geospatial intelligence capabilities, and the Communications Compatibility and Security Agreement (COMCASA) signed in 2018, which provides India with encrypted communications so that US and Indian military forces can communicate during peace and war. Both agreements are significantly advantageous for India's navy.[35] Although such measures are aimed at countering China's strategic entry into the Indian Ocean, intelligence sharing and technology transfer with India by the United States or Australia will likely need to be measured so as to not overly escalate regional tensions. For Australia and India, it is likely that in the short to medium term there will be ongoing challenges in sharing civilian intelligence beyond military exercises, given the underdeveloped nature of India's IC. For the next two years at least, a distracted and politically damaged Modi government – the result of its perceived mishandling of the COVID-19 pandemic – may create a political environment in New Delhi where India's national security apparatus is less likely to make progress, even on the less ambitious cooperation measures detailed earlier (e.g., joint intelligence assessments, regional intelligence workshops, strategic intelligence training). Cooperation efforts may be more feasible later, when global health security has become more stabilized and intelligence staff from New Delhi and Canberra can move freely between capitals.

What are the prospects for Australian and Japanese ICs to cooperate in the above-mentioned areas more broadly? As noted in contrast to India, Australia and Japan have already developed a broad and deep bedrock upon which further cooperation is possible on many initiatives, including the four previously mentioned. Despite the weaknesses in central integration of intelligence in Japan's CIRO – the institution responsible for developing all source assessments – ONI could play an influential role in encouraging more frequent joint intelligence assessments and strategic intelligence training. Eventually, post COVID-19, ONI could also sponsor visiting academic fellowships between Australia and Japan as well as regional workshops in which other Five Eyes partners and India could also participate.

The policy agendas of Shinzo Abe's successors, Yoshihide Suga and Fumio Kishida, indicate an ongoing willingness to expand aspects of military, national security, and intelligence cooperation with the United States and Australia, although Japan's current and projected economic outlook may constrain the development of some cooperation initiatives, including possibly less ambitious ones like regular intelligence workshops and analytical training. Suga and Kishida inherited Japan's worst economy since the Second World War, and the government's need to stimulate the economy in response to the COVID-19 pandemic will likely "leave Japan with a public-debt-stock-to-GDP ratio of nearly 270 per cent by the end of 2020, with little prospect of substantial improvement into the middle of the current decade."[36] However, the Biden White House has been more engaged than the Trump administration and will push Japan to invest more heavily in its military and intelligence capabilities, as well as in joint research and development on military technology.[37] Because of domestic pressure, Japan's government will continue to focus on rebuilding Japan's economy; in the meantime, Washington and Canberra will both be looking for further reform of the country's military and national security enterprise, not just in defence preparedness but also in terms of more effective counter-intelligence responses to China's civil/military fusion strategy.[38]

In addition, further comprehensive intelligence cooperation between Washington, Canberra, and Tokyo would be possible if Japan were to join the Five

Eyes intelligence partnership, making it the "Six Eyes." In recent years, there has been speculation that Japan will be invited to join the Five Eyes despite several intelligence capability gaps identified earlier, which would make integration with some Five Eyes technology and systems difficult. Nonetheless, as Japan has developed expertise in regional signals intelligence via its Directorate for Signals Intelligence, and given its proximity to China, North Korea, and Russia, it could be a valuable addition to the Five Eyes. In recent years, there has been some openness within the Japanese government to the idea of Tokyo joining the Five Eyes. For example, former defence minister Taro Kono has been enthusiastic about Japan doing so.[39] However, it is less clear whether current prime minister Fumio Kishida is interested in this option. Japan, like Australia and the United States, is increasingly subject to a hostile security environment, including state-sponsored cyberattacks emanating from China and other states. Furthermore, Russia's February 2022 invasion of Ukraine has increased concerns in Quad capitals that China may be emboldened to resolve the Taiwan issue militarily. Finally, the Quad nations' anxieties over China's recent more coercive diplomacy in the South Pacific that resulted in Beijing signing a security pact with Honiara (Solomon Islands) on 30 March 2022 underscore a deteriorating security situation in the Indo-Pacific.[40] A further sustained or substantive deterioration in the security environment may speed up decisions in Washington, Canberra, and Tokyo to create a "Six Eyes" intelligence partnership, but despite recent efforts we are not yet at this point. Some Five Eyes partners such as New Zealand have signalled that they do not want to propagate the perception that this long-standing partnership is designed to contain China on every regional security issue, which means that "adding" Japan may not be supported in Wellington.[41] That said, China's failed attempt in May 2022 to create a sweeping new agreement with ten Pacific nations, including on security, if it were to succeed in a different form in the future, would likely change views in Wellington and other Five Eyes capitals on even closer intelligence cooperation with Japan.[42]

In this chapter, I have identified some key areas where Australia's NIC, particularly its ONI, can expand intelligence cooperation both within the Five Eyes alliance and with two key strategic partners, Japan and India. As noted earlier, however, there are internal and external institutional challenges and constraints on how far Australia can expand on some intelligence cooperation measures – even those that may be less controversial, such as embarking on more regular joint intelligence assessments or academic outreach programs. Australia's NIC thus faces limitations on what it can do. However, by working in concert with its other Five Eyes partners, Australia can continue to identify areas where cooperation can progress within the network and with key strategic partners. The kinds of intelligence cooperation initiatives suggested in this chapter are achievable with the right kind of political and bureaucratic will. They can act as confidence-building measures between Quad member-states and would support the overlapping vital national security interests of Five Eyes and non–Five Eyes countries in

Australia's National Intelligence Community   133

the Indo-Pacific. Delivering on modest intelligence cooperation measures is the best way to provide the necessary impetus for even more enhanced intelligence cooperation among all states. The Australian government is expected to shortly announce another independent review of the NIC. At this stage no terms of references have been released but the next review would be a good opportunity to take stock not only of recommendations made in the 2017 IIR but also of how the NIC has enhanced intelligence cooperation in the increasingly contested Indo-Pacific.

Appendix A: List of 2017 Independent Intelligence Review Recommendations Discussed in Chapter

Recommendation 1: An Office of National Intelligence (ONI) be established as a statutory authority within the Prime Minister's portfolio
Recommendation 5: Current Office of National Assessments analyst numbers be increased by at least 50 per cent to support the Office of National Intelligence's (ONI) intelligence assessment role, and that: a) ONI be responsible for preparing a morning Daily Brief for the Prime Minister on intelligence issues of significance; b) an ONI Assessment Consultation Board be established, chaired by the Director-General ONI and consisting of senior leaders from ONI, other intelligence agencies and relevant policy departments as well as individuals from business, non-government organizations, universities and think-tanks who can add relevant perspectives to intelligence assessment matters; and c) ONI develop a more intensive and substantive program of interaction with experts outside of government to inform assessments.
Recommendation 7: A Joint Capability Fund administered by the Office of National Intelligence be established to support the development of shared capabilities, with the total amount in the Fund being equivalent to the Efficiency Dividend levied on the intelligence agencies
Recommendation 14: The Office of National Intelligence lead a more structured approach to the National Intelligence Community's responses to technological change, with a high priority given to: a) establishing a National Intelligence Community Science and Technology Advisory Board; b) creating a National Intelligence Community Innovation Fund to support the development of prototypes for transitioning research outcomes into operational systems; and c) supporting a National Intelligence Community Innovation Hub to facilitate ways in which government, industry and academia could come together to address capability needs and solutions and create new linkages.

NOTES

1 Patrick F. Walsh, "Transforming the Australian Intelligence Community: Mapping Change, Impact, and Challenges," *Intelligence and National Security* 36, no. 2 (2021): 243–59.
2 Michael L'Estrange and Stephen Merchant, "2017 Independent Intelligence Review," Australian Government, Department of the Prime Minister and Cabinet, 12, https://www.pmc.gov.au/publications/report-2017-independent-intelligence-review.

134   Patrick F. Walsh

3 L'Estrange and Merchant, "2017 Independent Intelligence Review," 16.
4 Walsh, "Transforming the Australian Intelligence Community," 243–59.
5 Walsh, "Transforming the Australian Intelligence Community."
6 Walsh, "Transforming the Australian Intelligence Community," 243–59; Patrick F. Walsh and Mark Harrison MBE, "Strategic Intelligence Practice in the Australian Intelligence Community: Evolution, Constraints, and Progress," *Intelligence and National Security* 36, no. 5 (2021): 1–16; Glenn Withers, Elizabeth Buchanan, Liz West, Dylan Clements, and Greg Austin, "Social Science Research and Intelligence in Australia," *Academy of the Social Science in Australia* (September 2019): 1–33, https://socialsciences.org.au/publications/social-science-research-intelligence-in -australia.
7 Jean-Louis Tiernan, "The Practice of Open Intelligence: The Experience of the Canadian Security Intelligence Service," in *Strategic Analysis in Support of International Policy Making: Case Studies in Achieving Analytical Relevance*, ed. Thomas Juneau (Lanham: Rowman and Littlefield, 2017), 147–62.
8 Patrick F. Walsh, *Intelligence Leadership and Governance: Building Effective Intelligence Communities in the 21st Century* (New York: Routledge, 2020).
9 L'Estrange and Merchant, "2017 Independent Intelligence Review," 18–19.
10 AUKUS (Australia, United Kingdom and United States) is a new security partnership announced on 15 September 2021 between the three long-standing allies designed to discourage future bids by China for regional hegemony. The initial step for AUKUS is to equip Australia with advanced nuclear submarines. Other details of the partnership appear to be works in progress but are likely to include extensive cooperation on cyber, AI, and quantum computing.
11 Ashok Sharma, "The Quadrilateral Initiative: An Evaluation," *South Asian Survey* 17, no. 2 (2010): 237–53.
12 Sharma, "The Quadrilateral Initiative."
13 Rahul Roy-Chaudhur and Kate Sullivan de Estrada, "India, the Indo-Pacific, and the Quad," *Survival Global Politics and Strategy* 60, no. 3 (2018): 181–94.
14 Benjamin Reilly, "The Return of Values in Australian Foreign Policy," *Australian Journal of International Affairs* 74, no. 2 (2020): 116–23.
15 Carlos Ramirez, "Japan's Foreign and Security Policy under Abe: From Neoconservatism and Neoautonomy to Pragmatic Realism," *The Pacific Review* 34, no. 1 (2021): 146.
16 Christopher W. Hughes, Alesso Patalano, and Robert Ward, "Japan's Grand Strategy: The Abe Era and Its Aftermath," *Survival Global Politics and Strategy* 63, no. 1 (2021): 125–60.
17 Hughes, Patalano, and Ward, "Japan's Grand Strategy," 132; Jin Canrong, "From 'China Threat' to 'China Responsibility': Changing Perceptions about China in the Western Media and China's Response," in *China's Rise – Threat or Opportunity?*, ed. Herbert S. Yee (New York: Routledge, 2011), 270–9.
18 Reilly, "The Return of Values in Australian Foreign Policy," 116–23.

19 Rory Medcalf, "Imagining an Indian National Security Strategy: The Sum of Its Parts," *Australian Journal of International* Affairs 71, no. 5 (2017): 518.

20 Harsh V. Pant and Premesha Saha, "India, China, and the Indo-Pacific: New Delhi's Recalibration Is Underway," *Washington Quarterly* 43, no. 4 (2020): 187–206; Saikat Datta, "Natural Alliance: Enhancing India – US Intelligence Cooperation," in *The Future of US–India Security Cooperation*, ed. Sumit Ganguly and Chris Mason (Manchester: Manchester University Press, 2021), 242–60; Sufian Ullah, "Realignments and Evolving Nuclear Capabilities in the Indian Ocean: Effects on Security Environment," *Australian Journal of Maritime and Ocean Affairs* 13, no. 4 (2021): 1–12.

21 Hughes, Patalano and Ward, "Japan's Grand Strategy: The Abe Era and Its Aftermath," 139–140; Rushali Saha, "Positioning the Indo-Pacific in India's Evolving Maritime Outlook," *Indian Foreign Affairs Journal* 15, no. 2 (2020): 125–38.

22 Ullah, "Realignments and Evolving Nuclear Capabilities," 9.

23 Patrick F. Walsh and Jerry Ratcliffe, "Strategic Criminal Intelligence Education: A Collaborative Approach," *IALEIA Journal* 16, no. 2 (2005): 152–66, https://www .ojp.gov/ncjrs/virtual-library/abstracts/strategic-criminal-intelligence-education -collaborative-approach; Patrick F. Walsh, "Teaching Intelligence in the Twenty- First Century: Towards an Evidence-Based Approach for Curriculum Design," *Intelligence and National Security* 32, no. 7 (2017): 1005–21; Walsh and Harrison MBE, "Strategic Intelligence Practice in the Australian Intelligence Community," 1–16.

24 Carol V. Evans, "A Vision for Future US–India Intelligence Cooperation," in *The Future of US–India Security Cooperation*, ed. Sumit Ganguly and Chris Mason (Manchester: Manchester University Press, 2021), 219–41; Amitabh Mattoo and Rory Medcalf, "Thinktanks and Universities," in *The Oxford Handbook of Indian Foreign Policy*, ed. David M. Malone, C. Raja Mohan, and Srinath Raghavan (Oxford: Oxford University Press, 2015), 275–6; Rory Medcalf, "Imagining an Indian National Security Strategy," 518; Vikram Sood, "The Indian Intelligence System: Meeting the Challenges of a New World," in *Handbook of Indian Defence Policy: Themes, Structures, and Doctrines*, ed. Harsh V. Pant (New Delhi: Routledge, 2015), 341–2.

25 Medcalf, "Imagining an Indian National Security Strategy," 524.

26 Medcalf, "Imagining an Indian National Security Strategy."

27 Gurmeet Kanwal, ed, *The New Arthashastra: A Security Strategy for India* (Noida: HarperCollins, 2016), 18.

28 Yoshiki Kobayashi, "Assessing Reform of the Japanese Intelligence Community," *International Journal of Intelligence and CounterIntelligence* 28, no. 4 (2015): 717–33.

29 Kobayashi, "Assessing Reform of the Japanese Intelligence Community," 721.

30 Kobayashi, "Assessing Reform of the Japanese Intelligence Community," 722.

136 Patrick F. Walsh

31 Kobayashi, "Assessing Reform of the Japanese Intelligence Community."
32 Carlos Ramirez, "Japan's Foreign and Security Policy under Abe," 159–60.
33 Craig Mark, "From Five Eyes to Six? Japan's Push to Join the West's Intelligence Alliance," *The Conversation*, 22 April 2021, https://theconversation.com/from-five-eyes-to-six-japans-push-to-join-the-wests-intelligence-alliance-159429.
34 Patrick F. Walsh, "Improving 'Five Eyes' Health Security Intelligence Capabilities: Leadership and Governance Challenges," *Intelligence and National Security* 35, no. 4 (2020): 586–602.
35 Misbah Mukhtar, "India–US Military Agreement: BECA and Its Implications for Region," Institute of Strategic Studies Islamabad, 17 November 2020, http://issi.org.pk/wp-content/uploads/2020/11/IB_Misbah_Nov_17_2020.pdf. 1–2.
36 Hughes, Patalano and Ward, "Japan's Grand Strategy," 144.
37 Hughes, Patalano and Ward, "Japan's Grand Strategy," 146–7.
38 Hughes, Patalano and Ward, "Japan's Grand Strategy," 147.
39 Craig, "From Five Eyes to Six?"
40 Patricia Kim, "Does the China-Solomon Islands Security Pact Portend a More Interventionist Beijing?," Brookings Institution, 6 May 2022, https://www.brookings.edu/blog/order-from-chaos/2022/05/06/does-the-china-solomon-islands-security-pact-portend-a-more-interventionist-beijing.
41 Patrick Wintour, "New Zealand's stance on China has deep implications for the Five Eyes alliance," *The Guardian*, 23 April 2021, https://www.theguardian.com/world/2021/apr/23/new-zealands-stance-on-china-has-deep-implications-for-the-five-eyes-alliance.
42 Andrew Tillet, "China overreach in pushing for Pacific Pact," *Australian Financial Review*, 2 June 2022, https://www.afr.com/politics/federal/china-overreached-in-pushing-for-pacific-pact-20220602-p5aqiq.

7 Enhanced ISR: The Paradox of Pursuing Strategic Advantage and Strategic Stability

NANCY TEEPLE

The two champions went one towards the other slowly, and keeping a good watch on one another, and wondering at one another's arms ... They thought it likely there would soon be battle.[1]

The competition for dominance within the emerging multipolar international system emphasizes peer adversaries seeking advantage over one another in the information domain. This is characterized by faster intelligence collection, fusion, and assessment, as well as sharing with key stakeholders to reduce vulnerabilities, avoid strategic surprise, and achieve near-perfect knowledge of rival states' intentions and capabilities. Within great power competition, the development of offensive weapons systems, especially advanced missiles, underscores the important role of intelligence and information sharing, both of which impact overall strategic stability by producing advantages for one state while creating vulnerabilities for its adversaries. Technological methods of intelligence for counterforce[2] have evolved alongside innovations in advanced missile targeting capabilities employing stealth, speed, precision, accuracy, and conventional as well as low-yield nuclear warheads.

From the Cold War to the present, the United States pursued counterforce dominance through superiority in weapons technology and intelligence. Critics of US counterforce doctrine argue that threatening an adversary's strategic deterrence assets is provocative and risks generating pre-emptive action or

---

This chapter was prepared in its original form for presentation at the 2019 ISA Convention Intelligence Studies section panel on "The Evolution of TECHINT," 28 March 2019, Sheraton Centre, Toronto. A revised version of this work was presented at the RAS-NSA virtual conference on Intelligence Cooperation in a Multipolar World on 6 May 2021. The author would like to acknowledge the valuable feedback and insights provided by Peter Gizewski, Strategic Analyst at DRDC-CORA, CALWC, Kingston, ON. This chapter comprises research conducted prior to my position at DRDC and does not represent the position of DRDC-CORA or the Canadian government.

138   Nancy Teeple

other asymmetric responses. In the current era, this issue concerns the increasing entanglement of nuclear and non-nuclear technologies, including adversaries' developments in dual nuclear and conventional delivery systems and advances in remote sensing to locate and target an adversary's nuclear forces as well as its command, control, communications, and intelligence (C3I). Such advances concern sea, air, and land strike platforms and, increasingly, the space and cyber domains.

Under great power competition, nuclear weapons and destabilization are at the forefront of the strategic stability discussion, as evidenced by Russia's resort to nuclear threats and targeting of nuclear facilities in its war against Ukraine,[3] both of which carry the risk of escalation. Recent Chinese military exercises around Taiwan, including live ballistic missile drills over the island into the waters of the northeast and northwest coasts,[4] also pose a potential escalation risk. This chapter explores the intelligence, surveillance, and reconnaissance (ISR) dimension of counterforce and deterrence by denial within the entanglement paradigm. As conventional and nuclear forces become intertwined, and the space and cyber domains become more salient, strategic competition becomes more complex and destabilizing. The quest for counterforce dominance through information superiority creates asymmetries that generate responses through countermeasures to exploit vulnerabilities by kinetic and non-kinetic means.

This chapter evaluates the extent to which enhanced ISR contributes to strategic instability, leading strategic peer competitors to rely on hybrid methods for denial of access and target the informational and cyber capabilities of the United States and its allies. These challenges create an opportunity for deeper cooperation in multilateral intelligence sharing to address Western vulnerabilities in these domains. Indeed, the war in Ukraine demonstrates the value of Western intelligence cooperation, which entails leveraging the resources of allied nations in conjunction with the dominance of US ISR capabilities. There are both positive and negative strategic outcomes of ISR superiority, but the advantages outweigh the disadvantages in terms of reinforcing transparency, reducing the margin of error and miscalculation, and enhancing deterrence by detection.

This discussion begins by addressing today's strategic stability debate, particularly the challenge of counterforce to traditional deterrence and the complexities introduced by entanglement. This discussion is followed by a look at new developments in ISR, cataloguing the evolution of capabilities since the Cold War. Following this is an assessment of the advantages and disadvantages of ISR superiority, using examples of key strategic issues of concern to Western powers, and in particular highlighting the challenges posed by countermeasures undertaken by strategic competitors. Paradoxically, the integration of domains aimed at providing greater interoperability and networked systems to enhance situational awareness and information sharing creates new vulnerabilities.

The Paradox of Pursuing Strategic Advantage and Stability   139

Gaps remain in near-perfect intelligence, particularly in terms of the human element, and vulnerabilities can be exploited, such as back door cyber channels, or kinetic anti-space capabilities, which are designed to destroy assets and disrupt the collection and transmission of strategic and tactical information. The findings of this research suggest that although superiority in ISR is provocative to strategic competitors, particularly in its role in US counterforce doctrine, it also provides advantages that can significantly increase strategic stability.[5]

This chapter is an extension of previous research exploring the nuclear postures of the United States and the Russian Federation oriented for deterrence by punishment (traditional deterrence) and deterrence by denial (counterforce and other disruptive approaches). It evaluates the intensity of the nuclear security dilemma based on the extent to which these two countries' nuclear strategies and capabilities are offence- versus defence-dominant.[6] In the current strategic context defined by great power competition, new developments in nuclear delivery systems are contributing to increasing destabilization of relations between the United States and its allies, and their competitors Russia and China, with an intensity not seen since the Cold War. Capabilities developed for strategic advantage are being supplemented by intelligence technologies intended to seek out and potentially target other countries' nuclear assets. The United States clearly enjoys superiority in both delivery technologies and ISR, although Russia and China are rapidly catching up. The asymmetry the United States has created through its advantage inspires insecurities in its nuclear competitors, generating responses to fill the vulnerability gap by asymmetric means.

This chapter explores the impact of new developments in ISR on strategic stability as a result of the asymmetries thereby created. It focuses primarily on ISR relating to US strategic advantages, including advantages in intelligence cooperation with allies, relative to its peer competitors. It addresses works that discuss ISR for battlefield awareness to the extent that such capabilities apply to the strategic level of competition. Complete information about ISR capabilities and sharing among allies and partners, as well as certain details about weapons systems, are not publicly available; therefore, this research relies on data from open sources.

Strategic Stability and the Twenty-First Century Strategic Environment

Tensions between the West and its strategic competitors are intensifying as a result of the NATO–Russia standoff in Eastern Europe, particularly Russia's invasion of Ukraine, as well as the deterioration of Western–Chinese relations arising from China's manipulation of international maritime law to expand into the South and East China Seas and potentially move against Taiwan. Russia and China continue to modernize their nuclear arsenals in response to the US upgrades to its own nuclear triad, including missile defences.

In the early 2000s the US upgrades were stated to be in response to North Korea's nuclear program and the threat of a nuclear-armed Iran; nevertheless, they created tensions with Russia and China. Increased deterrence for allies in Europe and Asia complicates the picture with deployments of the Aegis sea- and land-based missile defence system. In addition, the evolution of North American defence includes new strategic concepts for deterrence by denial, with the potential expansion into offensive roles for traditionally defensive commands like NORAD. Today's strategic context is more complex than the bipolar US–Soviet stand-off, with threats posed by myriad states and non-state actors, new domains of warfare – particularly cyber – and enhanced capabilities in the material domains of sea (maritime surface and subsurface), air, land, and space.

Deterrence Stability

The issue of strategic stability has returned to the debate about nuclear competition in the twenty-first-century strategic environment. This debate focuses on the interplay of political/military relationships and competition in offensive weapons technology.[7] The strategic stability debate itself began during the Cold War with an emphasis on deterrence of nuclear weapon use: if one side used them, the other would use them back harder. Put another way, if states could threaten unacceptable damage in retaliation (i.e., damage against high-value targets such as economic, industrial, political, and population centres), then rational states (i.e., the US and USSR) would not strike first with nuclear weapons or even engage in conventional aggression, which could escalate to nuclear use. The stalemate created by traditional deterrence is stabilizing because the balance of threat (and terror) strongly discourages nuclear use.

From the 1960s onward, strategy relied on this concept of assured destruction – and mutually assured destruction (MAD) after the Soviets were able to threaten a second strike – in conjunction with strategies that attempted to target the other side's nuclear forces, leadership, and command and control (C2). These same counterforce strategies targeted secure second-strike forces to avoid punishing retaliation. Deterrence by denial deters states by demonstrating the capability to deny the adversary's ability to use its strike capabilities, mainly through the threat of destruction of its launch platforms or through hardening of intended targets.[8] Thus, states' fear of losing their nuclear assets – their bargaining capability – prevents aggressive action. Long and Green address US policy and strategy on the use of intelligence assets to find and target Soviet ballistic missile submarines (SSBNs) and road-mobile intercontinental ballistic missiles (ICBMs), which constituted Russia's "secure" retaliatory nuclear capabilities.[9] Through a detailed empirical analysis, they demonstrate that as a result of developments in US intelligence, adversaries' second-strike assets are not

The Paradox of Pursuing Strategic Advantage and Stability   141

as secure as previously believed, thus negating the logic of MAD in favour of counterforce advantages.

Counterforce targeting, as incorporated into nuclear warfighting strategies, includes flexible options involving nuclear exchanges, surviving, and prevailing in a limited nuclear war. The issue with counterforce, according to critics, is that it contributes to arms races as each state attempts to overcome its perceived vulnerability relative to its competitor. In addition, there are these concerns: (1) intelligence may not be able to find and target all of the other state's nuclear assets, with the result that some missiles may get through; and (2) incentives for pre-emption are created if there is a perception – real or miscalculated – that intelligence is capable of locating and targeting the other side's second-strike forces.

Deterrence is central to the strategic stability debate, and experts stress that the strategic deterrence of the twentieth century was not the same as that of the twenty-first century. This is particularly true in today's multipolar, multi-domain strategic environment in which the concept of integrated deterrence has emerged. Dale and Herbeck argue that "deterrence must leverage all six domains of warfare,"[10] namely sea, air, land, space, cyber, and, more recently, the human mind – the cognitive domain.[11] The cognitive dimension involves the influence of perceptions and misperceptions on strategic doctrine and policy.[12] Perceptions influence the strategic balance of nuclear and conventional weaponry in these circumstances: (1) The adversary's systems are perceived as posing a threat to a state's arsenal and C2, so it pursues some asymmetric offset to the superior state's advantage in order to close the vulnerability gap. (2) A state perceives its capabilities as providing it with a strategic advantage over its adversaries, so it pursues an offensive strategy to achieve its global ambitions, supported by a powerful military that would deter the resistance of other states. Both these perceptions influence doctrine that favours offensive strategies

Critics of the US drive for global primacy point to (a) developments in the new nuclear triad following the US withdrawal from the 1972 Anti-Ballistic Missile (ABM) Treaty in 2002 in response to the threat that rogue states might seek to acquire nuclear capability and ballistic missile technology, and (b) the rise in weapons-of-mass-destruction (WMD) terrorism.[13] Russia and China condemned the US withdrawal as provocative and as a mistake. The abandonment of a cornerstone of Cold War strategic stability saw the US move forward with modernizing its nuclear arsenal with upgrades to its sea, air, and land legs; it also added new conventional counterforce capabilities, pursued layered missile defences, including national missile defence,[14] and enhanced its ISR capabilities. These modernizations have allowed the US to pursue unprecedented counterforce advantages. Lieber and Press affirm that counterforce is the domain of the powerful[15] and that the advantage of a successful first strike against Russian and Chinese arsenals is held by the United States.[16] The US has

142   Nancy Teeple

attempted to make itself invulnerable to state and non-state threats through a diverse arsenal of capabilities and an ambiguous posture that keeps its adversaries uncertain of its intentions.

Integrated Deterrence: An Evolving Strategy for Denial

The increasing emphasis on deterrence by denial and the need for expanding information systems for situational awareness, information processing, and decision-making advantage led to the development of the new strategic concept of integrated deterrence,[17] introduced in July 2021. US Defence Secretary Lloyd Austin describes integrated deterrence as "using every military and non-military tool in our toolbox, in lock-step with our allies and partners. Integrated deterrence is about using existing capabilities, and building new ones, and deploying them all in new and networked ways ... all tailored to a region's security landscape, and in growing partnership with our friends."[18]

Integrated deterrence is slated to be featured in the new National Defence Strategy. According to an unclassified fact sheet released in March 2022, "integrated deterrence entails developing and combining our strengths to maximum effect, by working seamlessly across warfighting domains, theaters, the spectrum of conflict, other instruments of U.S. national power, and our unmatched network of Alliances and partnerships. Integrated deterrence is enabled by combat-credible forces, backstopped by a safe, secure, and effective nuclear deterrent."[19]

Undersecretary of Defence (Policy) Colin Kahl affirms that integrated deterrence will "inform everything we do," highlighting that integration across domains involves conventional, nuclear, cyber, space, and informational; across theatres of competition and potential conflict; and across the spectrum of conflict from "high intensity warfare to the grey zone." The concept also involves the integration of all instruments of national power and, especially, integration "across our allies and partners, which are the real asymmetric advantage that the United States has over any other competitor or potential adversary."[20] In emphasizing the need for integration across all domains of conflict, Secretary Austin insists on "knocking down barriers to organizational cooperation along the way"; this will require integrating networks with US allies and partner nations in Europe and the Asia-Pacific.[21]

Thus, a key feature of integrated deterrence involves enhancing networking with allies and partners; for this, intelligence cooperation is imperative in order to coordinate timely detection, deterrence, and responses to deny the adversary advantage across the spectrum, from below-the-threshold grey zone and hybrid activities to conventional and nuclear behaviour. Technological obstacles and formal agreements remain a challenge to integrating multiple processes of information collection, fusion, dissemination, and communication across

The Paradox of Pursuing Strategic Advantage and Stability   143

military branches, commands, agencies, and national boundaries. Integrated deterrence intends to reduce silos and mitigate systemic constraints on information sharing in real time. US dominance in ISR is expanding to encompass a global Western framework of intelligence cooperation that could significantly outpace and disadvantage adversaries.

Crisis Stability

Strategic competitors fear a surprise disarming attack. This fear, under the right conditions, creates an incentive to strike first – to seize the advantage and not be the one to go second.[22] This is the motivation for hardening stationary land-based missiles and relocatable mobile missiles. This is also the motivation for protecting national leaders and ensuring their ability to communicate with their counterparts in adversary states, in addition to pursuing arms control and transparency to limit arms races and contribute to strategic stability. The "Moscow–Washington hotline" provides US and Russian leaders with a direct line of communication during a crisis to reduce the risk of escalation.[23] The Biden administration is considering the establishment of an encrypted hotline to Chinese leaders to share information about sudden military activities as well as warnings about cyberattacks.[24]

With large and diverse arsenals, there is a risk of accidents, miscalculations, and inadvertent launches. During times of crisis these risks increase, for tensions are high and systems are on a hair trigger. Perceptions of vulnerability create incentives to launch when there is a warning that the adversary is getting ready to strike. A pre-emptive strike is more likely under ambiguity – for example, when launch-on-warning doctrine is disguised as launch-under-attack. This ambiguity in US nuclear doctrine is deliberate, for it creates uncertainty and second-guessing by the adversary, thus increasing instability, especially crisis instability, which risks pre-emption. Under these conditions, competitors enter a spiral of mutual fear that affects judgment, calculations, and concerns that backing down will embolden the other, which in turn requires states to demonstrate credibility in asserting nuclear threats.

Crisis instability generates risks of escalation, whether deliberate,[25] inadvertent,[26] or accidental. A conventional crisis, or nuclear stand-off, could escalate to nuclear use. In such cases, deterrence fails and competing states seek to gain advantage or risk losing everything. The US maintains a range of asymmetric strengths to ensure superiority and "manage risks of escalation through dominance" by exploiting the asymmetric vulnerability of its opponent and by imposing unacceptable costs for its actions. The 2018 Nuclear Posture Review provides a framework for escalation control, to deny the adversary the ability to win in a nuclear exchange.[27] Flexible warfighting options have provided the US with solutions for addressing a range of contingencies; however, these have

144   Nancy Teeple

never actually been tested. There remains the possibility that limited nuclear strikes intended to buy time for "cooler heads to prevail" may not in fact remain limited.

Entanglement

The issue of entanglement has been emphasized in recent debates about strategic stability,[28] which includes the enhancement of ISR for counterforce advantages. New, non-nuclear technologies are being developed and integrated into the nuclear architecture. James Acton states that "entanglement describes how military and non-nuclear capabilities are becoming dangerously intertwined."[29] This is particularly concerning with the development of conventional counterforce alternatives to nuclear weapons that can strike at an adversary's nuclear arsenal and C2 systems. As discussed, this threat could incentivize a country to use its nuclear weapons before it loses them. Developments in technological capabilities also increase the chances that a conventional conflict will escalate into a nuclear exchange.

Debate continues regarding the extent to which increasing entanglement risks escalation triggered by the vulnerability of nuclear forces to a strike; however, experts agree that escalation resulting from threats to nuclear C3I is the more serious concern.[30] The threat posed by entangled systems lies in the realm of perception of what might be possible and influences how actions are interpreted. Acton states that "technological developments are increasing the likelihood of a conventional conflict *inadvertently* escalating into a nuclear war."[31]

Acton identifies five types of rapidly evolving non-nuclear technologies that blur the line between nuclear and non-nuclear assets and threaten competitors' nuclear forces and C3I infrastructure. These technologies are the following:

- information-gathering technologies, including cyberespionage tools and remote-sensing technologies;
- information processing systems, including AI;
- non-nuclear offensive weapons, including high-precision conventional,[32] anti-satellite capabilities, and cyber weapons;
- non-nuclear air and missile defences; and
- dual-use delivery systems that could accommodate nuclear and conventional warheads, "nuclear delivery systems that are superficially similar to non-nuclear systems," and dual-use C3I capabilities.[33]

Notably, integrated information-gathering technologies "enhance a state's ability to track an opponents' mobile nuclear forces and the corresponding countermeasures being deployed."[34] Information gathering involves the use of multiple systems for both nuclear and non-nuclear operations, such as satellites

The Paradox of Pursuing Strategic Advantage and Stability   145

and radars that can provide early warning of a nuclear strike and trigger nuclear and conventional missile defence interception. Advanced information processing systems, including AI, could process "vast quantities of data collected by new information-gathering technologies."[35] Advanced ISR capabilities thus supplement developments of new technologies that threaten other states' nuclear arsenals and C3I infrastructure. An asymmetric ISR advantage oriented to find concealed mobile second-strike forces can thus contribute to increasing strategic instability.

Evolving Intelligence Cooperation through Adaptive Technical Means

Advances in technological ISR capabilities have accompanied the evolution of intelligence cooperation among Western nations, including their allies in other geopolitical regions (such as Asia and the Middle East). This in turn has led to the integration of networked systems and the development of means for increasing data fusion and sharing for the purpose of achieving information dominance over adversaries (commonly agreed to be Russia, China, North Korea, and Iran). The Anglosphere has maintained intelligence cooperation since the Second World War, during which the US, the UK, and Canada collaborated on high-level intelligence sharing, particularly signals intelligence. This arrangement evolved into today's Five Eyes, with the US as the leader among the other four partners: the United Kingdom, Canada, Australia, and New Zealand. Post-war and Cold War intelligence cooperation also led to "intelligence sharing frameworks" within NATO, NORAD, and the EU, in addition to other bi- and multi-lateral arrangements among US partners around the world.[36] As the international security environment changes, intelligence cooperation adapts. The most recent development in intelligence cooperation has been the AUKUS (Australia–UK–US) arrangement, which involves sharing nuclear submarine propulsion technology with the non-nuclear state Australia; it also includes enhancing intelligence sharing on security and defence developments in the Indo-Pacific region.[37]

These intelligence cooperation frameworks, enhanced through adaptive technical means, signals/communications, human intelligence (HUMINT), and advanced analytical methods, create advantages over adversaries, which often find themselves on their own or in partnerships of circumstance with states and other actors that also view the US and the West as rivals. It is unknown to what extent mutual trust and intelligence sharing among such actors compares to that of the West (at least not in open sources), but it can be assumed that the West's arrangements remain stronger, based on history and capabilities, although notwithstanding the challenges of vulnerabilities owing to reliance on networked systems and potential security breaches, leaks, or "unplanned disclosures."[38] Adversaries, whether alone or in cooperation with other state or

146 Nancy Teeple

non-state actors, are seeking to catch up through advances in their own technologies, especially in the cyber domain and through infiltration (and sometimes outright purchase) of Western industry, defence technology, and other research institutes, particularly universities. Recently, experts have reported on the increasing Sino-Russian cooperation on high-tech research, driven by mutual interest in undermining US hegemony, although scepticism remains about the "long-term trajectory of this evolving partnership."[39]

Nuclear/conventional entanglement involving enhanced ISR includes developing a joint all-domain command and control (JADC2) capability as part of an evolving North American defence concept to achieve information dominance and decision superiority. This NORAD and USNORTHCOM concept outlines a global network of integrated layered sensors and advanced data processing systems utilizing machine learning and AI.[40] The objective is to close the gaps and seams in North American defence created by advances in adversaries' conventional strike systems, such as hypersonic glide vehicles, next-generation cruise missiles, unmanned aerial systems, and unmanned undersea systems. Many of these systems are dual-capable – that is, they can carry either nuclear or conventional warheads, or both. The US response emphasizes deterrence by denial, exploring options for offensive operations that include potentially targeting adversaries' platforms (the archers) while missile defences target incoming missiles (the arrows).[41] The entanglement concerns the blurring of roles between the Shield (North American defence via NORAD and USNORTHCOM) and the Sword (Strategic Command – STRATCOM). STRATCOM performs counterforce and countervalue targeting, whereas the Shield undertakes the integrated air and missile defence role, which may include counterforce targeting under the new deterrence-by-denial function involving "left of launch."[42] These functions are to be enabled by enhanced domain awareness and JADC2 for information dominance.

JADC2 reflects the US objective to "achieve integration between all its services, from land to space ... to shorten its decision-making cycles and improve its target collection functions." However, Cranny-Evans notes that "the rest of NATO has only made limited approaches towards this goal," which could impact the West's ability to deter Russia. He notes the importance of NATO's shift from deterrence by punishment to denial in order to deny Russia's success in its unprovoked invasion of Ukraine. Integration efforts include enhanced situational awareness, rapid sharing of information among NATO ground forces, layered air defence to increase resilience, long-range strike systems, and coordinated electronic warfare and offensive cyber capabilities to degrade the adversary's air defence networks and CNI.[43]

The potential blurring of offensive and defensive missions, in addition to advances in ISR capabilities and information sharing with allies and partners – such as the Five Eyes, NATO, and NORAD – intended to close the vulnerability gap in North American defence, may be perceived as threatening by near-peer adversaries. A globally integrated network of advanced ISR systems could enable and incentivize offensive actions, in addition to drawing allies and partners into US-led offensive postures through participation in the intelligence-sharing arrangements that enable them. This could also create vulnerabilities through reliance on networked information-sharing systems. Adversaries' advances in offset technologies to target Western vulnerabilities provide them with bargaining power and influence. US efforts to close those gaps create conditions for further refinements in long- and intermediate-range strike platforms intended to threaten targets in North America, as well as allies in the European and Pacific theatres.

Space and Cyber

Nuclear deterrence remains the cornerstone of US deterrence strategy; however, the US National Security Strategy and the Nuclear Posture Review both affirm that it is not "a one-size-fits-all solution to today's challenges."[44] The new approach requires an expansion of deterrence into multi-domain operations, including the cyber and space domains. These provide non-nuclear options as part of deterrence in both the nuclear and non-nuclear dimensions.[45] New advances in the realm of computing relate to quantum computing, AI, and combat cloud services. The latter provide computer information sharing to increase decision-making efficiency without requiring human decision-makers. All have uncertain outcomes and come with potential risks.[46]

The US is not the only nuclear state to entangle its nuclear with non-nuclear assets. China's Integrated Strategic Concept focuses on the non-military aspects of national power, combining diplomatic, economic, scientific, and technological with strategic deterrence, which includes space and cyber.[47] Its grand strategy, which has been referred to as Unrestricted Warfare,[48] applies an indirect approach that encompasses the non-military dimensions of national power: political, economic, diplomatic, cultural, and psychological, in conjunction with the multiple branches of the military domain, so that war can be conducted in the non-war spheres.[49] Militarily, China is expanding its conventional and missile forces as well as its cyber and anti-satellite capabilities. It is advancing its nuclear arsenal, including missile defences and tactical missiles, in an attempt to promote its strategic interests in the South China Sea and to challenge US nuclear forces.[50]

Russia's employment of hybrid tactics in the grey zone below the threshold of conflict utilizes kinetic and non-kinetic means not only to influence military decisions but also to destabilize Western democracies. Through "cross-domain coercion," Russia can show Western states that they are not immune to cyberattacks and information warfare that weaponizes mis- and disinformation and

148   Nancy Teeple

manipulates narratives by exploiting both mass and social media. Cyberattacks can have material-level effects as they target government institutions, financial institutions, civil infrastructure, communications technologies, and other networked systems.[51] Used in conjunction with special operations forces and strategic strike systems, these capabilities could have devastating effects. Cyberattacks could be launched against nuclear weapons systems through malware or viruses, compromising systems and influencing decision-makers with false information. This increases the risk of escalation.[52] The advantage to actors operating in the cyber domain is that confirming attribution is difficult if not impossible. Also, effects may not be detected until the damage is done. In the cyber realm, it is easier to attack than to defend. Russia can thus go after soft targets while staving off conventional confrontation against a NATO country that would engage the nuclear alliance. Like China, Russia is modernizing its nuclear and conventional offset capabilities in response to the US strategic advantage. These dual-capable systems introduce ambiguity into the nuclear deterrence calculus.

Thus, strategic deterrence has expanded to include cyber capabilities, missile defence, space systems, and electronic warfare. As part of integrated deterrence, the adversary may be deterred not only by nuclear weapons but also by the threat that its economic stability will be degraded or destroyed through cyber operations and that its information operations will be destabilized.[53] The space and cyber domains pose new challenges to deterrence involving the threat not only of nuclear action but also of disruption, degradation, deception, and destruction through these new domains. Considering these emerging challenges, advances in integrated ISR systems could reduce uncertainty through near-perfect intelligence, providing opportunities for earlier detection and possibly attribution. At the same time, near-perfect intelligence, combined with superior strike capabilities, could paradoxically jeopardize strategic stability, as US-led intelligence cooperation ensures Western dominance despite a multipolar international system. However, as noted, a key challenge of achieving near-perfect intelligence and information dominance is identifying and filling exploitable gaps and vulnerabilities posed by the multi-domain character of modern warfare.

New Developments in ISR

The purpose of intelligence is to reduce the fog and friction of war and provide forewarning, to the advantage of the side employing it. Fog and friction introduce uncertainty and thus some degree of constraint on both sides. Improved ISR need not mean an increase in express nuclear threats, since the deterrent power of these forces cannot be underestimated.[54] But the need for knowledge about other states' abilities to achieve new technological advantages remains a preoccupation of strategic thinking among peer and near-peer competitors.

When the Bush administration pursued the modernization of the "new" nuclear triad, intelligence and planning were part of the architecture that blurred nuclear and non-nuclear missions.[55] Goure indicates that the revolution in ISR "platforms, sensors, analytic capabilities, organizations, emerged from the wars in Afghanistan and Iraq."[56] These systems, designed for counter-insurgency warfare and to counter the global terror threat, saw significant investment and evolution to confront the new challenge that rogue states were acquiring, or seeking to acquire, nuclear weapons and ballistic missile delivery platforms (namely North Korea and Iran). These systems also provide knowledge about the activities of strategic peer competitors such as China and Russia.

In the US, ISR has undergone rapid development in the past decade, resulting in an evolving paradigm called distributed ISR operations, which are integrated with unmanned aerial systems as well as air, space, and cyberspace infrastructure, linking platforms and sensors to enhance network-centric warfighting.[57] Lieber and Press describe rapidly advancing technological developments in remote sensing, data processing, and communication. Regarding what they refer to as an age of "unprecedented transparency," the authors list five trends in remote sensing capabilities for counterforce targeting:[58]

(1) more diverse sensor platforms;
(2) more techniques for collecting signals intelligence (SIGINT);
(3) remote sensing platforms that increasingly provide persistent observation;
(4) steady improvement in sensor resolution; and
(5) a significant increase in the speed of data transmission.

These advances are described as transformative, particularly as they are employed together, providing a degree of transparency not seen before. What is notable is that these capabilities are not "proliferating around the world evenly." The US "seems to have exploited new sensing technologies more intensively than other countries."[59] The three critical roles of strategic intelligence in sensing missions are described as:

(1) intelligence preparation of the battlefield;
(2) detection – sensing possible targets; and
(3) identification – after a possible target is detected, other platforms are cued to identify and precisely locate the target.[60]

Like Long and Green, Lieber and Press argue that the sensing revolution has implications for the survivability of the nuclear arsenals of all countries. Hersman and colleagues state that beyond detecting survivable systems, future "strategic SA [situational awareness] architectures have the potential to provide unprecedented insight into an adversary's capabilities, actions and intentions such that decisionmakers can not only react to crises but also anticipate them. Taken together, these capabilities offer a range of characteristics – namely vantage and range, speed, detectability, precision, persistence, and resiliency and reliability – that allow them to detail the strategic operating environment in new and transformative ways."[61]

These objectives are reflected in the planned SHIELD concept for North American defence, which would integrate all-domain awareness (sensors), JADC2, and defeat mechanisms.[62] The recently released NORAD and USNORTHCOM Strategy (Executive Summary) outlined requirements to "deter in competition, de-escalate in crisis, and deny and defeat in conflict," through global integration for domain awareness, information dominance, and decision superiority.[63] The planned globally networked system is intended to bring down silos between military branches and other government departments, in addition to enhancing information sharing among allies and partners. In North America, this involves Canadian partners, Mexico, and the Bahamas, with more global implications for NATO allies and Five Eyes partners through plans for a globally integrated network that could bring allies into the US-led strategic posture. The Pathfinder Initiative is a key component of information collection, processing, storage, and access. Canada, as a leader in quantum computing, data analytics, AI, and machine learning, as well as a provider of sensing capabilities via its North Warning System, space-based and air assets, and undersea detection capabilities,[64] invested $5 million (USD) in the initiative between October 2020 and September 2021.[65] Pathfinder is a data ecosystem built with accessible digital cloud storage that synthesizes various streams of information into one operating picture, providing faster processing than current C2 systems for air defence. The system applies machine learning "to classify objects and predict threats more quickly," and this allows operators to "shift focus to decision making rather than data and signal analysis." Pathfinder helps the Commands share information with the military for faster response. The sensors pick up data that used to be left "on the cutting room floor," making more use of it than previously, and can continue to use old sensors, thus saving costs for replacements.[66] The initiative includes plans to add data from land, space, and sea surveillance platforms. USNORTHCOM and NORAD are engaging in prototyping partnerships with firms in Silicon Valley (particularly Kinetica) and have tested the system with the US Air Force Advanced Battle Management Systems, with plans to hand Pathfinder over to the Air Force in the next few years.[67] JADC2 and Pathfinder are prime examples of technological innovation to improve intelligence cooperation and sharing with key allies, such as Canada.

The US drive for information dominance in partnership with its allies and partners may create incentives for adversaries to seek vulnerabilities to exploit

The Paradox of Pursuing Strategic Advantage and Stability   151

in systems as they come online, while at the same time reinforcing deterrence by detection as enabled by enhanced ISR capabilities. Indeed, Gizewski suggests that the enhancement of ISR may create "an action-reaction cycle that re-introduces a new version or dimension of 'fog,'" in which vulnerabilities in the systems and the ability of adversaries to exploit them reduce confidence in the certainties the systems are intended to provide.[68] Hersman and Younis warn that the integration of situational awareness, warning, and communications tasked with both conventional and nuclear missions creates an escalation risk, particularly if an adversary believes that persistent capabilities tasked with conventional missions place their strategic nuclear assets at risk.[69] Undoubtedly, plans for a globally integrated network linking sensors, rapid data processing, and cloud computing, involving the sharing of information with allies and partners, such as NATO and the Five Eyes, would be perceived as increasingly provocative by adversaries. This matter could erupt into a particularly contentious issue as a result of NATO activity near Russia's borders in Eastern Europe and expanded exercises with NATO and its partners in Northern Europe in and around the Barents Sea, close to Russia's Northern Fleet and second-strike assets on the Kola Peninsula. It could also contribute to escalating tensions with China in the South and East China Seas, and over the status of Taiwan.

Advantages and Disadvantages of Enhanced ISR

The US-led superiority in ISR – enhanced by cooperation with its Western allies – provides a number of advantages to promote its global power projection and the ability to identify challenges to these ambitions. Such challenges include threats posed by adversaries' deployment of new unconventional methods of warfare, including asymmetric offsets to American strategic advantages.

The integration of nuclear and non-nuclear technologies allows for a level of networking never seen before, providing advantages in real-time imagery, communications, and other sensor data. However, this integration also reveals unanticipated vulnerabilities. For instance, the US reliance on space-based systems to enable terrestrial forces comprises a largely undefended infrastructure to be exploited by adversaries. The cyber domain, being networked into multiple land, sea, air, and space-based systems, also creates vulnerabilities, as activities in the cyber domain are difficult to detect and attribute and can cause devastating effects in the political, military, economic, and social realms, including civil infrastructure.

Disadvantages arise from American ISR enhancements because of the vulnerabilities they create in their adversaries. These vulnerabilities encourage deception and misinformation by the inferior competitor at one end of the spectrum, with aggressive, potential pre-emptive action at the other. Morgan and colleagues suggest that because they lack comparable capabilities, adversaries

152 Nancy Teeple

may be prompted to escalate in ways below the threshold of conflict, to which the US cannot respond proportionately.[70]

Disadvantages

(1) Countermeasures: In seeking to close the vulnerability gap created by US superiority in counterforce capabilities and ISR, strategic competitors like Russia and China have started exploiting US vulnerabilities asymmetrically through space, cyber, and other methods. This poses a challenge to intelligence cooperation, as allied nations are increasingly reliant on networked systems to collect and share intelligence. For such a network to be reliable, each participating nation must be trusted to prevent exploitable gaps from emerging. For instance, government collaboration with private industry on networked systems with defence partners must include decisions that consider the security needs of *all* participating states, such as decisions on 5G network providers.[71]

Space-based sensors and long-range radars provide early warning against nuclear attack. US missile defence relies on these systems, which may tempt adversaries to use counterspace weapons. Attacks on these systems, multi-purpose C2, and dual-use missile systems can be interpreted as a prelude to a nuclear first strike,[72] creating incentives for US pre-emptive action. According to the 2018 Nuclear Posture Review (NPR), the US will respond to attacks on its early warning system with nuclear weapons. Acton writes that early warning systems are increasingly vulnerable to non-nuclear threats, such as anti-satellite weapons (ASATs), conventional missiles, and cyber weapons (e.g., viruses and malware).[73] Communications systems and radars are also vulnerable to electromagnetic attacks, which can disrupt or disable the transfer of early warning information. Efforts to blind the US involve developing "countermeasures to thwart advanced sensor and strike systems,"[74] which include countering the threat posed by the offensive systems themselves. Such countermeasures include deploying radar jammers, anti-satellite capabilities, and decoys, as well as timing movements to elude satellites and minimizing communications to thwart SIGINT efforts.[75]

ASAT weapons may threaten satellites in all orbits, including geostationary and highly elliptical, both of which are critical to nuclear operations. High-precision conventional weapons can target ground-based systems such as radars and communication transmitters. According to Acton, dual-use C3I systems employed for nuclear and non-nuclear operations could be targeted in order to suppress conventional operations, thus degrading the nuclear C3I system as well. This kind of "incidental attack" could be misinterpreted as preparations for nuclear war, creating an escalation risk.[76]

Margolis notes that in contrast to geospatial intelligence (GEOINT), imagery produced by satellites is communicated as SIGINT, which makes it vulnerable since the feeds can be hacked by cyber actors.[77] Such interception provides adversaries with information that could reveal a state's interests and intentions; it also allows adversaries to respond with counter-methods without being detected. Indeed, an adversary can surreptitiously supplement the intelligence collected about it with falsified and misleading information, all the while seeking to conceal further images/information and identifying where US/Western intelligence is directing its efforts. In this way, adversaries can infer what concerns Western powers about them, providing ideas on where the US/West might seek to close its own vulnerabilities vis-à-vis the targets of its SIGINT efforts.

Additional countermeasures include deploying capabilities to deny access to strategic regions. Exclusion zones have been implemented by Russia around the Kaliningrad and Baltic areas and to defend strategic assets in and around the Kola Peninsula. By deploying S-400 surface-to-air systems, K-300 Bastion anti-ship missiles, and nuclear-capable SS-26 Iskander systems, Russia hopes to deny or at least limit NATO activities close to Russia.[78] China has deployed "counter-intervention" anti-access area-denial assets in the Western Pacific aimed at countering American air-, land-, and sea-based power – especially aircraft carriers, cruise missiles, and long-range bombers – and threatening kinetic and cyberattacks against satellites passing overhead.[79] As a result of these new anti-access/denial developments, ISR assets are required to operate in "an increasingly hostile air and electronic environment."[80] Besides presenting these kinetic challenges to military forces, China has placed ISR systems at risk. Non-kinetic risks remain a challenge. Increasing reliance on unmanned aerial vehicles (UAVs) creates new vulnerabilities – drone guidance systems can be jammed, and networks compromised.[81]

(2) Concealment: The US's ISR advantages over peer competitors and other hostile actors may spur the latter to seek new, innovative ways to conceal their strategic-military activities. The point of improving ISR to the level of near-perfect intelligence is to identify covert activities; however, adaptation by adversaries is to be expected. The concealment of mobile ICBMs and SSBNs was intended to prevent the US from detecting them so as to be able to target them. In 2015, Russia "leaked" information about its Poseidon submarine-launched torpedo drone, which had the ability to covertly bypass North American defences and detonate near a port city.[82] This innovation demonstrates an adaptation to offset American superiority in strategic defences and offensive capabilities.

(3) Human element: ISR presents other challenges beyond technological ones, such as the vagaries of the human element, which include the enduring problem of cognitive bias and decision-making pathologies. Intelligence that has been collected is subject to the potential biases of the analysts, commanders, and policy-makers when being interpreted, including as it relates to the purposes for which the intelligence is being used. JADC2, which enables most processes to be carried out by machines, and creates space for humans in

154   Nancy Teeple

the loop to better understand the battlespace, thus facilitating more informed decisions, may reduce the risks associated with bias, political manipulation, and disregard of contradictory information. However, questions about human oversight of machine-enabled processes should remain a concern, for AI and machine-learning systems themselves may develop their own biases or impose values distinct from those of commanders using the processed information to respond to various scenarios.

(4) Exploiting HUMINT: As the US increasingly relies on the technical aspects of intelligence, surveillance, and reconnaissance, its adversaries will deploy capabilities asymmetrically where they have experience. Over the past twenty years, Russian intelligence officers have sometimes been arrested in the US and repatriated to Russia in exchange for their Western counterparts. There has been a surge in Chinese espionage in North America, especially on the West Coast. These human intelligence assets are directed to seek out information that might benefit the People's Republic of China (PRC) – for example, about Western economic competitors and political-strategic developments. China has a strong interest in industrial technology, a great deal of which has military applications (e.g., jet engine technology).[83] Much of China's espionage is conducted in the cyber realm – by hacking into networks – but human actors may also be able to gain access to industry, including military and military-adjacent technologies, thus compromising key weapons systems.

Advantages

Advances in ISR toward near-perfect intelligence reduce uncertainty and errors related to unreliable and unverifiable information on an adversary's behaviour, capabilities, and locations of activity. This knowledge may strengthen strategic stability by ensuring compliance with arms control agreements, reducing arms race incentives, preventing nuclear launches due to accidents and false warnings, and deterring hostile actions.

(1) (i) Advances in ISR facilitate arms control verification[84] and transparency: Strategic stability is associated with mechanisms to constrain arms racing and proliferation through bi- and multi-lateral arms control agreements such as the Non-Proliferation Treaty (NPT) (1968), the Intermediate Nuclear Forces (INF) Treaty (1987), and the New Strategic Arms Reduction Treaty (New START) (2010). Ensuring that signatories comply with treaty provisions involves verification and transparency measures, including systems for reporting and inspections. These processes are intended to reduce uncertainty and build trust, confidence, and security among state actors, as well as to reduce the risks of misunderstanding and

miscalculation. Articles I and II of the NPT concern the sharing of classified nuclear weapon information. The concern, however, is whether states
can be trusted when they report their own compliance.

(ii) Monitoring for treaty violations and deployment of offensive systems:
There have been cases of states violating bi- and multi-lateral arms control
regimes. Concealment of prohibited nuclear programs and deployment
of treaty-violating capabilities have occurred in recent times, calling into
question the extent to which international regimes can constrain a state
bent on achieving its nuclear ambitions.

Advantages in imagery and communications technologies make it possible
to discover that a state is violating arms control agreements. The US initiated
withdrawal from the INF Treaty after reciprocal accusations by the US and Russia that each was violating the treaty by deploying prohibited systems.[85] Under
current conditions of deteriorating relations between the US and Russia, the US
may be unable to rely on Russian statements that it is not deploying forbidden
systems. Unverified accusations of violation can significantly affect strategic
stability through the breakdown of arms control – not only the INF but also
New START – so as to remove constraints on the arms race and perpetuate the
spiral of vulnerability, fear, and uncertainty.

Intelligence cooperation among international stakeholders – that is, states,
international organizations, and signatories to bi- and multi-lateral arms control agreements – interested in maintaining strategic stability and arms control
involves technical and procedural methods for verification and transparency,
including the following:

- routine monitoring and on-site inspection of nuclear material activities
  at facilities (International Atomic Energy Agency [IAEA], NPT, INF, New
  START);
- establishment of monitoring systems, including to detect unauthorized
  actions at nuclear facilities, such as the movement of objects, material, and
  personnel, as well as the destruction of material. For instance, the International Monitoring System within the Comprehensive Test-Ban Treaty
  (CTBT)[86] monitors for acoustic signatures on earth, in the oceans, and
  in the air, and also detects airborne radioactive particles and noble gases.
  Monitoring tools include capabilities to measure radionuclides, seismologi-
  cal data, and geophysical parameters associated with nuclear explosions
  (NPT, CTBT);[87] and
- national and multinational aerial and satellite reconnaissance of declared
  sites, in addition to on-site inspections, data exchanges,[88] telemetry
  exchanges, and detection of concealed objects or facilities. Aerial wide area/
  persistent surveillance involves aircraft, balloons, airships, and satellites.[89]

156   Nancy Teeple

Satellite-based observation systems provide overhead monitoring using optical or radar sensors and include sensors to detect atmospheric nuclear explosions.

(2) Prevention of nuclear launches based on false warning or accidents: The risk of nuclear escalation due to an accident, inadvertent launch, or false warning resulting from human or technical error can be mitigated through enhanced intelligence. Verification by triangulating information from imagery, signals, and communication with the state in which the error occurred can prevent wrong targeting, the unintended crossing of boundaries, and the sending of false signals. The challenge is how to verify for leadership, within the short time period available, the information needed to make the correct decision about whether to respond with a nuclear launch.

(3) ISR as deterrent (deterrence by detection): Enhanced ISR may serve to deter aggression by peer competitors, rogue states, and non-state actors. This involves triangulating knowledge about when, where, and how a state plans to move forward with annexing territory, deploying offensive systems that signal hostile intentions, or engaging in violence against its citizens (e.g., suppression of political unrest, genocide). The deterrent effect of enhanced ISR relies on communication between the defending state and the aggressor state – communicating that one has knowledge of its activities and will take action in response to the aggression (i.e., communicating red lines).

In summary, the advantages to enhancing ISR capabilities outweigh the disadvantages by way of reducing variables that contribute to uncertainty, miscalculation, and accidents, thus increasing stability via deterrence. Key advantages to enhancing intelligence cooperation within an integrated framework include that it closes gaps in the sources, methods, and scope of information collected, fused, analysed, and shared. Moreover, measures may be implemented to reduce the risks associated with shared intelligence, in ways that reflect the perspectives and priorities of the state providing the intelligence assessments. However, intelligence sharing could also be applied selectively so as to justify support for investments in costly global battlespace awareness networks and offensive weapons systems that contribute to provocation and instability among adversaries. A focus on shared values and interests, and objective assessment of perceptions versus actual threats communicated among intelligence partners, may help mitigate such challenges.

Conclusion

High-precision and stealth technologies supplemented by enhanced ISR to locate and target an adversary's conventional and nuclear assets creates asymmetries that impact strategic stability. Strategic advantage achieved through dominance in counterforce creates a security dilemma between the dominant state and its weaker peer competitors. It also creates dilemmas for allies and partners under the US-led nuclear umbrella, including their increasing alignment with US offensive postures through enhanced integration of systems for all-domain awareness and data-sharing networks as part of the evolution of intelligence cooperation. The role of ISR in the entanglement of nuclear and non-nuclear counterforce weapons creates instability that leads adversaries to deploy asymmetric countermeasures against Western vulnerabilities in multiple domains, including space and cyber. These actions increase the risk of pre-emption, especially when early warning systems are compromised. On the other hand, advantages arise from faster information processing and dissemination at the speed of relevance. As integrated systems enhance information dominance, moving decisions further left could prevent escalation by providing a range of options for engaging the adversary before the threat materializes. The advantages of ISR outweigh the disadvantages that encourage countermeasures and concealment, because they enhance knowledge and transparency to dissuade nuclear violations, prevent accidental or inadvertent launch, and deter aggressive regional behaviour. Intelligence cooperation, driven by partners' shared interests in strategic stability, strengthens the ability to deter adversaries' hybrid activities below the nuclear threshold – even below the threshold of armed conflict – that could escalate into a nuclear crisis. With advances in missile delivery technologies, in addition to hybrid methods in the grey zone of competition, traditional deterrence has shifted to an integrated full-spectrum deterrence concept as part of the evolution of strategy to counter or prevent aggressive adversary activity in multiple domains.

At this time, closing the gaps in situational awareness remains a challenge, particularly when it comes to integrating formerly siloed systems and addressing gaps in capabilities in geographical regions with uniquely challenging atmospheric conditions, such as the Arctic. As the US seeks to close the gaps in partnership with its Western allies, adversaries will continue to seek out vulnerabilities to exploit. Indeed, it is likely that superior ISR enhanced through intelligence cooperation will paradoxically generate instability as well as stability in the strategic competition in the years ahead.

NOTES

1 Lady Augusta Gregory, "The Coming of the Tuatha De Danaan," in *Irish Myths and Legends* (Philadelphia: Running Press), reprinted from *Gods and Fighting Men* (London: John Murray, 1910). Excerpts from pages 28 and 29.
2 Such as targeting the adversary's nuclear platforms and Command and Control (C2).

3 Schlosser's research reveals that "the risk of nuclear war is greater today than at any other time since the Cuban missile crisis." In addition to Hermann Kahn's escalation ladder, Schlosser describes the risk of nuclear use as a result of Christopher Yeaw's escalation vortex, which describes (in addition to Khan's vertical escalation) "a horizontal movement among various domains of modern warfare – space, cyber, conventional, nuclear," in which the vortex resembles a tornado where the worst outcome occurs at the widest part of the funnel. Eric Schlosser, "What if Russia Uses Nuclear Weapons in Ukraine?," *The Atlantic*, 20 June 2022, https://www.theatlantic.com/ideas/archive/2022/06/russia-ukraine -nuclear-weapon-us-response/661315. See also William Potter, "The Fallout from Russia's Attack on Ukrainian Nuclear Facilities," *War on the Rocks*, 10 March 2022, https://warontherocks.com/2022/03/fallout-from-russias-attack-on-ukrainian -nuclear-facilities-military-environmental-legal-and-normative; and Natalia Zinets and Max Hunder, "Ukraine, Russia trade blame for nuclear plant shelling amid global alarm," 8 August 2022, https://www.reuters.com/world/europe /un-chief-demands-international-access-ukraine-nuclear-plant-after-new -attack-2022-08-08.

4 Alys Davies and Yaroslav Lukov, "China fires missiles near Taiwan after Pelosi visit," BBC News, 4 August 2022, https://www.bbc.com/news/world-asia-62419858.

5 Rebecca Hersman, Bernadette Stadler, and Lizamaria Arias address the stabilizing effect of enhanced strategic situational awareness in the nuclear age in "When Is More Actually Less? Situational Awareness, Emerging Technology, and Strategic Stability," Center for Strategic and International Studies, 29 July 2019, https:// ontheradar.csis.org/analysis/overview.

6 Nancy Teeple, "Offensive Weapons and the Future of Arms Control," *Canadian Journal of European and Russian Studies* 14, no. 1 (2020): 79–102, https://doi .org/10.22215/cjers.v14i1.2695; Nancy Teeple, "Arms Control on the Eve of Destruction? The Prospects for an Arctic Nuclear Weapons-Free Zone in an Age of Counterforce Dominance," PhD diss., Simon Fraser University, 19 December 2017, http://summit.sfu.ca/item/17631.

7 See Teeple, "Offensive Weapons and the Future of Arms Control."

8 Deterrence by denial more broadly refers to the ability to deny the adversary the possibility of achieving their objectives through a range of capabilities – from counterforce targeting, to midcourse or terminal phase missile defences, to resilience and risk management and diplomatic tools – to dissuade adversary actions to the left or right of an attack (i.e., before or after the action is taken).

9 Austin Long and Brendan Rittenhouse Green, "Stalking the Secure Second Strike: Intelligence, Counterforce, and Nuclear Strategy," *Journal of Strategic Studies* 38, nos. 1–2 (2015).

10 Aryan Dale and Brendon Herbeck, "21st Century Strategic Deterrence: Beyond Nuclear," *Over the Horizon*, 26 March 2018, https://othjournal.com/2018/03/26/21st -century-strategic-deterrence-beyond-nuclear.

The Paradox of Pursuing Strategic Advantage and Stability   159

11 Although experts note that information operations have always been part of warfare – informing and shaping "perceptions, attitudes, behaviours, and understanding through the circulation of information" – today that circulation often utilizes the cyber platform. Chloe Diggins and Cline Arizmendi, "Hacking the Human Brain: The Next Domain of Warfare," *Wired*, 11 December 2012, https://www.wired.com/2012/12/the-next-warfare-domain-is-your-brain; Chloe Diggins and Clint Arizmendi, "Is war in the sixth domain the end of Clausewitz?," *Blogs of War*, December 13, 2012, https://blogsofwar.com/is-war-in-the-sixth-domain-the-end-of-clausewitz.

12 Robert Jervis, *Perception and Misperception in International Politics* (Princeton: Princeton University Press, 1976).

13 Recent developments include the US withdrawal from the 1987 INF Treaty, the JCPOA, and the Open Skies Treaty, and concerns remain regarding whether a new treaty will be negotiated to replace New START when it expires in 2026.

14 Ground-based midcourse defence (GMD).

15 Keir Lieber and Daryl Press, "The New Era of Counterforce: Technical Change and the Future of Nuclear Deterrence," *International Security* 41, no. 4 (2017): 46.

16 Lieber and Press, "The New Era of Counterforce," 7–44.

17 There remains debate over the scope of the concept of integrated deterrence: it seems to be defined broadly to include all military domains, in addition to multiple dimensions utilizing all instruments of foreign policy – political, diplomatic, informational, economic, legal (international law), and financial. See also Frank Hoffman, "Conceptualizing Integrated Deterrence," Lawfare – Duke University, 8 January 2022, https://sites.duke.edu/lawfire/2022/01/08/guest-post-dr-frank-hoffman-on-conceptualizing-integrated-deterrence.

18 Remarks by Secretary of Defense Lloyd Austin at the 40th International Institute for Strategic Studies Fullerton Lecture (As Prepared), 2 July 2021, Singapore. See also James A. Russell, "Flexible Response and Integrated Deterrence at Sea in the 21st Century: Implications for the US Navy," *Military Strategy Magazine* 8, no. 1 (Summer 2002), https://www.militarystrategymagazine.com/article/flexible-response-and-integrated-deterrence-at-sea-in-the-21st-century-implications-for-the-u-s-navy; and Maj Justin Magula, "The Theater Army's Central Role in Integrated Deterrence," *Military Review* (May–June 2022), 77–89. https://www.armyupress.army.mil/Portals/7/military-review/Archives/English/MJ-22/Magula/Magula.pdf.

19 The NDS classified version was transmitted to Congress on 28 March 2022. United States Department of Defense, National Defence Strategy 2022 Fact Sheet, 28 March 2022, 2, https://media.defense.gov/2022/Mar/28/2002964702/-1/-1/1/NDS-FACT-SHEET.PDF.

20 Jim Garamone, "Concept of Integrated Deterrence Will be Key to National Defense Strategy, DoD Official Says," US Department of Defense, 8 December 2021, https://www.defense.gov/News/News-Stories/Article/Article/2866963/concept-of-integrated-deterrence-will-be-key-to-national-defense-strategy-dod-o.

21 US Department of Defense, "Secretary of Defense Remarks for the INDOPACOM Change of Command," 30 April 2021, https://www.defense.gov/News/Speeches /Speech/Article/2592093/secretary-of-defense-remarks-for-the-us-indopacom -change-of-command.

22 Thomas C. Schelling, *The Strategy of Conflict* (Cambridge, MA: Harvard University Press, 1960); Thomas C. Schelling, "The Reciprocal Fear of Surprise Attack," RAND Corporation, 16 April 2007, 1, https://www.rand.org/content/dam/rand /pubs/papers/2007/P1342.pdf.

23 With the rise of ambiguity in grey zone activity, the utility of this hotline may require re-evaluation and revision to address the challenges posed by actions unattributable in the multidomain environment, particularly the cyber and information domains.

24 A military-only hotline to China is located at the Pentagon but is rarely used. Kylie Atwood, "Biden administration looks to set up 'Red Phone' to China for emergency communications," CNN Politics, 14 July 2021, https://www.cnn .com/2021/07/14/politics/biden-red-phone-china-xi/index.html.

25 A state increasing the intensity or scope of an operation to gain advantage or avoid defeat signals an intention to coerce or punish. Morgan E. Forrest, Karl P. Mueller, Evan S. Medeiros, Kevin L. Pollpeter, and Roger Cliff, "Dangerous Thresholds: Managing Escalation in the 21st Century," RAND Corporation, 2008, https://www .rand.org/content/dam/rand/pubs/monographs/2008/RAND_MG614.pdf.

26 Actions that the actor does not realize are escalatory but that are interpreted as such by the adversary. Forrest et al., "Dangerous Thresholds."

27 Forrest et al., "Dangerous Thresholds"; US Department of Defense, "Nuclear Posture Review," Office of the Secretary of Defense, February 2018, https://media .defense.gov/2018/Feb/02/2001872886/-1/-1/1/2018-NUCLEAR-POSTURE -REVIEW-FINAL-REPORT.PDF.

28 John Steinbruner first used the term "entanglement" in 2000 to describe the intersection of nuclear and conventional capabilities. James M. Acton, "Why Is Nuclear Entanglement So Dangerous?," Carnegie Endowment for International Peace, 23 January 2019, https://carnegieendowment.org/2019/01/23/why-is -nuclear-entanglement-so-dangerous-pub-78136.

29 Acton, "Why Is Nuclear Entanglement So Dangerous?"

30 Simons Foundation, "Repairing the U.S.-NATO-Russia Relationship and Reducing the Risks of the Use of Nuclear Weapons," Report of the Simons Forum, 27–28 September 2018, 31, https://www.thesimonsfoundation.ca/projects/repairing-us -nato-russia-relationship-and-reducing-risks-use-nuclear-weapons.

31 James Acton, "Issues Affecting Strategic Stability," prepared for the conference on Repairing the U.S.-NATO-Russia Relationship and Reducing the Risk of the Use of Nuclear Weapons, 26–28 September 2018.

32 This includes hypersonic weapons that can deliver multiple payloads globally and circumvent missile warning and missile defence. Dale and Herbeck, "21st Century Strategic Deterrence."

The Paradox of Pursuing Strategic Advantage and Stability   161

33 Acton, "Issues Affecting Strategic Stability."
34 Acton, "Issues Affecting Strategic Stability."
35 Simons Foundation, "Repairing the U.S.-NATO-Russia Relationship," 31.
36 Sylvain Rouleau, "The Value of Intelligence Sharing for Canada: The 'Five Eyes' Case," *Canadian Army Journal* 21, no. 1 (Winter 2020): 30–1.
37 AUKUS includes technology integration beyond submarines: "AUKUS seeks to win the technology competition with China by pooling resources and integrating supply chains for defense-related science, industry, and supply chains" as it seeks to "seize advantages in artificial intelligence, quantum computing and cyber technology." Arzan Tarapore, "AUKUS Is Deeper than Just Submarines," Stanford Freeman Spogli Institute for International Studies, 29 September 2021, https://fsi .stanford.edu/news/aukus-deeper-just-submarines.
38 Rouleau, "The Value of Intelligence Sharing for Canada," 32.
39 Such technological developments include the fields of information and communication technology, AI, and the "Internet of Things" – with an emphasis on "big data, AI, and cloud computing." Samuel Bendett and Elsa Kania, "The Resilience of Sino-Russian High Tech Cooperation," *War on the Rocks*, 12 August 2020, https://warontherocks.com/2020/08/the-resilience-of-sino-russian-high -tech-cooperation. See also Brad D. Williams, "STRATCOM Commander Warns of China–Russia Coordination; Report Details AI Collaboration," *Breaking Defense*, 3 September 2021, https://breakingdefense.com/2021/09/stratcom -commander-warns-china-russia-coordination-report-details-ai-collaboration.
40 Developing these capabilities includes binational Global Information Dominance Experiments (GIDE). See General Glen D. VanHerck, "New Tools to Create Time and Information: Building the Bike While We Ride It," *War on the Rocks*, 6 July 2021, https://warontherocks.com/2021/07/new-tools-to-create-time-and -information-building-the-bike-while-we-ride-it.
41 General Terrence J. O'Shaughnessy and Brigadier-General Peter M. Fesler, "Hardening the Shield: A Credible Deterrent and Capable Defense for North America," Wilson Center – Canada Institute, September 2020, 12–14, https://www .wilsoncenter.org/publication/hardening-shield-credible-deterrent-capable-defense -north-america; Andrea Charron and James Fergusson, "NORAD and the Evolution of North American Defence," Macdonald-Laurier Institute, 24 May 2017, https://www.macdonaldlaurier.ca/norad-and-the-evolution-of-north-american -defence-andrea-charron-and-james-fergusson-for-inside-policy; Nancy Teeple, "The Future of Canadian Participation in Missile Defence," in *The Sword and the Shield: Canada's Role in NORAD Modernization*, NAADSN Engage Series no. 4, ed. Nancy Teeple and Ryan Dean, (Peterborough: Trent University, 2021), 127–8.
42 "Left of launch" is generally understood as preventing an adversary from launching an offensive strike against the launch platform by kinetic means. Some debate considers whether the concept applies to both the pre-boost and post-boost phases of a missile launch. "Right of launch" otherwise refers to intercepting the missile

in its midcourse or terminal phase. Left-of-launch options, however, may be non-kinetic – including disabling a launch system by other means (cyber disruption, for example), or even engaging in diplomacy and dialogue to prevent a crisis from emerging. Teeple, "The Future of Canadian Participation in Missile Defence," 125–6.

43 Samuel Cranny-Evans, "Integrated Effects: Deterring Russia through Multi-Domain Operations," *Army Technology*, 25 July 2022, https://www.army-technology.com/analysis/integrated-effects-deterring-russia-through-multi-domain-operations.

44 US Department of Defense, "Nuclear Posture Review."

45 Dale and Herbeck, "21st Century Strategic Deterrence."

46 Dale and Herbeck, "21st Century Strategic Deterrence."

47 Dale and Herbeck, "21st Century Strategic Deterrence."

48 Produced in 1999 by Col. Qiao Liang and Col. Wang Xiangsui, translated into English under the title *Unrestricted Warfare* (*Chao Xian Zhan*, literally "War beyond Rules"). Tony Corn, "Peaceful Rise through Unrestricted Warfare: Grand Strategy and Chinese Characteristics," *Small Wars Journal* (2010): 2, https://smallwarsjournal.com/blog/journal/docs-temp/449-corn.pdf.

49 Corn, "Peaceful Rise through Unrestricted Warfare"; Qiao Liang and Wang Xiangsui, *Unrestricted Warfare* (Beijing: PLA Literature and Arts Publishing House, 1999), 141–2.

50 Anthony H. Cordsman, "China and the New Strategic Arms Race," Center for Strategic and International Studies, 14 November 2018, https://www.csis.org/analysis/china-and-new-strategic-nuclear-arms-race.

51 Dale and Herbeck, "21st Century Strategic Deterrence."

52 Beyza Unal and Patricia Lewis, "Cybersecurity of Nuclear Weapons Systems: Threats, Vulnerabilities, and Consequences," Chatham House: Royal Institute of International Affairs, January 2018, https://www.chathamhouse.org/sites/default/files/publications/research/2018-01-11-cybersecurity-nuclear-weapons-unal-lewis-final.pdf.

53 Unal and Lewis, "Cybersecurity of Nuclear Weapons Systems."

54 Peter Gizewski, Defence Scientist – Strategic Analyst, DRDC-CORA, Kingston, March 2019.

55 Hans M. Kristensen, Robert S. Norris, and Ivan Oelrich, "From Counterforce to Minimal Deterrence: A New Nuclear Policy on the Path toward Eliminating Nuclear Weapons," *Federation of American Scientists* 7 (April 2009): 17.

56 Dan Goure, "Evolving Threats and Strategies Will Require More and Better ISR," *National Interest*, 31 March 2017: https://nationalinterest.org/blog/the-buzz/evolving-threats-strategies-will-require-more-better-isr-19962.

57 David A. Deptula and James R. Marrs, "Global Distributed ISR Operations: The Changing Face of Warfare," *Joint Force Quarterly* 54, no. 3 (2009): 110–17.

58 Lieber and Press, "The New Era of Counterforce."

The Paradox of Pursuing Strategic Advantage and Stability   163

59 Lieber and Press, "The New Era of Counterforce."
60 Lieber and Press, "The New Era of Counterforce."
61 Hersman et al., "When Is More Actually Less?"
62 Strategic Homeland Integrated Ecosystem for Layered Defense – SHIELD. O'Shaughnessy and Fesler, "Hardening of the Shield"; Ryan Dean and Nancy Teeple, "NORAD Modernization Report Three: JADC2/JADO," CDA Institute, 28 October 2020, https://cdainstitute.ca/norad-modernization-report-three-jadc2-jado.
63 General (USAF) Glen D. VanHerck, "NORAD and USNORTHCOM Strategy," North American Aerospace Defense Command, 15 March 2021, 3, https://www.norad.mil/Francais/Article/2537173/commander-norad-and-usnorthcom-releases-strategic-vision.
64 Guillaume Cote, Kevin Budning, Hannah Diegel, and Sean Murphy, "The Making of Canadian Connected Battlespaces," NPSIA Report based on a virtual workshop in partnership with Collins Aerospace and MITACS Accelerate program, 2020, 12.
65 Pat Host, "US Air Force Contracts Kinetica for NORAD," Jane's, 23 April 2021, https://www.janes.com/defence-news/news-detail/update-us-air-force-contracts-kinetica-for-noradnorthcom-pathfinder-data-fusion-effort.
66 Comments by General Glen D. VanHerck at the House hearing "National Security Challenges and U.S. Military Activity in North and South America," Committee on Armed Services, House of Representatives, 117 Congress, 1st Session, 14 April 2021, US Government Publishing Office, https://www.congress.gov/event/117th-congress/house-event/LC67778/text?s=1&r=84.
67 Rachel S. Cohen, "Pentagon's Silicon Valley Hub Is Helping NORAD Monitor US Airspace," Air Force Magazine, 23 October 2020, https://www.airforcemag.com/pentagons-silicon-valley-hub-is-helping-norad-monitor-us-airspace; Theresa Hitchens, "NORTHCOM Developing, Testing AI Tools to Implement JADC2," Breaking Defense, 5 March 2021, https://breakingdefense.com/2021/03/exclusive-northcom-developing-testing-ai-tools-to-implement-jadc2.
68 Gizewski, Defence Scientist – Strategic Analyst, DRDC-CORA, Kingston, March 2019.
69 Rebecca K.C. Hersman and Reja Younis, "Surveillance, Situational Awareness, and Warning at the Conventional-Strategic Interface," Center for Strategic and International Studies, 15 January 2023, 2–3, http://defense360.csis.org/wp-content/uploads/2021/01/Hersman-and-Younis-ISR-Nuclear-Nexus.pdf.
70 Forrest et al., "Dangerous Thresholds."
71 Andy Blatchford, "Canada joins Five Eyes in ban on Huawei and ZTE," Politico, 19 May 2022, https://www.politico.com/news/2022/05/19/canada-five-eyes-ban-huawei-zte-00033920.
72 Jason H. Pollack, "Is Crisis Stability Still Achievable?," American Physics Society/James Martin Center for Nonproliferation Studies, 16 March 2017, https://www.aps.org/units/fps/newsletters/201707/crisis.cfm.

164   Nancy Teeple

73 Acton, "Why Is Nuclear Entanglement So Dangerous?"
74 Lieber and Press, "The New Era of Counterforce," 46.
75 Lieber and Press, "The New Era of Counterforce."
76 Acton, "Why Is Nuclear Entanglement So Dangerous?"
77 Gabriel Margolis, "The Lack of HUMINT: A Recurring Intelligence Problem,"
    Global Security Studies 4, no. 2 (Spring 2013): 48, https://www.iwp.edu/wp
    -content/uploads/2019/05/20170830_LackofHUMINTaRecurringProblem.pdf.
78 Leo-Paul Jacob, "Limiting Russia's Anti-Access/Area-Denial Strategy in the Baltic
    Sea," NATO Association, 22 February 2017, http://natoassociation.ca/limiting
    -russias-anti-accessarea-denial-strategy-in-the-baltic-sea; Herb Kemp, "Strategic
    Security in Northern Europe: The Implications of Russian Anti-Access/Area
    Denial Strategies in Developing Complex Environments," *Journal of Strategic
    Security* 14, no. 1 (2020): 78–91.
79 Dean Cheng, "Countering China's A2/AD Challenge," *National Interest*, 20
    September 2013, https://nationalinterest.org/commentary/countering-china's-a2
    -ad-challenge-9099.
80 Goure, "Evolving Threats and Strategies."
81 Goure, "Evolving Threats and Strategies."
82 Formerly STATUS-6. NATO reporting name: Kanyon. Michael Peck,
    "100-Megaton Nuclear Monster: How to Stop Russia's City-Killer Torpedo,"
    National Interest, 27 September 2018, https://nationalinterest.org/blog/buzz/100
    -megaton-nuclear-monster-how-stop-russias-city-killer-torpedo-32082.
83 James Andrew Lewis, "Responding to Chinese Espionage," Center for Strategic and
    International Studies, 2 November 2018, https://www.csis.org/analysis/responding
    -chinese-espionage.
84 UN Panel of Government Experts describes verification as "a tool to strengthen
    international security. It involves the collection, collation and analysis of
    information in order to make a judgement as to whether a party is complying with
    its obligations." UN, "Verification in all its aspects, including the role of the United
    Nations in the field of verification," Office for Disarmament Affairs, 2008, para. 9,
    https://www.sipri.org/sites/default/files/research/disarmament/dualuse/pdf-archive
    -att/pdfs/un-verification-in-all-its-aspects-including-the-role-of-the-united-
    nations-in-the-field-of-verification.pdf.
85 Russia was accused of violating the treaty by testing and later fielding a ground-
    launched cruise missile within intermediate ("prohibited") ranges (500–5500 km);
    this is the 9M729, a version of the Iskander-K cruise missile system. Russia in
    turn accused the United States of violating the treaty by testing missile defences
    in prohibited ranges, arming UAVs (which they categorize as prohibited ground-
    launched cruise missiles – GLCMs), and deploying the Mk-41 launcher on Aegis
    Ashore BMD systems. Russia argues that the latter could be outfitted with the
    Tomahawk cruise missile, which would also make the system a prohibited GLCM.
    The Special Verification Committee established by the treaty has been challenged

The Paradox of Pursuing Strategic Advantage and Stability   165

in its ability to verify these claims. Simons Foundation, "Repairing the US–NATO–Russia Relationship and Reducing the Risks of the Use of Nuclear Weapons," 41–2.

86 Not entered into force – the US has not ratified the treaty.

87 United Nations, "Disarmament Forum: Arms Control Verification," UN Institute for Disarmament Research, 2010, 3–6, https://www.unidir.org/files/publications /pdfs/arms-control-verification-en-320.pdf.

88 C.R. Wuest, "The Challenge for Arms Control Verification in the Post–New START World," Lawrence Livermore National Laboratory, 16 July 2012, https:// www.ipndv.org/wp-content/uploads/2012/07/Wuest_2012_The_Challenge_for _Arms_Control_Verification_in_the_Post_New_START_World.pdf.

89 "High altitude systems that can loiter over particular areas might provide added confidence through near-continuous monitoring of activities, possibly at a reduced cost when compared with satellite systems." Wuest, "The Challenge for Arms Control Verification," 15.

8 In Search of Trust: Challenges in UN Peacekeeping-Intelligence

SARAH-MYRIAM MARTIN-BRÛLÉ

The UN Peacekeeping-Intelligence Policy is a stepping stone to safer and more effective peacekeeping missions. It fulfils a dire and long overlooked need to link enhanced situational awareness to timely decisions and actions to ensure the safety and security of personnel and the protection of civilians. Developed in the wake of the Cruz Report (2017) and the Action for Peacekeeping initiative (2018), it represents a paradigm shift from intelligence conceived as an inherently sovereign matter toward a rigorous approach to gathering information and making forward-looking assessments in the UN context.

The challenge of developing Peacekeeping-Intelligence is how to do intelligence and how to get it "right" in a UN context. If each member-state has developed its own way to do intelligence with its own technology, what should intelligence look like for an international organization that promotes transparency, impartiality, and efficiency? How can the best practices be developed, and on which bases?

UN peace operations are home to an intense and multifaceted struggle for influence among member-states, and peacekeeping-intelligence is yet another site and channel for great power competition.[1] The policy on Peacekeeping-Intelligence confronted divisions among member-states. The divide mirrored – and exacerbated – both the competition and the "division of labour" in UN peacekeeping between funders and troop contributors. For many European states, the experience with NATO in Afghanistan had convinced them of the value of multidimensional intelligence units, leading them to push for the

---

This chapter is based on the arguments developed in Sarah-Myriam Martin-Brûlé, "Finding the Way on UN Peacekeeping-Intelligence," IPI, and in Sarah-Myriam Martin-Brûlé, "Competing for Trust: Challenges in United Nations Peacekeeping-Intelligence," *International Journal of Intelligence and CounterIntelligence*, https://10.1080/08850607.2020.1798153 with additional fieldwork material.

168   Sarah-Myriam Martin-Brûlé

intelligence policy. Conversely, many members of the Non-Aligned Movement, which provide most of the troops for peacekeeping missions, were suspicious that European states had ulterior motives and concerned about further European intervention in international peace and security and the "NATO-ization" of peacekeeping. Other troop contributors were reported to have remained largely silent on the policy, however, including several countries that had lost peacekeepers and had a longer-term interest in a strong intelligence capability in peacekeeping operations.[2]

This chapter examines the challenges in implementing the UN Peacekeeping-Intelligence Policy and creating trust among member-states, units, and personnel in a growing multipolar context. If intelligence is driven by a need to know, this chapter highlights an additional need: the need to trust. The main challenges stem from the lack of trust in the structures/mechanisms put in place to securely share intelligence within peacekeeping missions and at the headquarters, the lack of familiarity with the UN way of doing intelligence, the lack of expertise of the personnel hired to do peacekeeping intelligence, the political sensitivities linked to the postings, the hiring process in UN Peacekeeping-Intelligence units, linguistic barriers within the organization and with the locals, and, finally, the capacity of the UN to (re)act in a timely manner to the intelligence that is shared. To study peacekeeping-intelligence-sharing mechanisms at the UN, this chapter draws from official documents as well as from field research at the UN headquarters and in four peacekeeping missions: the UN Organization Stabilization Mission in the DR Congo (MONUSCO), the UN Multidimensional Integrated Stabilization Mission in the Central African Republic (MINUSCA), the UN Multidimensional Integrated Stabilization Mission in Mali (MINUSMA), and the UN Mission in South Sudan (UNMISS) over 2017–19.

UN Intelligence

The UN has always recognized that it needs intelligence. Its first two Secretaries-General, Dag Hammarskjöld and U Thant, decried the organization's lack of knowledge, understanding, and anticipation of the environment.[3] The term "intelligence" was first used in the context of the 1960 UN Operation in the Congo (ONUC), when a military information branch was created to collect information by intercepting messages, conducting aerial surveillance, and interrogating detainees. Yet intelligence remained in the military realm and was mostly the prerogative of specific national contingents; there was no integrated approach to intelligence gathering within missions.

In 1993, Secretary-General Boutros Boutros-Ghali established a Situation Centre within what was then the Department of Peacekeeping Operations (DPKO) to facilitate information flows among the civilian, police, and military

Challenges in UN Peacekeeping-Intelligence 169

components. In the 1990s, the UN created intelligence-oriented offices: the Office for Research and Collection of Information and the Information and Research Unit. Both were later dismantled due to member-states' suspicions that the information collected could be used outside of UN missions. Tragedies in Rwanda and Srebrenica then triggered new questions about the need for institutional mechanisms to enhance situational awareness and provide early warning both to missions and to UN headquarters.[4]

In 2000 the Information and Strategic Analysis Secretariat was put in place at the UN headquarters to combine existing entities and personnel working on situational awareness and policy planning related to peace and security. Its objective was to support the Secretary-General, UN officials, and troop- and police-contributing countries in assessing risks in areas where personnel and troops would be deployed.[5] In 2003, the bombing of the UN offices in Baghdad made it clear that missions needed the capacity, including both human and material resources, to conduct integrated analysis. The Department of Safety and Security (DSS) was created as "a dedicated risk and threat assessment unit at Headquarters with dedicated links at the field level [and] a 24-hour operations centre."[6]

As an *ad hoc* response to gaps in analytical capacities in the UN missions in Afghanistan, Darfur, the DRC, Haiti, and Liberia, the UN first put in place Joint Mission Analysis Centres (JMACs) in 2005. In 2006, the JMACs were officially incorporated into UN doctrine as a core unit in missions. JMACs were meant to provide mission-wide analysis to support strategic, operational, and tactical decision-making. Later that year, DPKO released the first official policy directives on JMACs, which also covered Joint Operations Centres (JOCs).

The following year, member-states launched an initiative to establish a central situational awareness unit that would combine existing entities at headquarters. This led to the creation of the UN Operations and Crisis Centre (UNOCC) in 2013, which brought together DPKO's Situation Centre, DSS's Communications Centre, and staff from the Department of Political Affairs (DPA), Department of Public Information (DPI), Office for the Coordination of Humanitarian Affairs (OCHA), Office of the High Commissioner for Human Rights (OHCHR), and UN Development Programme (UNDP). UNOCC became responsible for supporting and following up on implementation of JMAC policy. It was also meant to be a hub for innovation on new system-wide approaches to improve the situational awareness of peacekeeping operations, such as the UN Situational Awareness and Geospatial (SAGE) program.[7]

Despite the establishment of these units, the 2015 report of the High-Level Independent Panel on Peace Operations (HIPPO) found that "an effective system for the acquisition, analysis and operationalization of information for peace operations in complex environments is lacking."[8] In 2016 the UN General Assembly's Special Committee on Peacekeeping Operations (C34) confirmed

170   Sarah-Myriam Martin-Brûlé

the need for "a more cohesive and integrated United Nations system for situational awareness that stretches from the field to the Headquarters."[9]

Beginning in 2016, efforts to improve the flow of information became increasingly linked to the safety and security of UN personnel and the protection of civilians. A high-profile attack on a UN base in the DRC that killed several uniformed peacekeepers in 2017, together with the high casualty rate in MINUSMA, prompted the Secretary-General to commission a report on the safety and security of UN peacekeepers in 2017. Later that same year, the Cruz Report emphasized the need for intelligence "to prevent casualties" and decried that missions "lack the basics, especially human intelligence, networks of informants, situational awareness, and capacity to communicate with the population."[10]

The Secretary-General's Action for Peacekeeping initiative (A4P), launched in 2018, further stressed the link between improved analysis and the safety and security of peacekeepers and the protection of civilians. Referring to A4P, the Under-Secretary-General for Peace Operations, Jean-Pierre Lacroix, emphasized the need for peacekeeping intelligence, along with specialized equipment like helicopters, to achieve the overall goal of "reconfiguring Missions to be more mobile and more proactive."[11] The UN General Assembly's Special Committee on Peacekeeping Operations (C34) confirmed the need for "a more cohesive and integrated United Nations system for situational awareness that stretches from the field to the Headquarters."[12] In 2017 the first UN Peacekeeping Intelligence Policy was approved, but it was not implemented. Member-states, mainly members of the Permanent Five (P5), continued to disagree over the extent of intelligence and the purpose for which it should be implemented. Peacekeeping-Intelligence was meant to be developed exclusively in the context of multidimensional integrated stabilization missions and initially to support the mission's mandate. Yet member-states feared that the comprehensiveness of missions' mandates could be used as an excuse to extend peacekeeping-intelligence-related activities to tasks that were too specific to each member-state's own national benefit. This fear of instrumentalization of peacekeeping operations fuelled the competition for information between the great powers involved in the missions. The debates over Peacekeeping-Intelligence hence became less focused on the development of the policy *per se* than on its scope, that is, whether it should cover all activities related to the mandate or be narrowed to focus on the security and safety of UN personnel along with the protection of civilians.

Defining Peacekeeping Intelligence

In 2017, Peacekeeping Intelligence was defined as "the non-clandestine acquisition and processing of information by a Mission within a directed Mission intelligence cycle to meet requirements for decision-making and to inform operations related to the safe and effective implementation of the Security

Council mandate."[13] Through a consultative process, the then UN Department of Peacekeeping Operations – now called the Department of Peace Operations (DPO) – thus accomplished a tour de force in forging agreement among member-states on the urgent need to institutionalize methods for intelligence gathering while adhering to the UN principles of impartiality, transparency, and efficiency.

In 2019, the policy was revised, rebranded as UN Peacekeeping-Intelligence Policy, with the hyphen to emphasize the distinction between national intelligence and the UN specificity of such policy.[14] Member-states remained hesitant to endorse the definition and wondered how the scope of intelligence could be limited so as to solely "inform operations related to ... effective implementation of the Security Council mandate."[15] Peacekeeping operations' mandates are characterized by their comprehensiveness and refer to a wide spectrum of activities and tasks (from "stabilization" to security sector reform and protection). For some member-states, letting Peacekeeping-Intelligence cover all aspects of the mandates[16] would be too broad and could lead to intelligence activities detrimental to their own interests. Making a point that the term "peacekeeping" itself had never been officially defined by the UN, the member-states agreed to remove the definition.[17]

In place of a definition, the document provided seven principles for Peacekeeping-Intelligence. It should be (1) rules-based, (2) non-clandestine, (3) conducted within designated areas of application, (4) respectful of state sovereignty, (5) independent, (6) executed by accountable and capable authorities and, and (7) secure and confidential. The process would be akin to a standard intelligence cycle: decision-making, assessment of requirements, tasking, and issuing of direction; acquisition; examination and collation; analysis; and dissemination.[18] The policy detailed how the information would be classified, handled, shared, and used and with which mechanisms and tools it was to be managed. It defined the roles and responsibilities of mission actors from the head of mission down. In addition to replacing the definition of Peacekeeping-Intelligence with principles, the policy toned down the link between the methods used and missions' mandates. Peacekeeping-intelligence was thus presented as "a critical enabler to permit Missions to operate safely and effectively," with a threefold aim to "support a common operational picture ... to provide early warning of imminent threats ..., and to identify risks and opportunities."[19] All of this was meant to enhance the situational awareness of mission leaders, allowing them to better gauge the stakes in terms of the safety and security of personnel and the protection of civilians.[20]

The UN initially turned to the member-states to provide the organization with best practices in the intelligence realm. Yet member-states provided limited know-how, for two main reasons: (1) national intelligence systematically entails both clandestine practices and classified information, which are inherently not part of peacekeeping-intelligence, and (2) each state has its own way of doing intelligence. The Division of Policy, Evaluation and Training thus initiated a preliminary assessment of how intelligence could be used in peacekeeping operations. The conclusion was that an intelligence policy should be developed by the organization and remain careful to avoid adopting one member-state's way of doing intelligence over another's. Also, it would not use any tools, tactics, or procedures that would involve either clandestine practices or information that was classified at the national level.

Standardizing Peacekeeping-Intelligence Practices

The UN's efforts to standardize Peacekeeping-Intelligence methods were concretized through the development of policy, guidelines, and handbooks. Mission-specific standard operating procedures were put in place to supplement UN-wide Peacekeeping-Intelligence handbooks developed through close consultation with member-states. Those volumes included the Military Peacekeeping-Intelligence Handbook; the Peacekeeping-Intelligence, Surveillance, and Reconnaissance (ISR) Staff Handbook and Units Manual; and the Police Peacekeeping-Intelligence Handbook. Each handbook was meant to complement the others, contributing to the overall picture of Peacekeeping-Intelligence. Member-states involved in developing these handbooks recognized that their own national personnel would be the end users and would be using the handbooks in their pre-deployment training. The handbooks were thus intended to be both for UN staff and for the police and military personnel deployed by member-states. However, reaching agreement on the content of these handbooks among member-states was a challenge.

Over the two years (2017–19) when these handbooks were being developed, the member-states involved went back and forth providing documents and justifications for why the different methodologies they were putting forward would best serve peacekeeping missions while meeting member-states' expectations. Some member-states pushed for approaches that resembled NATO's, while others raised concerns about that model. The fear was that some member-states would use UN peace operations as instruments for engaging in intelligence activities to further their own national agendas.

After the multinational working groups completed the Peacekeeping-Intelligence Policy, the UN revised it to ensure that its content aligned both with the unique nature of UN peace operations and with UN doctrine. To that end, UN officials inserted human rights considerations and situated the military component within the larger civilian-led structure of the UN and the structure of peace operations specifically.

The UN policies and guidelines define the role of each unit involved in Peacekeeping-Intelligence during peacekeeping missions. Hence, according to the Peacekeeping-Intelligence Policy, the substantive units responsible for

Challenges in UN Peacekeeping-Intelligence 173

Peacekeeping-Intelligence are the Joint Mission Analysis Centres (JMACs), the Force and Police Components, the UN Department of Safety and Security (UNDSS), and the Joint Operations Centres (JOCs), in partnership with other sections such as the Political Affairs Division, the Protection of Civilians program, the Office of the Legal Adviser, and the Human Rights Division.[21]

Challenges in Implementing the Policy and Creating Trust[22]

As is the case in national settings, during UN peacekeeping missions, information and analysis are to be shared on a need-to-know basis and, in exceptional circumstances, on a need-to-share basis. The need-to-*know* principle has it that one must justify the need and have the authority to receive the information requested. The intention here is to prevent the unauthorized disclosure of sensitive information. The need to *share* applies when the Head of Mission surmises that the information is necessary in order to keep colleagues safe.[23] These needs are instilled in an environment in which the analysts trust the sharing environment, the people in that environment, and the infrastructures that enable them to take in the information.[24] If intelligence is driven by a need-to-know basis, I highlight an additional need: the need to *trust*. That encompasses trust between the member-states in sharing practices and know-how toward common objectives, which include the safety and security of personnel and the protection of civilians, as well as respective national interests.[25]

"Trust is key to intelligence sharing".[26] Trust is reinforced through exchanges of intelligence – its timing, sequence, frequency, and value – and that reinforcement then increases the value of intelligence. Frequent sharing fosters interpersonal, interorganizational, and international networks.[27] Trust can be analysed at the organizational and personal levels and in terms of the states within an organization. When implementing policy about sharing information, the UN has faced challenges creating trust both among member-states and *among* and *within* units.

Lack of Trust between Member-States

The multinational composition of UN missions has long been identified as the main reason why states resist sharing intelligence with those missions as well as within them. During the war in the former Yugoslavia, NATO refused to share sensitive intelligence with the UN Protection Force because the mission's commander was from India, a non-NATO country.[28] The multinational composition of troops was associated with fears that intelligence would be instrumentalized for domestic purposes at the expense of the peacekeeping operation's mandate. Chesterman and Dorn have highlighted that, because states bring different interests to the UN's process of gathering, sharing, and using intelligence,

174   Sarah-Myriam Martin-Brûlé

interveners could use that intelligence to influence or bluntly manipulate the UN. Put another way, there is a danger that intelligence may be gathered selectively and presented in such a way as to influence the intervention so that it favours the interveners. As one example, "one permanent member in favour of intervention provided intelligence showing large numbers of displaced persons in wretched conditions; a second permanent member opposing intervention offered intelligence suggesting a far smaller number of people subsisting in more reasonable conditions."[29]

Abilova and Novosseloff have pointed to weaknesses in the UN intelligence system to explain why member-states refuse to share intelligence with the organization "except when they have an interest to do so."[30] The mistrust of member-states toward information-sharing mechanisms within peacekeeping missions has been highlighted as an impediment to optimal information flow. One UN personnel explained how, in peacekeeping missions,

> the fundamental problem is that the member-states of NATO do not want to share information. If drone imagery cannot be shared, NATO applies to the Afghan model, whereas the African contingents would have much more to contribute. As long as we don't share information (between the TCCs [Troop and Police Contributors]). The problem of rotation of staff is a clear problem. We need intelligence, but there is a reluctance of member-states. There is a better acceptance now but with clear hurdles. We need to see that over five to ten years.[31]

The Peacekeeping-Intelligence Policy addresses the sharing of information between the UN and its member-states. It is meant to regulate the disclosure and release of sensitive information.[32] The policy details how the DPO receives information from the member-states, as well as how that information is shared and according to which information-handling and classification standards. In peacekeeping missions, the special representative of the Secretary-General (SRSG) ultimately decides with which non-mission UN and or non-UN entities information will be shared. Information sharing is authorized to be discussed on a need-to-share and need-to-know basis with "UN partners" (e.g., G5 Sahel, French forces, EU mission, TCCs).[33]

Stiles highlights the key role played by the institutionalization of practices in fostering trust among states, "even when their interests are fickle and fluid."[34] Indeed, the reluctance exhibited by member-states vis-à-vis peacekeeping-intelligence stems from the lack of secure, clear, and standardized procedures in the UN Peacekeeping-Intelligence-sharing system. Even if the UN has a system for classifying information, "this system, however, is not linked to any prosecution procedures, as in most countries, NATO, or the EU."[35] Moreover, there is no central and secure system that enables actors to stock or save sensitive information. As one UN personnel interviewed summarized: "One of the main paradoxes is that, in Missions, we are hiding information from one another while in New York, they share everything. They have access to each unit's code cables for example."[36] Given these weaknesses in the UN intelligence structure, when information is exchanged through official means, those exchanges may be more transparent, but that transparency comes at the cost of poorer quality and utility of the information shared among actors.

Lack of Trust Between Substantive Units

The concept of interorganizational trust highlights the relationships between units within UN peace missions. Interorganizational trust manifests itself through interactions between offices/entities within the peacekeeping mission. Intelligence is optimal when states trust one another in providing complementary approaches to similar issues through specialization. UN peace operations have high potential for intelligence efficiency, given the task division between its different offices. Yet however distinct their different roles, the encompassing nature of the peacekeeping missions' mandates[37] and the complexity of the context blurs the division of tasks among units. The result is that despite there being set policies for each office, the bureaucratic organization of UN peacekeeping missions remains for many "inherently ambiguous."[38]

Substantive units have the mandate to report and analyse various aspects of intelligence pertaining to the mission (for example, JMACs focus on integrated and forward-looking analysis to implement the mandate, DSS focuses on the security and safety of personnel, U2 on military intelligence, and JOC on information reporting). Hence, one would expect intelligence to be of better quality when entities trust one another to exchange intelligence focusing on different aspects of the same issues. However, my field research indicates that a lack of trust has impeded Peacekeeping-Intelligence sharing among substantive units. This stems from four challenges: (1) unclear tasking by senior leadership, (2) overlapping mandates of substantive units and ensuing duplication of work, (3) perception of insecure handling/storing/labelling of information, and (4) competition among units.

UN personnel interviewed complained that the senior leaders of their mission (D1, D2, USRSGs, and SRG) were not all equally aware of the role of each unit; this resulted in a lack of clear tasking of these entities.[39] Senior leaders themselves, when interviewed, admitted that while each unit played a key role in peacekeeping missions, their input into decision-making was neither consistent nor clear. The lack of clear tasking for each unit created confusion and led to each office planning its own work following its own interpretation of what was relevant to the mandate rather than focusing on senior leadership's needs.[40] This generated overlap in the work of units, duplication of reports, and, ultimately, information overload for the leadership. Ironically, the multiplication of Peacekeeping-Intelligence products often has the counterproductive effect of diminishing each individual unit's influence.[41] The more reports are produced and the less crucial or relevant their information, the harder it is for senior leadership to rely on the products delivered to them, and this limits the credibility and predictive value of the delivered output.[42] The resulting lack of trust in the information provided by the units undercuts that information's value when decisions are being made and, ultimately, the impact of the units on the mission. Also, the gap between the headquarters' expectations and the field offices' requirements leads to tension: the peace operations "often reflect the political agreement reached between member states of the Security Council rather than the functional and operational requirements of the situation on the ground."[43]

To senior leadership's lack of trust of in the various units, add the lack of trust *among* the units, which stems from the very design of Peacekeeping-Intelligence structures within peace missions. These structures were put in place to facilitate flows of information and to optimize information sharing. Yet for many, the work of missions is still done in silos. Units working on their own reports tend to be reluctant to share information, especially when it is a challenge to secure information.

Analysts also highlighted the often intense competition among peacekeeping-intelligence units, due notably to the blurriness of tasking and the ensuing overlap in the division of work. According to analysts interviewed, these tensions lead to suboptimal sharing of information and or to its entire absence.

Lack of Interpersonal Trust

Interpersonal trust can generate networks when there is a lack of interorganizational trust.[44] Interpersonal trust relates to the ties individuals forge with one another – ties that are central to the creation of informal networks. Interpersonal trust can stem from a similar intelligence culture, long experience working together, a similar professional background, or a common nationality. The lack of interpersonal trust remains a key challenge to effective Peacekeeping-Intelligence-sharing, for five key reasons: (1) mission leaders', and staff's, lack of familiarity with peacekeeping-intelligence policy, including with its guidelines and handbooks; (2) the absence of clear and relevant professional experience requirements when intelligence analysts are being recruited; (3) the multinational composition of intelligence staffing; (4) inadequate linguistic skills; and (5) negative views of sharing information held by the international staff or the local population, or both.

Lack of Familiarity and Expertise

Trust grows out of predictability, but the UN's peacekeeping-intelligence policy is still new, and sharing mechanisms are still not set. To overcome this problem, the UN has produced handbooks to provide guidance:

Military Peacekeeping-Intelligence: The Peacekeeping-Intelligence, Surveillance, and Reconnaissance (ISR); and Police Peacekeeping-Intelligence. These documents provide overall general guidance with regard to practices; however, they are not equally adaptable to the realities of each mission. Peacekeeping-Intelligence handbooks are meant to provide guidance, but many of them reflect unfamiliarity with the concepts and practice of peacekeeping-intelligence.

Akin to national intelligence, UN peacekeeping-intelligence follows the cycle of planning/tasking, acquisition, collation/examination, analysis, and dissemination. With regard to planning and tasking, members of mission leadership (D1 and above) interviewed were hard-pressed to articulate what UN peacekeeping-intelligence meant and how it could be used to support them in their decision-making. Similarly, many staff admitted to a blurry understanding of what they should expect of leadership and what peacekeeping-intelligence meant for their own work in the peacekeeping mission.

Intelligence in a peace operation is thus still done in a multidimensional, high-stakes environment in which there are few trained intelligence experts. The difficulty in implementing such procedures arises from a lack of expertise in sharing intelligence in a UN context in which intelligence is characterized by its "non-clandestineity." The Peacekeeping Intelligence Policy (now the Peacekeeping-Intelligence Policy, with the hyphen emphasizing the creation of a unique UN concept) was first adopted only in 2017, so the organization has not yet developed the required expertise. This is in part because the UN system for hiring civilian, police, and military personnel has failed to attract or create a pool of qualified candidates.

Politically Sensitive Postings and Hiring Process

The UN promotes diversity and representativeness; hence its recruitment system is meant to be neutral, impartial, and based on peace operations' needs. Difficulties in targeting candidates with intelligence experience highlight general hurdles within the system as well as hurdles more specific to peacekeeping-intelligence.

One challenge is that on *Inspira,* the official UN hiring platform, job descriptions and terms of reference are standardized in such a way that it is impossible for recruiters to specifically call for candidates who have previous intelligence experience, let alone test candidates' actual skills and abilities to do peacekeeping-intelligence work. A UN official explained:

> Another restriction is the informal holds some member-states have on posts. For example, in MINUSCA, the JMAC is systematically composed of an American, a French, and a Portuguese staff member (the Americans rarely speak French, while

178   Sarah-Myriam Martin-Brûlé

the French are rarely trained as analysts), and in UNMISS, British and Norwegian personnel hold key posts in the JMAC. These national holds on posts create a two-fold problem. First, they make it harder to target and attract the most qualified personnel for the job. Second, they pose questions about what information these personnel might be sharing with their embassies or capitals, leading analysts to take a cautious approach that some believe has an impact on the intelligence products.[45]

So a balance must be struck between personnel put forward by member-states and the criteria prioritized by the UN in the selection process. One UN official suggested that more targeted recruitment required a partnership between the UN and member-states. Also, at the mission level, recruitment becomes politically sensitive in terms of units' part in the peacekeeping-intelligence. The head of a peacekeeping-intelligence unit explained:

With the new recruitment process in place you ... have a number of stages where you are blind to the candidate ... For instance, for obvious reasons I can never recruit ... from [the neighboring country] ... With all the implications of ... [that neighbouring country], in this country I cannot ... And they are probably very well, people very, you know, with the right skills.

When we opened for recruitment a few years ago we had [more than thirty] candidates from [the neighbouring country] applying ... for the post and it is a real effort of ... [that neighbouring country] intelligence to penetrate us, and that you cannot screen people out, because of their nationality, it is forbidden in the UN, so how do I do? You see, so I think that you know, they have put in place several things in the recruitment process that coming from maybe from like, private sectors which work well with Coca-Cola, or you know, McDonald's but not necessarily fulfil our requirements you know, particularly in these shops. I'm not saying that I mean we are not must, more important than anybody else but this is very sensitive area, and then so it is sometimes we find these challenges and it is not easy to handle.[46]

In addition to all this, the selection of analysts to perform a given task is a politicized process that seems to prioritize informal national rapport with TCCs or member-states over the peace operations' needs.[47] Another restriction is the informal holds some member-states have on posts. For example, on certain missions, the units are systematically composed of a mix of pre-selected nationalities, such as in the examples presented earlier of the JMAC at the MINUSCA being composed of an American, a French, and a Portuguese, with British and Norwegian personnel in UNMISS. For the U2, Americans are systematically assigned as Chief U2 at MINUSCA and as Deputy Chief U2 at MINUSMA.

"These national holds on posts create a twofold problem. First, they make it harder to locate and attract the most qualified personnel for the job. Second,

Challenges in UN Peacekeeping-Intelligence   179

they pose questions about what information these personnel might be sharing with their embassies or capitals, leading analysts to take a cautious approach that some believe has an impact on intelligence products. As one official lamented, "it means we end up having to put less and less in written documents."[48] The lack of written documents reinforces informal as opposed to formal intelligence sharing.

Linguistic Barriers

Language itself is key in intelligence sharing. People who do not understand any of the local languages and that hold key positions in peacekeeping-intelligence usually face communication problems. "Forces' peacekeeping-intelligence branches ... frequently do not have the capacity or the appropriate language skills to gather information from, and build relationships with, their ... counterparts or other stakeholders."[49] English is the working language of most missions operating in francophone countries (MINUSCA, MINUSMA). English is the operational language for the force, yet many staff officers are unilingual francophones. In addition, French is the operational language for the police, notably at the MINUSMA.

In an interview, an anglophone officer complained that Scandinavian counterparts would share information with one another either in Swedish or Norwegian, thus excluding their anglophone and francophone colleagues from the conversations. Even more problematic is that locals speak mostly French and various local languages, whereas the vast majority of the staff speak neither French nor any of these local languages. Linguistic barriers between the mission and the locals, and within the mission itself, hinder efficiency in the peacekeeping-intelligence cycle and reinforce informal mechanisms among individuals who speak the same language.

Lack of Trust in Timely (Re)action

Lack of trust between the locals and the mission as a whole also stems from the lack of trust that the mission will respond in a timely manner in the event of an attack, as well as from the lack of protection offered to those who would speak to the mission's staff. Séan Smith explains that "several MINUSMA officials noted that Malian stakeholders do not wish to provide information to the Mission for fear of reprisals." Moreover, the UN military is suspicious of information shared by locals; they fear "being lured into an ambush."[50]

Conclusion: Trusting the Process

A few years ago, UN intelligence was still mocked by some as an oxymoron. Intelligence remained taboo until 2017; today, the UN Peacekeeping-Intelligence Policy is being implemented convincingly enough on all peacekeeping missions

180   Sarah-Myriam Martin-Brûlé

that we can safely say it is there to stay. The development and implementation of standardized peacekeeping-intelligence processes has led to more efficient practices within missions. Mission-wide Peacekeeping-Intelligence acquisition plans and mission Peacekeeping-Intelligence coordination mechanisms are being implemented, enhancing the sharing of information and improving the general situational awareness of mission leaders. Challenges remain for headquarters and missions to optimally align and adapt Peacekeeping-Intelligence implementation so as to stay relevant to each mission's context and constraints. Missions' personnel and units testify to the enhanced efficiency of information-sharing mechanisms, yet member-states remain wary. The member-states deploying their staff on missions keep an eye on the process of acquiring and sharing intelligence as part of the Peacekeeping-Intelligence process and on the extent to which information acquired through the missions' Peacekeeping-Intelligence cycle makes its way back to each national capital. Another key issue relates to the opportunities and drawbacks arising from the formalization of practices. For now, the policy has opened the way for improving each stage of the Peacekeeping-Intelligence cycle, to better recruit, train, and retain personnel and, overall, to improve sharing mechanisms. Trust remains to be earned for member-states, units, and personnel for this new Peacekeeping-Intelligence mindset to best ensure the safety and security of their personnel and the protection of civilians.

NOTES

1   Sarah-Myriam Martin-Brûlé, Lou Pingeot, and Vincent Pouliot, "The Power Politics of United Nations Peace Operations," in *International Institutions and Power Politics*, ed. Anders Wivel and T.V. Paul (Washington, D.C.: Georgetown University Press, 2019), 149–66.
2   Sarah-Myriam Martin-Brûlé, "Finding the UN Way on Peacekeeping-Intelligence," International Peace Institution, 9 April 2020, 4 https://www.ipinst.org/2020/04 /finding-the-un-way-on-peacekeeping-intelligence.
3   Haidi Willmot states that "the UN's Second Secretary-General, Dag Hammarskjöld, viewed the absence of a situational awareness system as a 'serious handicap'" and that his successor, Secretary-General U Thant, "was of the view that the lack of authoritative information, without which the Secretary-General cannot speak … was one of the two 'insuperable obstacles' he faced during his tenure." Haidi Willmot, "Improving UN Situational Awareness: Enhancing the UN's Ability to Prevent and Respond to Mass Human Suffering," Stimson Center, 2017, 14, https:// www.stimson.org/wp-content/files/file-attachments/UNSituationalAwareness_ FINAL_Web.pdf.
4   Military information officers were trying to apply the intelligence cycle, but in a non-integrated manner, with only "improvised/ad hoc" access to information

Challenges in UN Peacekeeping-Intelligence   181

gathered by missions' civilian components. Personal communication with officials in UN missions, 2019.

5 Willmot, "Improving UN Situational Awareness: Enhancing the UN's ability to prevent and respond to mass human suffering."

6 United Nations, "Report of the Independent Panel on the Safety and Security of UN Personnel in Iraq," UN Digital Library, 20 October 2003, https://digitallibrary .un.org/record/529406?ln=en.

7 The UN SAGE software is an incident-reporting and situational-awareness tool.

8 UN Secretary-General, "The Future of United Nations Peace Operations: Implementation of the Recommendations of the High-Level Independent Panel on Peace Operations," UN Digital Library, 2 September 2015, https://digitallibrary .un.org/record/802167?ln=en.

9 United Nations, "Report of the Special Committee on Peacekeeping Operations," UN General Assembly, 15 March 2016, https://www.securitycouncilreport.org/atf /cf/%7B65BFCF9B-6D27-4E9C-8CD3-CF6E4FF96FF9%7D/a_72_19.pdf.

10 United Nations, "Statement to the UN Peacekeeping Ministerial," Under-Secretary-General for Peace Operations Jean-Pierre Lacroix, 29 March 2019, https:// peacekeeping.un.org/sites/default/files/pk-ministerial-usg-dpo-asdelivered_.pdf.

11 Lacroix, "Statement to the UN Peacekeeping Ministerial." This statement was also referring to Hervé Ladsous's take on investing in force multipliers, whether equipment such as helicopters or mechanisms such as analytical structures akin to peacekeeping-intelligence.

12 United Nations, "Report of the Special Committee on Peacekeeping Operations," para. 52.

13 UN Peacekeeping-Intelligence was then revised and approved in May 2019 with a change in the definition and in the label. From then on UN Peacekeeping-Intelligence policy was to stress the non-clandestine requirement of information acquired and to emphasize the difference with non–Peacekeeping-Intelligence. United Nations, "Peacekeeping-Intelligence Policy," 1 May 2019, https://www.confluxcenter.org/wp -content/uploads/2018/11/2017.07-Peacekeeping-Intelligence-Policy.pdf .

14 UN Department of Peace Operations, "Peacekeeping-Intelligence Policy."

15 UN Department of Peace Operations, "Peacekeeping-Intelligence Policy."

16 The term "Christmas tree mandate" is often used to illustrate the range of tasks requested for the peacekeepers to perform. Paul D. Williams, "The Security Council's Peacekeeping Trilemma," *International Affairs* 96, no. 2 (2020): 479–99, https://doi.org/10.1093/ia/iiz199.

17 Interview of the author, 2018.

18 Benjamin Oudet highlights that "it is worth noting that the collection phase – the most sensitive phase of secrecy and espionage for state intelligence – must be 'effective, responsible, and ethic' in UN missions." Oudet, "The UN Intelligence Function," in *The Conduct of Intelligence in Democracies: Processes, Practices, Cultures*, ed. Florina Cristiana Matei (Boulder: Lynne Rienner, 2019), 161. In

182   Sarah-Myriam Martin-Brûlé

fact, the UN does not use the term "collection." Rather, it refers to the concept of "acquisition of information" to emphasize that its work is distinct from that of national intelligence mechanisms. Oudet concludes that "the crucial information on 'personalities,' 'motives' and 'intent' can only be obtained through traditional HUMINT means" (163). Yet the United Nations officially does not acknowledge doing "human intelligence." Again, to emphasize that its work is distinct from that of national intelligence, the UN has instead developed guidelines on the "acquisition of information from human sources." See Martin-Brûlé, Pingeot, and Pouliot, "The Power Politics of United Nations Peace Operations."

19   Martin-Brûlé, "Finding the UN Way on Peacekeeping-Intelligence."

20   United Nations, "Peacekeeping-Intelligence Policy"; Martin-Brûlé, "Finding the UN Way on Peacekeeping-Intelligence."

21   United Nations, "Peacekeeping-Intelligence Policy."

22   This idea inter- and intra-organization trust was developed in Sarah-Myriam Martin-Brûlé, "Competing for Trust: Challenges in United Nations Peacekeeping-Intelligence," *International Journal of Intelligence and Counterintelligence* 34, no. 3 (2020): 494–524.

23   For example, information that was distributed after the Baghdad bombing when staff needed to understand the security situation. A security alert to all staff is a classic example of a need to share. United Nations, "Information Sensitivity Toolkit Version 1," Peacekeeping Information Management Unit DPKO, 24 February 2010, https://archives.un.org/sites/archives.un.org/files/RM-Guidelines/information_sensiti vity_toolkit_2010.pdf.

24   Hence, for Cotter, "the prevalence of the 'need-to-know' mentality and the importance placed on secrecy in the intelligence community suggests that intelligence organisations may resist inputting sensitive information into digital information networks." Ryan Cotter Sinclair, "Police Intelligence: Connecting-the-Dots in a Network Society," *Policing and Society* 27, no. 2 (June 2017): 173–87. "Additionally, intelligence officers may be resistant to the time-consuming and rule-bound formal procedures associated with formal digital networks, preferring instead to exchange information via methods less easily audited. In this context, intelligence officers may rely on informal communication via personal networks to share sensitive intelligence information." Peter Gill and Mark Phythian, *Intelligence in an Insecure World* (Cambridge: Polity, 2006), 3.

25   Martin-Brûlé, "Competing for Trust," 5.

26   Martin-Brûlé, "Competing for Trust," 5; Stéphane Lefebvre, "The Difficulties and Dilemmas of International Intelligence Cooperation," *International Journal of Intelligence and Counterintelligence* 16, no. 4 (2006): 527–41; Derek S. Reveron, "Old Allies, New Friends: Intelligence-Sharing in the War on Terror," *Orbis* 50, no. 3 (Summer 2006): 453–68.

27   For Whelan, the two are intrinsically linked. "When asked to identify which level of trust – interpersonal or inter-organisational – is more important for the functioning of security networks, most interviewees selected interpersonal

trust. This is despite the strong foundations of institutional trust that exist in this security field. By definition, the very fact that an individual or organisational unit has a security clearance is supposed to mean that individual or unit can be trusted. But the effects of such mechanisms in promoting trust require much further analysis. In theory, they should be capable of promoting trust between parties in the complete absence of personal or organisational relationships as well as be scalable to accommodate institutional environments of any size. In practice, however, while these processes help to promote trust, this research would lead us to preliminarily conclude that they are no comparison for relational trust. The relationship between the different levels and forms of trust requires considerably further attention across the security field." Chad Whelan, "Informal Social Networks Within and Between Organisations: On the Properties of Interpersonal Ties and Trust," *Policing: An International Journal of Police Strategies and Management* 39, no. 1 (2016): 145–58.

28 Martyn explains that "attempting to utilize intelligence within multinational PSOs has created ludicrous situations such as when Indian Lieutenant-General Satish Nambiar, commanding the United Nations Protection Force (UNPROFOR) in the former Yugoslavia was denied North Atlantic Treaty Organization (NATO) intelligence being provided to his staff." Robert Martyn, "Beyond the Next Hill: The Future of Military Intelligence in Peace Support Operations," in *Peacekeeping-Intelligence: New Players, Extended Boundaries*, ed. David Carment and Martin Rudner (London: Routledge, 2007), 23; Hugh Smith, "UN Peacekeeping," in *Secret Intelligence: A Reader*, ed. Christopher Andrew, Richard J. Aldrich, and Wesley K. Wark (New York: Routledge, 2009), 495–509.

29 Simon Chesterman, "Intelligence Cooperation in International Operations," in *Accountability of International Intelligence Cooperation*, ed. by Hans Born, Ian Leigh, and Aidan Wills (New York: Routledge, 2011), 829.

30 Olga Abilova and Alexandra Novosseloff, "Demystifying Peacekeeping-Intelligence: Toward an Organizational Doctrine," International Peace Institute (July 2016): 20, https://www.ipinst.org/wp-content/uploads/2016/07/1608 _Demystifying-Intelligence. pdf.

31 Interview by author, 2017.

32 United Nations. "Peacekeeping-Intelligence Policy."

33 The need to know refers to information that can be requested based on a need to take action, when information needs to be acted upon and is necessary for one to complete a job. The need to share refers to information that can be shared for a wider benefit such as lessons learned, but not acted upon.

34 Kendall W. Stiles, *Trust and Hedging in International Relations* (Ann Arbor: University of Michigan Press, 2018).

35 Abilova and Novosseloff, "Demystifying Peacekeeping-Intelligence: Toward an Organizational Doctrine."

36 Interview by author, 2017.

37 Denis M. Tull, "The Limits and Unintended Consequences of UN Peace Enforcement: The Force Intervention Brigade in DR Congo," *International Peacekeeping* 25, no. 2 (2018): 167–90.

38 Joel Gwyn Winckler, "Exceeding Limitations of the United Nations Peacekeeping Bureaucracy: Strategies of Officials to Influence Peacekeeping Activities within the United Nations Mission in Liberia and the Department of Peacekeeping Operations," *International Peacekeeping* 22, no. 1 (2015): 44, https://www.stimson .org/wp-content/files/file-attachments/UNSituationalAwareness_FINAL_Web.pdf.

39 Interview by author, 2016.

40 Interview by author, 2019.

41 Interviews by author 2017, 2018.

42 Interview by author, 2015.

43 Winckler, "Exceeding Limitations of the United Nations Peacekeeping Bureaucracy," 44.

44 Gill and Phythian, *Intelligence in an Insecure World*; Cotter, "Police Intelligence"; Whelan, "Informal Social Networks Within and Between Organisations." Martin-Brûlé, "Competing for Trust", 7.

45 Martin-Brûlé, "Competing for Trust", 11; Interview by the author, 2019.

46 Interview by author, 2017.

47 Interview by the author, 2019.

48 Interview by the author, 2019.

49 Séan Smith, "Early Warning and Rapid Response: Reinforcing MINUSMA's Ability to Protect Civilians," *Center for Civilians in Conflict* (April 2021): 12, https:// civiliansinconflict.org/wpcontent/uploads/2021/04/CIVIC_Peacekeeping_EWRR _Report_EN_BAT_web.pdf.

50 Smith, "Early Warning and Rapid Response," 11.

Conclusion

DANIEL JEAN

The theme of this edited collection is relevant and timely. In this conclusion, I demonstrate that intelligence cooperation – which transcends the inner circles of governments and traditional security and intelligence agencies – is more than ever required for America's allies to navigate this complex multipolar world. I begin by highlighting some key features of the current international environment to provide the context for what they mean for the intelligence function and specifically for intelligence cooperation. I then discuss how these elements should inform intelligence priorities, activities, and behaviours. Finally, I focus in a more targeted way on what intelligence cooperation that transcends the inner sanctums of government may mean for US allies.

A Multipolar World, but with a Major Geopolitical/ Geoeconomic Bipolar Confrontation at Centre Stage

It may be true that we live in a multipolar age in which power resides in more than two nation-states with dominant military, cultural, and economic influence. Yet we are also witnessing at centre stage a major competition and confrontation between two giants – the United States and the new contender, China. In this confrontation, geopolitical and geoeconomic interests are closely intertwined. This strategic competition is in play everywhere: in accessing key transportation routes, critical infrastructure, and data (the new currency in a wired world). There is also competition over standards governing a number of these realms and in developing or acquiring the next technological advances from universities and state-of-the-art companies.

While we should not underestimate military considerations in this confrontation, the race for economic and technological advantages is paramount and in fact often serves military ambitions. The Cold War between the United States and the Soviet Union had no comparably significant economic dimension. In such a context, both sides wish to pursue their range of strategic interests without triggering a conflict, which would be devastating.

186 Daniel Jean

While the two giants, China and the United States, will remain at centre stage for the foreseeable future, we also observe the resurgence of Russia. It may not be the major military threat that it was in the past, and it has never been a key competitor in the economic arena. In February 2022, to the surprise of many Western states, Russia launched a new war against Ukraine. As it has turned out, Russia's military weaknesses, the astonishing resilience of the Ukrainians, and the rapid military support the latter have received from NATO has resulted in a prolonged conflict and a weakened Russia. Nevertheless, Russia remains a major disruptive power, having resorted to hybrid warfare and proxy activities. It is difficult to imagine, for example, that the Ukraine crisis and the annexation of Crimea by Russia in 2014 or Moscow's involvement in the Syrian war did not undermine the pivot to Asia begun by the Obama administration.

Through actions such as the cyberattack on the World Anti-Doping Agency (WADA) in 2016, meddling in foreign elections, and cyber hacks like Solar-Winds, and with Russia tolerating if not encouraging attacks by cyber mercenaries on Western critical infrastructure, Russia is demonstrating how a relatively low investment in the cyber domain coupled with traditional intelligence instruments can serve its intelligence needs and threaten the democratic institutions of its rivals. Nancy Teeple addresses this topic in chapter 7, in which she describes how new domains such as cyber offer significant strategic opportunities even while opening new vulnerabilities.

The COVID-19 pandemic and the ensuing competition to develop vaccines, as well as the competition for strategic resources such as the rare earths on which so many new technologies depend, have reminded us of the dangers of overreliance on uncertain supply chains. International scientific cooperation has been at the heart of the rapid development of several effective COVID vaccines, and that knowledge will now support the fight against other diseases, while the world slowly grapples with the reality that the pandemic is not over.

This is not simply a reminder that global crises such as pandemics and climate change require concerted global responses. It is also a warning that national governments are no longer the only location where the intelligence function operates.

This is a rather sombre picture of this emerging multipolar world. There are, nevertheless, some encouraging signs.

The US–China Confrontation

Coalitions and alliances of the like-minded are back in style and are showing their strength, as demonstrated by the pushback against Huawei as a supplier of 5G telecommunications networks in Western countries. This reflects a realist approach to the risks posed by China as well as the election in 2020 of a new US

Conclusion   187

president, Joe Biden, who seeks and nurtures alliances more than his predecessor had. All of this has created an opportunity for transatlantic cooperation that encourages normative behaviours, intelligence sharing on threats, and, when necessary, punishment of excesses. One particular challenge for these like-minded states is how to conduct concerted pushback on China without being at the mercy of the US, a more benevolent but no less ambitious titan. In the present era, multilateralism remains fragile and some of the new international vectors of power, such as technological platforms and data, are operating without frontiers and with little governance. This highlights how important it is for some actors, notably the EU, to pursue strategic autonomy, as Bjorn Fägersten describes in chapter 2, and to give themselves the means to do so by pursuing a European intelligence strategy, as Adriana Seagle discusses in chapter 3.

Struck by the phenomenal growth of Chinese power over the past three decades, too many observers have fallen into the linear extrapolation syndrome, as others had done with the United Kingdom at the time of the Industrial Revolution and with Japan in the 1980s during the manufacturing revolution. In a world where many strategic advantages are the result of technological innovation, some of the constraints inherent in authoritarian regimes could hamper China's ability to move further up the supply chain continuum, notwithstanding the huge progress it has made so far. Modern history also reminds us that one should never underestimate the capacity of the US to re-emerge from its struggles through the power of innovation and entrepreneurship. At the heart of the China–US confrontation is the common imperative to generate wealth for domestic redistribution, in order to perpetuate one-party rule (in China's case) or to depolarize society (in that of the US).

Russian Hybrid Warfare

Some of the surprise effects of Russia's earlier use of hybrid warfare tactics such as foreign election meddling are gone. The new challenge for democratic states is to expand their defensive capacities to increase their resilience in the face of similar tactics, such as state-sponsored disinformation. The SolarWinds hack is a reminder that the US and its allies still have a long way to go to prevent and deter espionage, but now, at least, they have a better appreciation of the threat and of the need to continue working closely with technology companies to address these vulnerabilities and develop better protections.[1] A growing challenge in this domain may be that cyber mercenaries enjoy impunity in Russia, where they can launch ransom attacks on critical infrastructure abroad. Deterrence will come partly from better awareness and cyberdefences; beyond that, the US and its allies need to work together to promote better behaviour by Russia through incentives and disincentives.

188   Daniel Jean

What Does This New International Environment
Mean for the Intelligence Function?

Governments and their key assets are no longer the only targets of foreign state actors; conversely, intelligence agencies no longer have a monopoly on the collection, assessment, and dissemination of intelligence.

With regard to collection, various chapters in this volume have shown that security and intelligence agencies need to expand their networks of sources beyond traditional covert signals (SIGINT) and human intelligence (HUMINT) so as to encompass new sources, including open ones. For example, the major business intelligence firms, consulting groups, and international media often have a global presence that includes access to governments, business entities, and key civic actors. Intelligence agencies need to tap these sources of information more deliberately without compromising their independence or safety.

Regarding intelligence assessment, ongoing engagement with non-governmental contacts is essential to better understand both threats and possible mitigation strategies. In a world in which many targets are non-governmental, those targets must be actively engaged in the assessment process. Some non-governmental actors may be more inclined to work with the government on non-traditional threats, especially if they can benefit from that cooperation.

In terms of dissemination, security and intelligence agencies need to expand their client base to better equip these non-governmental partners, be they universities, large and small technology companies, or civil society actors such as the media and regular citizens, notably in the battle against state-sponsored disinformation. The public release of intelligence by the US and the UK related to developments in the run-up to the Russia–Ukraine war, in combination with sensitive information accessed by hacktivist groups like "Anonymous," has served as a successful counteroffence to sophisticated disinformation campaigns.

When it comes to intelligence cooperation, the US and its allies must appreciate that their respective national interests are better served when they combine their efforts to gather and share intelligence and when they develop and deploy common actions. Such efforts are more likely to encourage the right behaviours when it comes to peace and security and adherence to international norms such as territorial integrity, freedom of navigation, fair economic competition, and respect for fundamental human rights. These concerted actions call on the traditional arsenal of diplomatic levers, including incentives and deterrence. The US and its allies must also be prepared to consider more muscular actions when responding to transgressions that are more serious when traditional diplomatic levers fail. The delicate balance that NATO members have struck in offering rapid and unequivocal military support to Ukraine while resisting measures that would lead to a broader conflict serves as a strong message to Russia but

Conclusion   189

also to China, should it consider action against Taiwan. The US's inaccurate claims in 2003 that Iraq possessed weapons of mass destruction serves as a sad reminder of the importance of building and maintaining trust among allies regarding the reliability of their intelligence. Such trust is vital in order to sustain the possibility of mounting concerted actions.

Alliances and coalitions such as NATO and the Five Eyes remain vital to the collection, assessment, and sharing of intelligence. For example, the Five Eyes is a mature work-sharing model that allows its members – Australia, Canada, New Zealand, the UK, and the US – to share their unique skills and knowledge in complementary ways. The value of the contributions of smaller members, like Canada, rests in the quality and complementarity of the craft and products they bring rather than the sheer volume.

China's increasing assertiveness beyond its borders has led to the creation of new economic instruments and regional alliances. The Trans-Pacific Partnership (TPP), now known as the Comprehensive and Progressive Agreement for Trans-Pacific Partnership (CPTPP), was initially an essential element of the US pivot toward Asia, in that it offered alternative trade opportunities for Asia-Pacific states. The agreement remains central to the regional security agenda of countries like Japan and Australia, despite the US withdrawal under the administration of former President Donald Trump. Patrick Walsh, in chapter 6, provides valuable context on how the Quadrilateral Security Dialogue (Quad) initially emerged as a security dialogue and has evolved more recently to include joint military exercises by the US, Japan, Australia, and India as an expression of their desire to counter China. The recent three-party security pact between Australia, the UK, and the US (AUKUS) represents an additional step in developing interoperable capacities in the region.

In that same chapter, Walsh describes the challenges that intelligence sharing poses for countries like Japan and India, which, unlike the Five Eyes countries, do not benefit from an enduring relationship of trust or that, in the case of India, may not be completely aligned with the US. Sarah-Myriam Martin-Brûlé, in chapter 8, expands on this challenge: countries that lack an intelligence-sharing tradition face additional obstacles to developing joint intelligence in support of the conduct of UN peace missions.

Technology is a new theatre of conflict and calls for new forms of cooperation between like-minded states. One need only look at the extensive work the European Commission has engaged in to procure sensitive technologies, as well as the efforts of some of its member-states, to appreciate that transatlantic cooperation on this front serves the geopolitical and economic interests of both the EU and North America.

Institutions in the security and intelligence community need to better engage and leverage non-intelligence government institutions. Such horizontal engagement is critical to intelligence collection, assessment, and dissemination, but it

190   Daniel Jean

is also crucial to the development of policies that can better integrate prosperity and security objectives. This expanded theatre calls for the intelligence community to develop new competencies to supplement its traditional ones. A new breed of intelligence experts must have the ability to conduct outreach externally with actors such as major corporations, technology start-ups, and excellence centres in universities. Universities and other professional development programs, for their part, will need to expand their multidisciplinary approach to graduate learning to include technology literacy. This is not to suggest that security and intelligence experts must all be engineers, but rather that they must acquire better technology literacy to allow for meaningful exchanges with external interlocutors and the development of relevant and timely assessment products.

What Does Intelligence Cooperation That Transcends the Inner Sanctums of Government Mean for American Allies?

In response to the US–China confrontation, the nefarious activities of countries such as Russia, and the challenges faced by the international rules-based order, some experts emphasize that US allies, who for years have benefited from that alliance, no longer live in a world in which failing to anticipate threats or making mistakes has limited consequences. Thomas Juneau, for example, argues that Canada no longer lives in a benevolent world, the implication being that Ottawa – and the same case can be made about other close American allies – needs better intelligence to support its national interests.[2] In Canada's case, for example, the challenge will be to protect its national interests in the Arctic by finding a balance between the pursuit of continental security in cooperation with the US and the increased desire by many states, including allies, to exploit new ocean transportation routes and increasingly accessible natural resources in Canada's North.

The business case for intelligence has never been so clear for America's allies. Yet being partly exempted from threats has meant that their cultures, ecosystems, and security and intelligence awareness are often limited, particularly outside government (e.g., think tanks, media, and public discourse more generally). The evolving threat environment has seen a targeting of key national interests such as the ability to generate wealth through innovation and to protect critical infrastructure and sectors against cyberattacks or other nefarious activities. Even democratic institutions are being threatened by outsiders. All of these factors should help make the intelligence realm more visibly relevant.

In this context, the ability of security and intelligence agencies to offer value to the private sector and to civil society, through the protection of democratic values, is what will best enable them to develop a constituency in support of their work. There are some encouraging signs. The Canadian Security

Conclusion 191

Intelligence Service (CSIS), for example, has been making a significant effort to connect with the private and academic sectors, and the Communications Security Establishment (CSE), Canada's signals intelligence agency, has seized on the need during the pandemic to make Canadian businesses and citizens more resilient to cyberthreats.[3] In doing so, these agencies had to come out of the shadows; this is a positive development, but these new partnerships must still mature through iterative and systemic engagement. A sound value proposition would be one in which businesses and citizens benefit from government expertise on threats, methods, and potential mitigation strategies. These non-governmental actors might also be willing to share information with the government, thus enhancing the development of knowledge and mitigation strategies. This calls for behavioural changes, and in this regard, security and intelligence communities among US allies could do a much more proactive job of "sanitizing" intelligence products about evolving threats, while protecting craft and sources, for external audiences to act on in a more informed way. This area too is ripe for much more cooperation among American allies.

Another challenge for US allies that has been raised by the implications of global power shifts relates to their ability to collect foreign intelligence. Those allies – especially the Five Eyes partners – benefit significantly from cooperative arrangements. How confident can they be that the status quo will always continue? In Canada, the absence of a foreign human intelligence agency is a cause for concern for some. Yet Thomas Juneau and Stephanie Carvin in chapter 4 and Reg Whitaker in chapter 5 make the case that more "Canadianization" of intelligence collection and assessment may be the preferable course, unless the country is prepared to make significant investments in creating a new agency. To varying extents, many other US allies will have to explore the same question.

The last issue to discuss here is structural change. Some of the most successful horizontal initiatives often have little to do with structure but rather owe their success to good governance that generates sufficient common purpose to leverage the capacities and expertise of the various actors where it resides – that is, in the mandated departments and agencies. Success, in other words, is the ability to conjure strengths in pursuit of common causes and objectives. Great analytical talent at the centre of government is certainly necessary to synthetize interdepartmental contributions into strategic advice for the country's leadership, but the successful implementation of a strategy must reside with the empowered and relevant organizations that support common causes and that have the legal instruments and authorities as well as the capacity and expertise. This type of approach is far more promising than wasting energy on creating additional structures that may already be outdated by the time they are functional.

To sum up, the world may be becoming more multipolar, but its chief characteristic is a live confrontation between two giants, China and the US. Unlike the previous confrontation between the US and the Soviet Union, this competition is as much economic as it is geopolitical. And this time, the two superpowers often confront each other in theatres outside the realm of government. As the chapters in this volume show, US allies need to rethink how, and with whom, they share intelligence, and seek new partners among both state and non-state actors.

NOTES

1 On SolarWinds, see Dina Temple-Raston, "A 'Worst Nightmare' Cyber-Attack: The Untold Story of the SolarWinds Hack," NPR, 16 April 2021, https://www.npr .org/2021/04/16/985439655/a-worst-nightmare-cyberattack-the-untold-story-of -the-solarwinds-hack.
2 Thomas Juneau, "Canada will Pay the price for neglecting our foreign policy," *Globe and Mail*, 7 June 2020, https://www.theglobeandmail.com/opinion/article-canada -will-pay-the-price-for-neglecting-our-foreign-policy.
3 Stephanie Carvin, "Canadian National Security Operations during COVID-19," in *Stress Tested: The COVID-19 Pandemic and Canadian National Security*, ed. Leah West, Thomas Juneau, and Amarnath Amarasingam (Calgary: University of Calgary Press, 2021), 107–26.

Contributors

Stephanie Carvin is an associate professor at the Norman Paterson School of International Affairs at Carleton University.

Björn Fägersten is senior research fellow at the Swedish Institute of International Affairs and CEO of the geopolitical risk consultancy Politea.

Daniel Jean is former National Security and Intelligence Advisor to the Prime Minister of Canada and former Deputy Minister of Foreign Affairs. He is now a Senior Fellow at the Graduate School of Public and International Affairs at the University of Ottawa.

Thomas Juneau is an associate professor with the Graduate School of Public and International Affairs at the University of Ottawa.

Sarah-Myriam Martin-Brûlé is Full Professor in the Department of Politics and International Studies at Bishop's University and Non-Resident Fellow at the International Peace Institute, New York.

Justin Massie is Full Professor of Political Science at the Université du Québec à Montréal and Co-Director of the Network for Strategic Analysis.

Marco Munier is a PhD candidate in Political Science at the Université du Québec à Montréal and an emerging scholar at the Network for Strategic Analysis.

Adriana Seagle is Associate Professor and Program Director of Intelligence and Security Studies at Bellevue University.

Nancy Teeple is a research associate and adjunct assistant professor at the Department of Political Science and Economics at the Royal Military of College

194   Contributors

of Canada. She is a Strategic Analyst at Defence Research and Development Canada's Centre for Operational Research and Analysis (DRDC CORA).

Damien Van Puyvelde is Assistant Professor and Intelligence and Security at the University of Leiden.

Patrick F. Walsh is a former Australian intelligence analyst and Professor, Intelligence and Security Studies, at Charles Sturt University, Australia.

Reg Whitaker is Distinguished Research Professor Emeritus at York University and Adjunct Professor of Political Science at the University of Victoria.